THE GREATEST WORK IN THE WORLD

The Greatest Work in the World

EDUCATION AS A MISSION OF EARLY
TWENTIETH-CENTURY CHURCHES OF CHRIST

*Letters of Lloyd Cline Sears
and Pattie Hathaway Armstrong*

Edited by
Elizabeth C. Parsons

Foreword by
Richard Hughes

Afterword by
Larry Long

WIPF & STOCK · Eugene, Oregon

THE GREATEST WORK IN THE WORLD
Education as a Mission of Early Twentieth-Century Churches of Christ
Letters of Lloyd Cline Sears and Pattie Hathaway Armstrong

Copyright © 2015 Elizabeth C. Parsons. All rights reserved. Except for brief quotations in critical publications or reviews, no part of this book may be reproduced in any manner without prior written permission from the publisher. Write: Permissions. Wipf and Stock Publishers, 199 W. 8th Ave., Suite 3, Eugene, OR 97401.

Wipf and Stock
An Imprint of Wipf and Stock Publishers
199 W. 8th Ave., Suite 3
Eugene, OR 97401

www.wipfandstock.com

ISBN 13: 978-1-4982-0276-3

Manufactured in the U.S.A. 01/23/2015

For the ancestors, with gratitude and love.

Contents

Foreword by Richard Hughes | ix
Acknowledgments | xv
Chronology | xvii

   Introduction | 1
1 Summer 1915 | 35
2 Summer 1916 | 111
3 Summers 1917 and 1918 | 162
4 Academic Year 1920–21 | 167

Afterword by Larry Long | 217
Names Index with Annotations | 221
Bibliography | 249
Index | 253

Foreword

By editing and publishing this collection of letters, Elizabeth Parsons has done a favor of inestimable value for students of American history, American religious history, and especially the Churches of Christ, born and bred on the American frontier.

These letters, chiefly between Lloyd Cline Sears (1895–1986) and Pattie Hathaway (often called Pataway for short) Armstrong Sears (1899–1977) tell us much about the lives of ordinary white Americans in the American Southwest (Oklahoma) and Midwest (Kansas) during those years. For that reason alone these letters are worthy of preservation and analysis by historians interested in that region and that era.

Beyond that, these letters are a goldmine for students interested in the history of the Churches of Christ, one of three major denominations that trace their roots to Barton Stone and Alexander Campbell in the early years of the nineteenth century.

Stone and Campbell both believed that the New Testament documents offered a clear picture of the primitive church, and both sought to restore that church as a way to unify a badly fractured Christian world. But unity for them did not require agreement, and they disagreed on what constituted the essence of that church. Informed by the Anglo-American Enlightenment, Campbell viewed the biblical text through the lens of reason. Treating the Bible much as a scientist would treat evidence in a scientific experiment, Campbell sought to identify the forms and structures (proper organization, proper form of worship, proper observance of the sacraments, etc.) that he thought characterized the church in its earliest years. And the proper identification of those forms and structures, he believed, required significant learning, not only about the text itself but also about the historical and cultural contexts from which that text emerged. In a word, Campbell was a scholar. On the other hand, Stone was chiefly informed not by the Anglo-American Enlightenment but by the American revival tradition, especially the Great Awakening in the American Colonies (1734–1743) and the Second Great Awakening (1800–1830) in whose Cane Ridge, Kentucky, revival of 1801 he was a key participant.

As a result, Stone was less concerned with the "pattern" of the primitive church than with the sort of life he believed the gospel required. Central to Stone's understanding of the Christian gospel was Jesus' proclamation of the kingdom of God—a kingdom whose citizens abandoned self-interest for the sake of poor and marginalized people and whose allegiance to that kingdom required them to abandon the sword. In fact, Stone believed that allegiance to the kingdom of God precluded allegiance to any other kingdom or power on earth, and for that reason he refused even to vote. Believing that the kingdom of God would eventually triumph over all the earth, Stone and his colleagues sought to live their lives as if the kingdom had triumphed even in the here and now.

I argued in *Reviving the Ancient Faith: The Story of Churches of Christ in America* that Stone and his immediate colleagues launched within Churches of Christ a tradition—i.e., a sizable segment of Churches of Christ—that embraced those values from the early nineteenth century until World War I when the fervor of patriotic nationalism dealt that tradition a mortal blow. Key leaders in that tradition included Stone who birthed it, Tolbert Fanning who led in the second generation, David Lipscomb and James A. Harding who led in the third generation, and J. N. Armstrong and R. H. Boll who led in the fourth generation.

And once we name the third- and fourth-generation leaders of that tradition, we begin to realize why the letters contained in this volume are so important to the history of Churches of Christ, for Pattie Hathaway Armstrong was the daughter of J. N. Armstrong (1870–1944) and Ida Woodson Harding Armstrong (1879–1971) who, in turn, was the daughter of James A. Harding (1848–1922) and Pattie Cobb Harding (1853–1945). The couple whose lives these letters document stood, therefore, at the very heart of that strong tradition in Churches of Christ so committed to living out Jesus' vision of the kingdom of God.

These letters are also important for the light they shed on the extraordinary importance of education among Churches of Christ—a commitment that has characterized an important strand of those churches from the early nineteenth century until now. Today Churches of Christ produce biblical scholars in numbers far out of proportion to the size of the denomination, and some of the leading biblical scholars in the world come from that tradition. That reality can be traced squarely to Alexander Campbell whose passion to discover and grasp the truths of the biblical text led him to establish Bethany College in Bethany, Virginia (now West Virginia), in 1840. Bethany, in turn, stands at the forefront of a long line of colleges established by members of that tradition.

Campbell and Bethany College are important to the story told by the letters contained in this book since Pataway's maternal grandfather, James A. Harding, attended Bethany College as a young man and there imbibed the passion for biblical truth so characteristic of the Campbellian tradition. Then, in 1891, Harding joined with David Lipscomb to establish in Nashville, Tennessee, the Nashville Bible School—a college committed to biblical learning, secular learning, and especially the propagation of the biblical vision of the kingdom of God. The Nashville Bible School survives today as Lipscomb University in Nashville, Tennessee.

In 1901, Harding left Nashville to establish a similar school—Potter Bible College in Bowling Green, Kentucky, and J. N. Armstrong served on his faculty. In 1905, Armstrong left Bowling Green to help establish the Western Bible and Literary College in Odessa, Missouri. And in 1908, Armstrong became president of another school established by members of Churches of Christ—Cordell Christian College in Cordell, Oklahoma. It was there, as students at Cordell Christian College in Oklahoma, that Pattie Hathaway Armstrong and Lloyd Cline Sears first met.

In reading the letters in this collection, one quickly discovers how deeply committed Cline and Pataway were to the cause of Christian education—what Cline called in one of his letters to Pataway "the greatest work in the world," a phrase that inspired the title of this book. Indeed, Cline and Pataway typified the strong intellectual legacy that has been central to Churches of Christ since the days of Alexander Campbell. Both earned college degrees—Pataway with her BA degree in English and speech and Cline with his PhD in English—and committed their lives to enlarging the sphere of education in Churches of Christ.

But these letters also reflect an equally strong anti-intellectual tradition at work in Churches of Christ, a tradition that Cline encountered in some of the congregations he attended while a student, first at the University of Oklahoma and then at the University of Kansas. Alexander Campbell with his passion to discover biblical truth in order to restore the ancient church clearly stands at the fountainhead of the intellectual side of Churches of Christ. In a backhanded sort of way, he also stands at the fountainhead of the anti-intellectual tradition that so bedeviled Cline during his student days—a tradition that thrived among people who assumed that they had fully discovered biblical truth and fully restored the ancient church. For such people, there was nothing left to learn. Further, armed with the typical American passion for freedom and autonomy, many of these people feared that colleges would in time dominate the local churches. Accordingly, in some of the letters in this collection, Cline and Pataway comment on the opposition to colleges they encountered among some of their brothers and sisters in Churches of Christ.

While all the schools established by Lipscomb, Harding, and Armstrong—the Nashville Bible School, Potter Bible College, the Western Bible and Literary College, and Cordell Christian College—promoted education and the life of the mind, each of them also promoted the biblical vision of the kingdom of God and graduated scores of preachers who kept that vision alive among Churches of Christ for many years. And because the Nashville Bible School stood at the fountainhead of that educational tradition, editor Elizabeth Parsons speaks in this text of the Nashville Bible School Tradition, NBST for short. The letters in this text clearly illumine the commitment of both Cline and Pataway to the biblical vision of the kingdom of God and testify to the fact that they stood squarely in the Nashville Bible School tradition.

Of all these schools, the story of Cordell Christian College is especially poignant. President Armstrong, the board of trustees, the faculty, and the students virtually all embraced the biblical vision of the kingdom of God which for them meant that they could not participate in human warfare. But that commitment collided head-on with the euphoric patriotism and passionate war fever generated by World War I, once the United States entered that war in 1917. Accordingly, Cline reported in a letter dated August 16, 1918, that "the school has closed. We have had such severe persecution from brethren and the county Council of Defense [i.e., local selective service office] that we have had to discontinue." Cline's reference to "persecution from brethren" testifies to the fact that by 1918, the biblical vision of the kingdom of God commanded the allegiance of an ever-shrinking minority among Churches of Christ.

All the schools that stood in the Nashville Bible School tradition were precursors to Harding College in Searcy, Arkansas, today a major academic institution serving Churches of Christ, and Lloyd Cline Sears in time would serve as both professor of English and academic dean at that institution. He retired from the deanship in 1960.

Many students who were fortunate enough to attend Harding College in the 1940s and 1950s, and even into the 1960s, can recall the way the biblical vision of the kingdom of God informed that institution through the teaching and example of professors like Lloyd Cline Sears, his son and biologist Jack Wood Sears, Bible professor Andy T. Ritchie, and Greek professor Leslie Burke, to name but a few.

Beyond the two themes that dominate these letters—the commitment of the letter writers both to Christian education as "the greatest work in the world" and to the biblical vision of the kingdom of God—these letters reveal other important themes as well. Among those themes are attitudes toward race, class, and gender that typified the American Southwest in the early twentieth century. Because editor Parsons has explored those themes—and others—quite fully in her introduction, there is no need for me to explore them here.

The only thing now left for me to say is how immensely grateful I am to Elizabeth Parsons for inviting me to play a small role in this book by writing this Foreword. She has honored me, indeed.

Richard T. Hughes
Messiah College
Grantham, Pennsylvania

Acknowledgments

This project could not have reached its present level of precision and dissemination without the consistent encouragement of Thomas H. Olbricht of Pepperdine University, who has wisely shepherded both it and me. His direct knowledge of my forebears and involvement in the production of this work have made the difference at every point along the way. With that involvement has come the hospitable, insightful presence of Dorothy Olbricht. Memories of times spent with them in fellowship, interspersed with work, are very dear to me.

Richard T. Hughes of Messiah College and Larry R. Long of Harding University have supported the research, writing, and presentation of material over an extended period of time. Given heavy professional responsibilities, their writing of foreword and afterword respectively especially honors me. No doubt their involvement would make the letter writers smile.

The inspiration of my mentor at Boston University School of Theology, Dana Robert, helped me realize the value of these letters when I first stumbled on them. Dana's support of the project through the Center for Global Christianity and Mission has also given this work a reach it would not otherwise have had.

There are others who deserve public thanks, as well. Early in the research phase, Don Haymes of Christian Theological Seminary went to lengths I cannot fully appreciate to identify people named in the letters. He also generously helped me think through the initial project proposal, doing so from an atypical, stimulating perspective. My primary contact in

Oklahoma, Janis Donley Hall, provided introductions that led to insights I never would have had otherwise. She and her husband, Van, offered exceptional hospitality during a research trip to Cordell and I remain grateful for their friendship. Wayne Boothe of the Washita County Museum granted lengthy interviews, freely sharing information that proved vital to understanding the letters' contexts. Kristy Spaulding of the Oklahoma State University Extension office cheerfully helped with some technical matters. Penny Carpenter of Clinton helped make a variety of connections clearer. That she is the granddaughter of my grandmother's good friend imparted a full circle feeling to our time together. Various members of the Oklahoma Christian University community in Edmond have given generous, ongoing assistance. Tamie Willis, Jennifer Compton, Kathleen Fuller, and April Ford of the University's library and archives provided research space, advice, technological access, and permissions of various kinds. Their involvement has significantly enlivened and clarified this work. William Kooi, professor of Bible who is investigating angles of the Cordell Christian College story himself, has provided encouragement and camaraderie. In Norman, Jacquelyn Slater of the University of Oklahoma enthusiastically offered access to their Western History Collections while Magen Bednar of the University's Bizzell Library tracked down an obscure, pertinent record. Also from Norman, Don Symcox provided background on a family often mentioned in the letters. From Odessa, Missouri, Lisa Ziegler filled in some knowledge gaps about Western Bible and Literary College. At Harding University in Searcy, Arkansas, Nancy Tackett diligently searched for and found another obscure, pertinent record. From Abilene, Texas, Darryl and Anne Tippens (whose forebears and mine were close friends and colleagues) have shared information and wisdom, providing more full circle experiences. Matthew Wimer and others at Wipf and Stock have been most pleasant, professional, and prompt in all dealings.

My cousin, Pattie Sue Sears, read the manuscript, answered questions, and has shown remarkable support. My siblings, Sarah Louise Sears, Anne Harding Logan, and Robert Kern Sears saw to it that funding to complete this project was made available just when it was most needed. They have also good-naturedly fielded a slew of preoccupied emails from me in the midst of their own responsibilities these past few years. Additionally, Sarah read through the entire manuscript and has provided technical assistance with an artistic flair on a variety of fine points. My husband, Lin Parsons, has been encourager-in-chief on this project as he is in every aspect of my life.

Chronology

1891   David Lipscomb and James Alexander Harding establish the Nashville Bible School in Nashville, Tennessee.

1895   Lloyd Cline is born to James Matthias and Martha Ellen Sears in Odon, Indiana.

1898   Ida Woodson Harding and John Nelson Armstrong marry in Nashville.

1899   Pattie Hathaway is born to the Armstrongs in Nashville.

1900   The Hardings leave Nashville to establish Potter Bible College in Bowling Green, Kentucky. The Armstrongs accompany them.

1903   The Sears family moves to Kiowa, Kansas.

1905   The Armstrongs move to Odessa, Missouri, to establish Western Bible and Literary College.

1906   The Churches of Christ are listed separately from the Disciples of Christ for the first time in the federal religious census.

1907   Citizens and members of the Church of Christ in Cordell, Oklahoma open a Christian school. The Armstrongs leave Missouri due to his ill health and move to New Mexico. Later that year, J. N. Armstrong is invited to become president of Cordell Christian College.

1908   The Armstrongs move to Oklahoma.

Chronology

1909	Cline Sears enrolls in the high school at Cordell Christian College.
1912	Ill health forces J. A. Harding's resignation from Potter Bible College. The Hardings move to Atlanta, Georgia.
1913	Potter Bible College closes.
1915	Members of the Churches of Christ in Harper, Kansas, open a Christian school.
1916	Western Bible and Literary College closes. Cline graduates from Cordell Christian College.
1917	The United States enters World War I. Cline and Pataway marry in Cordell. David Lipscomb dies in Nashville.
1918	Pataway graduates from the high school at Cordell Christian College. Jack Wood is born to Pataway and Cline in Cordell. Cordell Christian College closes prior to the 1918–19 academic year. Cline obtains a teaching job at Harper College; the Armstrongs move to Harper as well. Nashville Bible School is renamed David Lipscomb College. World War I concludes.
1919	J. N. Armstrong assumes the presidency of Harper College. Cline receives his BA degree from the University of Oklahoma, Norman.
1920	James Kern is born to Pataway and Cline in Harper.
1921	Cline earns his MA in English at the University of Kansas, Lawrence. The school in Cordell reopens as a junior college under the name Western Oklahoma Christian College.
1922	J. A. Harding dies in Atlanta.
1924	Harper College and Arkansas Christian College in Morrilton, Arkansas merge to form Harding College. The Armstrong and Sears families move to Morrilton. J. N. Armstrong becomes president of the new school.
1934	Harding College moves from Morrilton to Searcy, Arkansas.
1935	Cline completes his PhD studies in English, with a specialization in Shakespeare, at the University of Chicago.
1936	J. N. Armstrong retires from the presidency of Harding College. George S. Benson succeeds him in the presidency.
1941	Pataway earns her BA in English and Speech at Harding College.
1944	J. N. Armstrong dies in Searcy.

1945	Pattie Cobb Harding dies in Atlanta.
1960	Cline retires from the academic deanship of Harding College.
1971	Woodson Armstrong dies in Searcy.
1977	Pataway dies in Searcy.
1979	Harding College becomes Harding University.
1986	Cline dies in Searcy.

Cordell Christian College administration and dormitory buildings
Photo credit: Oklahoma Christian University Archives, Cordell collection

Jack and Woodson Armstrong at Cordell
Photo credit: Oklahoma Christian University Archives, Cordell collection

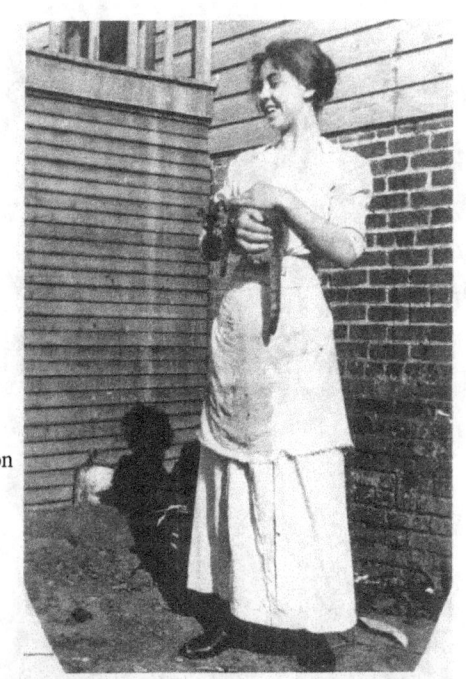

Pataway at Cordell
Photo credit: Oklahoma Christian
University Archives, Cordell collection

Cline at Cordell
Photo credit: Oklahoma Christian
University Archives, Cordell collection

Pattie Hathaway Armstrong
c. 1915

Pataway and friend Ira
Warlick at a school picnic
c. 1915

Young men preparing to preach c. 1914. Cline Sears, seated front row third from left; J. D. Armstrong, front row extreme right with Ben Randolph next to him; J. N. Armstrong, second row center; Homer Rutherford, second row extreme right
Photo credit: Oklahoma Christian University Archives, Cordell collection

Cline Sears, front row center, Dean of Harper College, 1920

Introduction

The Context

The Churches of Christ offer an approach to Christianity that rests, in part, on assuming a sense of corporate historyless-ness. The irony is that these churches actually have deep roots in the Christian spiritual and Western intellectual traditions.[1] Over the past few decades, historians, theologians, and sociologists—many also members of the Churches of Christ—have been piecing together this heritage[2] perhaps in the spirit of an African proverb that says, "You cannot know where you are going unless you know where you have come from."

A brief synopsis of where the Churches of Christ have come from includes "four sets of roots: (1) the biblical documents left by the primitive church . . . (2) the restorationist side of the Protestant Reformation . . . (3) the Enlightenment of the seventeenth and eighteenth centuries . . . and (4) the Stone-Campbell Movement of Barton Stone, Walter Scott, and the

---

1. On both the points of historyless-ness and rootedness, see Hughes, *Reviving the Ancient Faith*, 1–2, 4–8 and Hicks and Valentine, *Kingdom Come*, 15.

2. In addition to sources already cited, some of the most recent examples are: Williams et al., *Stone-Campbell Movement*, and Foster et al., *Encyclopedia of the Stone-Campbell Movement*. See also an older, but most valuable, work: Young, *History of Colleges*.

Campbells in nineteenth-century America."[3] The terms "Restoration Movement" and "Stone-Campbell Movement" have both served as shorthand ways of referring to this rich heritage with the Churches of Christ being one of the three contemporary branches of the whole. The other two branches are the Christian Church (Disciples of Christ) and the independent Christian Churches/Churches of Christ.[4]

Scholars examining the Stone-Campbell Movement have often concentrated their efforts on matters of public concern. This is not unusual. Societies and groups typically have public (or dominant) and private (or alternate) self-understandings with the public stances usually being the ones recorded for posterity. In the Churches of Christ's case, public self-understanding has tended to focus on doctrinal matters and corporate worship practices. So, if asked, "What characterizes the Churches of Christ?" someone raised in the tradition might well respond with examples such as trying to "speak where the Bible speaks"; practicing immersion baptism of adult believers; and using only *a capella* singing in worship. Extant materials reveal a fair amount about many of the men who argued these sorts of ideas via debates and circulars.[5] But information on the daily lives of members, especially in the early twentieth century when the tradition's distinctive identity was

---

3. Allen and Hughes, *Discovering Our Roots*, 6.

4. Separation of the Churches of Christ and the Disciples of Christ began largely along regional lines following the Civil War. Official recognition followed with the 1906 government census of churches. Foster et al., *Encyclopedia of the Stone-Campbell Movement*, 76. See also Hicks and Valentine, *Kingdom Come*, 9. Since the official distinction between these two branches took place only nine years before the correspondence in this volume began, the writers of these letters might have had a fluid understanding of the relationship between the Disciples of Christ and the Churches of Christ. The second major schism in the Stone-Campbell Movement involved the breaking off of the independent Christian Churches/Churches of Christ from the Disciples of Christ. This division, taking place in the 1920s and 1930s, generally revolved around differences of viewpoint on local versus institutional identity and control of resources. Foster et al., *Encyclopedia of the Stone-Campbell Movement*, 185. When referring to the overall tradition, the present work uses the term *Stone-Campbell Movement* in accord with the most contemporary research.

5. Women's public contributions in this arena have been far outnumbered by those of men and the subject of gender is addressed at a point further on in this text. Hughes has observed that written publications and their editors historically functioned in the Churches of Christ as bishops have in other denominations. By this he means that the transmission of theological concepts and shaping of adherents' ideals often have taken place via publications rather than through priestly or papal proclamations. Hughes, *Reviving the Ancient Faith*, 10. Similarly, Hicks and Valentine, *Kingdom Come*, 21, use the term *editor-bishops* to describe the role of publishers and editors in the Churches of Christ.

coalescing, is less available.[6] The disparity between accessible source materials is relevant to our current understanding because too much focus on public talk about matters of intellectual concern or corporate practice can affect how we understand the tradition's overall purpose and significance.

Fortunately, the tradition's public records also contain clues about what it has meant to *be* members of the Churches of Christ. The felt motives for what people in those early years did; what they held most dear; even where and how they lived—these things are occasionally discernible in public documents. For example, the published quarrels over particular practices or scriptural interpretations that may seem tedious or irrelevant today were frequently conducted with great passion. The passion itself is worth noting because it suggests that behind those intellectual interests were strong emotional commitments of the sort that saw God as having a powerful claim over the whole of life.

Since leaders of the tradition would have viewed the whole of life as encompassing an eternal soul and a temporal body, their doctrinal debates mattered. But so did the everyday world. In fact, it mattered so much that some in the Stone-Campbell Movement wanted to live as if the heavenly existence they anticipated had already begun on earth. For American Christians who had endured this country's bloody and disruptive nineteenth century, such a perspective could hold understandable appeal. But by the early twentieth century, earthly existence for many in the United States had begun to seem more inviting. Humanity generally appeared to be making great intellectual and material gains. America in particular was enjoying unprecedented political power and economic growth. So, focus on more temporal—rather than eternal—matters began to intrigue many, including large numbers of American Christians.

Such changing times presented opportunities and dilemmas for everyone as is true of our own era[7] and, because it really does help to know where we have come from, the letters transcribed here are significant. They give us a sense of what life was like a century ago—at least for one small region, according to one family powerfully committed to the kingdom of God. This collection of correspondence increases our knowledge of private, or everyday, life in that setting and offers some inspiration for the future.

6. Hooper declares 1906 to 1930 to be an era in which the Churches of Christ were looking for focus and direction. This happened in part because the generation that shaped the fertile period of the late 1800s was dying off. David Lipscomb, for instance, died in 1917 and J. A. Harding in 1922. Hooper, *Distinct People*, 66. The early twentieth century was also a time when the United States as a whole was trying to comprehend the country's rising international importance. Hicks and Valentine, *Kingdom Come*, 27.

7. See discussions of the ferment of the times in Williams et al., *Stone-Campbell Movement*, 3, as well as throughout Adams, *Epic of America*.

The Letter Writers

The correspondence contained here originates from a family that was prominent within the Churches of Christ for almost a century, from roughly the mid-1800s through the 1960s. The members of immediate interest are James Alexander Harding (1848–1922) and Pattie Cobb Harding (1853–1945); their daughter Ida Woodson (1879–1971) and her husband John Nelson, or Jack, Armstrong (1870–1944); but most especially Woodson and Jack's daughter Pattie Hathaway, or Pataway,[8] (1899–1977) and her husband, Lloyd Cline Sears (1895–1986).

James A. Harding was born in Kentucky to a family deeply involved in the Stone-Campbell Movement. He attended Bethany College in what is now West Virginia, a school founded by Alexander Campbell. Harding then went on to become a teacher and itinerant preacher. Pattie Cobb, also a Kentuckian by birth, was Harding's second wife, his first having died after only a few years of marriage. In 1891 Harding, with his now better-known colleague, David Lipscomb, founded the Nashville Bible School (NBS) in Nashville, Tennessee. Today the NBS is known as Lipscomb University, the oldest Churches of Christ college in continuous existence.[9] Some of the most recent research on the Churches of Christ designates the stream of thought these two leaders inspired as the *Nashville Bible School Tradition* (NBST). The NBST represented an attempt to chart a middle way between a form of conservatism originating with Texas leadership and the liberalism of the Disciples of Christ in the north.[10] Because the present work focuses on educational efforts of this family and their colleagues, the term NBST will occasionally appear here as well. James and Pattie Harding had several children, their first being Ida Woodson, who was born before the family moved from Kentucky to Tennessee. While a student studying expression at the Nashville Bible School,[11] Woodson met

---

8. The nickname *Pataway* came from a childhood friend who apparently found *Pattie Hathaway* too difficult to pronounce. Sears, *For Freedom*, 58.

9. Young, *History of Colleges*, 82.

10. Hicks and Valentine describe the intellectual tenets of the NBST over against those of a strain of thought they term the *Texas Tradition*. Hicks and Valentine, *Kingdom Come*, 17–18. They also assert that the NBST's dependence on particular personalities ultimately figured into the Tradition's decline toward the middle of the twentieth century. Ibid., 194. See also a description of the powerful influence of the Nashville Bible School and the institutions modeled after it. Hooper, *Distinct People*, 72–75. Other research on intellectual forces in the Churches of Christ identifies three dominant streams of thought: the *Tennessee Tradition* representing the general viewpoints of Lipscomb and Harding; the *Texas Tradition* inspired by the views of Austin McGary and colleagues; and the *Indiana Tradition* reflecting the views of Daniel Sommer. Williams et al., *Stone-Campbell Movement*, 89.

11. Expression was a course of study concentrating on "the systematic development

and later married her teacher, J. N. Armstrong, who specialized in biblical languages. Together, the Armstrongs established and ran several schools in the American South, Midwest, and Southwest all designed in the NBS mold. At one of these schools—Cordell Christian College in Cordell, Oklahoma— Woodson and Jack's only child, Pattie Hathaway, met and eventually married fellow student, Lloyd Cline Sears. In time, Cline became a professor of English and served for many years as academic dean of Harding College, now Harding University in Searcy, Arkansas.[12] Cline was also the principal biographer of Harding's and Armstrong's lives.[13] Pataway, whose college degree was in English and Speech, devoted many years to management and teaching at Harding as well. The Sears had two children, Jack Wood (1918–2007) and James Kern (1920–2003), both of whom became teachers and researchers in the sciences. Kern was my father.

Most of the letters in this collection were written by Pataway and Cline during the summers of 1915 and 1916. We also have one letter each from the summers of 1917 and 1918. During this time, the authors were in Cordell. An additional set of letters, written solely by Cline during the academic year 1920–21, also appears in the collection. By that time, the Sears and Armstrong families had moved to Harper College in Harper, Kansas. A few of the letters in the collection were written by Woodson and Jack. One was written by Pattie Harding.

The two shoeboxes containing this correspondence came to light around 2005 in a clean out of my parents' home in St. Louis. Notes in my grandfather's handwriting on the envelopes make it clear that he relied heavily on these letters to construct some chapters of his autobiography. Notes on the envelopes in my father's handwriting indicate that he read them at some point, too. But I had no knowledge of their existence until a few years ago.

My ancestors did not expect their correspondence to be published but I have done so because they make the lives of these leaders more tangible. They also contribute to the record of the Stone-Campbell tradition and to issues of American Christianity more broadly. Since their letters were not

---

of the powers of expression, voice, gesture and platform presence." Its objective was "to make better readers, better speakers, better thinkers." *Cordell Christian College Eighth Annual Announcement*, 31. Woodson oversaw expression studies at the schools where the Armstrongs served.

12. This institution was founded after the death of James A. Harding and named in his memory.

13. Sears, *Eyes of Jehovah* and Sears, *For Freedom*. Readers interested in more details of the letter writers' biographies may consult these works as well as Cline's autobiography. Sears, *What Is Your Life?*

envisioned for general readership, however, we are essentially eavesdropping on conversations that took place a century ago. Consequently, there is a certain amount of reading between the lines that goes into some of the analysis that follows. But even speculative inquiry can be valuable.

Illuminating an Alternate Perspective

This correspondence allows contemporary readers to glimpse lives lived by a family that was clear about their Christian viewpoint and purpose. Their letters illuminate a perspective that powerfully influenced the Churches of Christ during the early 1900s and then largely disappeared from public view a few decades later. Now being revisited by scholars, this perspective is often termed *apocalyptic*, meaning that "the believer gives his or her allegiance to the kingdom of God, not to the kingdom of this world, and lives as if the final rule of the kingdom of God were present in the here and now."[14] Since apocalypticism today tends to be associated with ideas of the second coming of Christ and end-times judgment, some further explanation is important. The apocalyptic worldview of the letter writers did not concern itself with Christians getting out of this world. But it was fixed on the idea that Christians should live in counterpoint to much that dominated society in those days. In this, they were heavily influenced by Barton Stone's skepticism of equating modern progress with the good, his distrust of human made institutions, and his rejection of popular cultural values.[15]

In contrast to the norms of their surroundings, Harding, Lipscomb, and their colleagues propagated a vision of the world in which God's children looked forward and lived into, God's generous reign. Doing so meant that their values had to be different from the non-Christians among whom they lived.[16] Drawing inspiration from biblical texts such as the Sermon on the Mount, they argued that Christianity had to make a difference in how people lived, not simply in how they worshipped.[17] Christians, of course, have largely maintained such a stance for two millennia, but the view at

14. Hughes, *Reviving the Ancient Faith*, xii. He also asserts that J. N. Armstrong was arguably the most prominent early twentieth-century defender of this apocalyptic tradition in ibid., 151. See also Williams et al., *Stone-Campbell Movement*, 77, on Harding's linking of Christian responsibility with apocalypticism.

15. Hughes, *Reviving the Ancient Faith*, 3.

16. Hicks and Valentine, *Kingdom Come*, 31. Hooper claims that living outside the cultural mainstream was a deliberate choice for the Churches of Christ. Hooper, *Distinct People*, 107–8.

17. In the NBST, responsibility reached beyond worship style concerns to encompass "non-conformity to secular values." Hicks and Valentine, *Kingdom Come*, 31–32.

the Nashville Bible School and its model schools made these ideals specific to the times and conditions. For example, Christians were to exhibit loyalty to God's world, avoiding nationalism and patriotism related to earthly governments. This meant that Christians were not to participate in civil government by taking elective office or voting.[18] Nor were they to support political efforts at empire building, especially when such endeavors involved military actions. Further, people working expectantly for God's reign were to avoid pursuing monetary gain in favor of trusting that they would always have enough of what they needed.[19] Their daily lives were to be punctuated by systematic Bible reading, prayer, and regular gatherings of the Christian community.[20] And their daily work was to exhibit compassion and care for those whom dominant society ignored. So, in sum and in language appropriate to our own era, this apocalyptic vision yielded in practice "a tradition of essentially left-wing sympathies for labor, the poor, and the downtrodden."[21]

Training people in such a way of life became essential, with the crucible for Christian formation being the school possibly even more than the local congregation. In fact, the authors of these letters envisioned God's mission as best enacted through education.[22] This, the "greatest

18. On these matters, leaders of the Nashville Bible School reflected values closely associated with Barton Stone's teaching. He held that Christians should not participate in government affairs because political participation could negatively affect Christian spirituality. Stone, moreover, felt that biblical principles gave sufficient guidance for how earthly societies should run. In his view, Christians did have a responsibility to pray for their governments and to be subject to laws that accorded with Christ's teachings. Williams et al., *Stone-Campbell Movement*, 41–42.

19. The "trust theology" or "trust theory" within the Stone-Campbell Movement is a concept particularly associated with Barton Stone who "downplayed material concerns and oriented his life toward supernatural and ethical interests." Hughes, *Reviving the Ancient Faith*, 93. Many of his followers developed a bias against wealth and J. A. Harding—who took Stone's teaching very much to heart—exhibited a powerful conviction that God would supply all material and spiritual needs. Hughes, *Reviving the Ancient Faith*, 131, 137–38. This stance was sometimes misunderstood and maligned. For example, a contemporary of Harding reportedly said, "Harding believes that all he has to do is open his mouth and God will drop the buttered biscuits in." Sears, "James A. Harding," 11. Harding, however, found a biblical basis for his trust theology in scriptures such as Ps 37:5. Hicks and Valentine, *Kingdom Come*, 49. Moreover, there is some evidence that antipathy toward wealth and status inspired the Nashville Bible School founders to see their educational efforts as offering an alternative to that city's elite Vanderbilt University. Williams et al., *Stone-Campbell Movement*, 89.

20. Hicks and Valentine, *Kingdom Come*, 18.

21. Hughes, *Reviving the Ancient Faith*, 156.

22. Young characterizes the Churches of Christ and their schools as having a "close" but "not organic" relationship. In his view, "the school is an adjunct to the home helping the Christian home carry out its responsibility to train its children. When the church wins more people to the Christian way of life there are more Christian homes desiring

work in the world"[23] was to be holistic, high quality, and equally available to women and men.[24]

Illustrating Christian Mission in Action

The intense commitment the letter writers felt for their Christian work meant that serious thoughts infiltrated even their personal correspondence. These letters, then, are more than simply casual chats—though much of that casual talk is quite interesting. They contain recurrent themes that hold clues as to how the authors conceived of their purposes as Christians. We will examine several of these interrelated topics as they emerge from the letters, paying particular attention to the correspondence of Cline and Pataway since it makes up the bulk of the collection.

---

the assistance of the school." Young, *History of Colleges*, 33. The letter writers would certainly have agreed that the home is the heart of the Christian community. But their correspondence strongly suggests they thought of themselves primarily as teachers, seeing their calling in education rather than, for instance, what we might today call *congregational development*. This seems to buttress Hooper's point that schools have consistently been important in the Churches of Christ as places for preacher education and church leader training. Hooper includes J. A. Harding and J. N. Armstrong in a short list of men whose names "are synonymous with education among Churches of Christ." Hooper, *Distinct People*, 72–75, 165. At a time when state-sponsored education was not equal to what could be offered privately, Harding and Lipscomb envisioned small schools springing up in every community where there were sufficient numbers of Christians to support them. Young, *History of Colleges*, 116.

23. See Cline's letter dated June 27, 1915.

24. Aspects of educational ideas expressed by the letter writers were likely influenced by American progressive education principles of that time. Many reforms arose from awareness that industrialization was causing human suffering. So, progressive educators viewed good schools as providing better antidotes to such suffering than would charitable and philanthropic interventions or political revolutions. Cremin, *Transformation of the School*, 8–9, 58. Progressive education movement leaders also saw public education as a means for infusing the notion of God's blessing within students who could then be molded into good citizens. In this view, proper education could "bring about a secular millennium, could make the United States quite literally God's country." Tyack and Cuban, *Tinkering toward Utopia*, 4, 16. The letter writers' perspectives on the importance of educating women also resonate with the views of Stone-Campbell Movement leader Silena Moore Holman who used some dominant assumptions about women's roles to argue in favor of women's education. If women were supposed to be good wives and mothers, she reasoned, then they needed to be educated. Williams et al., *Stone-Campbell Movement*, 73.

Mission and Missionaries

Although it was common in the Stone-Campbell Movement to think of Christians who left the United States for service in other settings as being missionaries,[25] *mission* itself was not confined to activities in foreign, exotic locales. The authors of these letters considered their domestic actions to be the work to which God called them. In that sense, even if they never designated themselves by the term, they were missionaries. Their purpose, or mission, "was to introduce the kingdom into a fallen world,"[26] by creating communities in which people could come to know God and to live exemplary lives. The specific mechanisms through which this mission was to be accomplished were schools, congregations, publishing houses, and often, orphanages.[27] Such small, semiautonomous, and cooperative entities all helped to create outposts of God's kingdom on earth. This model reflected rather standard NBST practice even though elements of the model are not original to the tradition.

Nonetheless, there were some distinctive characteristics of the missional-educational model envisioned by the letter writers. For instance, it was important that these organizations be simply and locally organized. God could be trusted to provide sufficient funds and support, so formal, complex structures would be unnecessary and counter to kingdom objectives.[28] Many of the Christians who came together on Sundays were the same people who filled the classrooms or staffed the schools during the week, but this overlap between school and congregation did not make either body redundant. What all this did, in fact, was provide a means of realizing the mission more fully.[29]

---

25. With the exception of Japan, the conservative wing of the Stone-Campbell Movement did not emphasize international mission work until after 1906. Later on, China and Africa attracted some missionaries but even by the late 1920s, the Churches of Christ had only about sixty-five missionaries in foreign countries. Hooper, *Distinct People*, 81, 84–85. Several of those who did go, including some individuals identified in these letters, were products of the Nashville Bible School Tradition. One of Armstrong's former students once said that he, "more than anyone else in his day, inspired people to go to foreign fields to preach." Bales, "J. N. Armstrong," 28.

26. Williams et al., *Stone-Campbell Movement*, 77.

27. David Lipscomb had established an orphanage in Nashville in 1883. Hooper, *Distinct People*, 79–80. Pataway, whose early letters show a desire to establish an orphanage, would have been familiar with this as well as the orphanage established on the grounds of Potter Bible College, Bowling Green, Kentucky after that institution closed.

28. Harding's practice of itinerant preaching and deliberate avoidance of a salaried job "became the model for the earliest missionaries of the Churches of Christ who would forego the secure support of missionary societies and rely on volunteer offerings." Daggett, "Lord Will Provide," 49.

29. Young asserts that there was "an essential emphasis upon education" in

The letter writers were aware that their model was not the only way that the kingdom of God could exist on earth. But they appear to have thought that other models carried more difficult challenges and possibly achieved less effective results. For example, secular universities that provided Christian houses or clubs had merit, but the odds of this method producing passionate, well-informed, and dedicated disciples seemed slim. This was because future generations of Christians could best be guided and molded by the wisdom of their elders when they lived close together, in smaller groups that variously interacted, maintaining their connections over time.[30] Secular universities could hardly structure themselves that way. Likewise, overarching organizations—such as mission, women's, and children's societies—established by more liberal members of the Stone-Campbell tradition were certainly popular. But they also could distract Christians from God's personal guidance, making ultimate success suspect.[31]

Alexander Campbell's approach to restoration of primitive Christianity. Young quotes Campbell as saying that adherents to his way of thinking should be "the greatest patrons of schools and colleges." He further notes that the Churches of Christ have particularly tried to maintain this attitude. Young, *History of Colleges*, 25. See also the whole of his chapter three on this subject. Olbricht also observes that Campbell viewed education as second only to the gospel in terms of its importance. His vision of who should be educated and how was decidedly progressive for his time. Olbricht, "Alexander Campbell as an Educator," 79–100. Moreover, Williams and colleagues directly relate the ability of Stone-Campbell congregations to attract and retain members to "the establishment of schools." Williams et al., *Stone-Campbell Movement*, 31. Cline had not envisioned becoming a teacher, but his experience at Cordell convinced him otherwise: "I decided that working in a Christian school was the way in which I could best serve the Lord." Sears, *What Is Your Life?*, 36.

30. Here, again, is most likely some influence of secular education philosophy from that era. Progressive educators, for example, saw public schooling as a mechanism for Americanizing immigrants. Cremin, *Transformation of the School*, 67.

31. Hughes, *Reviving the Ancient Faith*, 9, names antipathy to mission societies as one of the issues closely tied to Churches of Christ identity. Both of the Nashville Bible School's founders disliked such societies for several reasons. One rationale they gave publicly was that Alexander Campbell felt "extra-biblical organizations," including missionary societies, helped feed clericalism. Hooper, *Distinct People*, 4–5. David Lipscomb's antipathy also seems due, at least in part, to his objections to the public participation of women as was allowed in some Stone-Campbell mission societies. This objection arose from his taking a literalist approach to biblical texts about women. Ibid., 25–26, 32–33. J. A. Harding, whose trust theology strongly influenced his views of missionary societies, appears principally to have objected out of concern that such societies would divert a Christian's attention away from God's providence. He believed that when people devised specific organizations or institutions, they relied on human constructs rather than on God's faithfulness. Hughes, *Reviving the Ancient Faith*, 138. Both Lipscomb's and Harding's stances on this matter appear to reflect regional cultural influences. For example, by the late 1890s the public role of women in the churches had become an increasingly prominent topic of debate in the Stone-Campbell Movement

Educational Philosophy

Although the letter writers did not seem to apply the term *missionaries*, to themselves they were clear about their identities as educators. In this, they were inspired by the Churches of Christ's historical aversion to an ordained clergy with associated specializations and set apart seminaries. Christian education should be for all. It could also apply everywhere. Here, broader Stone-Campbell Movement interests in liberal arts education seem to have inspired them as well, for the schools they ran included a range of subjects similar to what secular institutions might offer under an arts and sciences heading.[32]

The letter writers were quite interested in the Churches of Christ schools being viewed as credible by secular liberal arts colleges and universities. Even though distinctive differences separated Christian schools from non-Christian ones, the letter writers knew they could learn from and even

---

with the Disciples tending to support women's inclusion. The rationale for doing so, Disciples leaders in the north said, was that biblical prohibitions against women were meant for that ancient time and place. This was a more liberal stance than Lipscomb could take. And even though Harding voiced different reasons for disliking mission societies, on the matter of women's roles generally, he aligned more closely with Lipscomb's than with the Disciples' views. Williams et al., *Stone-Campbell Movement*, 92–93. Moreover, the Disciples' American Christian Missionary Society (ACMS) took a strong anti-slavery, pro-Union position prior to the Civil War. That position seems to have alienated both Lipscomb and Harding, Southerners by birth. Ibid., 44–45. Much later, Harding's son-in-law J. N. Armstrong expressed strong anti-mission society sentiment, but his reasons for doing so seem to have shifted slightly from those of his predecessors. In a fund-raising letter distributed on behalf of a committee creating a memorial to Harding, Armstrong wrote: "It is a well known fact to all those acquainted with the great Middle West that when instrumental music was introduced into the worship and the organizing of various missionary societies in the Church began their destructive work, nearly all the strong churches departed from the faith." Correspondence in possession of the editor, 1922.

32. In the early 1940s, Frederick D. Kershner described differences in educational models employed by members of the Stone-Campbell movement as falling into three categories thusly: the "undifferentiated," "differentiated," and "standardized." The undifferentiated model provided a "broad liberal arts background with a considerable amount of Biblical instruction thrown in." Kershner as quoted in Richardson, "Models of Ministerial Preparation," 49. What we are calling here the NBST model of education would fit in the undifferentiated category. See the whole of the Richardson article for more details on Kershner's models. Although the letter writers referred to the schools as *Bible schools*, and a four-year curriculum in Bible was offered at Cordell, also offered were such things as a four-year program in English; four years of mathematics (including algebra, geometry, and calculus); courses of study in the visual, dramatic, and musical arts; the hard sciences (physics, chemistry, physiology, astronomy); some history, psychology and logic, as well as ancient and modern languages. Parks, *Cordell's Christian College*, 14–16. Similarly, Potter Bible College offered three areas of study leading to bachelor's degrees. These were the classic, the scientific, and the literary. Young, *History of Colleges*, 113.

be aligned (to some degree) with secular efforts.[33] Moreover, they were very aware that good pedagogy, curriculum, and organizational structure were crucial to successful education.

To achieve their objectives, teachers at Churches of Christ schools needed quality training. The best place to receive that level of expertise was at an established educational institution such as a state university.[34] This understanding inspired the decisions for Cline to attend the Universities of Oklahoma and Kansas.[35] There, he immersed himself in many experiences about which he wrote in his letters. Detailed descriptions of homework and extracurricular activities offer contemporary readers a sense of the good caliber instruction he received. Beyond the classroom, Cline investigated a Rhodes scholarship and some study-related travel. Eager to absorb everything he could and, supported in his efforts by Pataway, Cline also seemed intent on demonstrating that small Christian colleges could adequately prepare students for better known academic arenas. His letters contain, for instance, multiple references to seeking accreditation for both the Cordell and Harper schools.[36] Discussions of his own in-class performances suggest he felt a desire for personal credibility as well.

Most of the information we can glean from the letters about pedagogical, curricular, and organizational structure matters comes from Cline with Pataway's observations about her envisioned orphanage providing additional details. Both appear to have favored a teaching approach that was pragmatic yet heartfelt. Cline, for example, maintained that engaging students' passions for a subject was far more important than making sure

33. During this time the basic structures of what could be considered a *college*, including such things as the necessary numbers of faculty members, length of instructional periods, and admission requirements, were being decided. This was largely done via a foundation set up by Andrew Carnegie that included such members as David Starr Jordan of Stanford, Charles Eliot of Harvard, and Woodrow Wilson of Princeton. Tyack and Cuban, *Tinkering toward Utopia*, 91–92. Cline was exposed to the thinking of such educational leaders through his studies in Oklahoma and Kansas.

34. Sears, *What Is Your Life?*, 51, 89.

35. Cline began studies at the University of Oklahoma while still a student at Cordell in order to be qualified as a teacher there. Ibid., 50. We can think of this point about public credibility in contrast to Christian groups such as the Amish who have deliberately withdrawn from dominant American society. Credibility with the world, then, is not always something to be striven for in Christian communities. But the letters suggest it mattered at least on some level to their authors.

36. Cordell Christian College offered three years' worth of work according to officially accredited schools. Sears, *What Is Your Life?*, 88. The College entered into an agreement with the University of Oklahoma in 1917 that allowed advanced standing for transferring Cordell students. J. S. Buchanan, correspondence in possession of the editor, August 29, 1917.

they consumed enormous amounts of information—much of which they would simply forget. He also saw value in teaching students how to apply knowledge gained in the classroom to real life situations.[37]

Appreciation for practical application also may have influenced Cline's interest in starting a teacher training program at Harper College. Envisioned as an addition to standard liberal arts offerings and resonating with secular progressive educational values of the time, such a program would have responded to a long-recognized public need.[38] At the beginning of the twentieth century only one-half of the country's population ages five to nineteen was enrolled in school. Additionally, only about ten percent of youths between the ages of fourteen and seventeen enrolled in high school and, of that number, just around eight percent graduated.[39] Those who did go to public schools were only in the classroom for about ninety-nine days, roughly one-half of today's norm. Public secondary and tertiary educational systems west of the Mississippi also lagged considerably behind those back east,[40] while quality teacher education was scarce virtually everywhere. For example, roughly fifty percent of elementary teachers had only two years' worth of training beyond high school.[41] Aware that most of his peers encountered educational difficulties of these kinds, Cline took a personal interest in establishing an accredited, Bible-centered teacher training program.[42]

Not every aspect of education so engaged his enthusiasm, though. He particularly seems to have discriminated between education as being part of Christian mission and education as being an academic subject. In the latter

---

37. See remarks in his correspondence as well as in Sears, *What Is Your Life?*, 74. In all this he may have been influenced by the thinking of John Dewey who was in the midst of his influential career at the time. Dewey advocated pedagogical approaches that engaged students on multiple sensory levels. Cremin, *Transformation of the School*, 118.

38. Tyack and Cuban, *Tinkering toward Utopia*, 93.

39. Tyack and Cuban assert that, throughout the country generally, high school education outside of urban areas was often more of an elementary school extension than anything else, offering few teachers and few subjects. Statistics in ibid., 21, 47–48.

40. Adams, *Epic of America*, 273.

41. Sears, "Short History of United States Education," 95. Problems would have been especially notable in rural areas where many teachers were untrained and the teaching method often prescribed rote memorizing of outdated materials. Cremin, *Transformation of the School*, 20. See also Tyack and Cuban, *Tinkering toward Utopia*, 49–51. Public school teachers at the time would likely have been educated at normal schools, later known as teacher's colleges. Many teacher's colleges evolved into today's state colleges and universities. James Madison University, "What's a Normal School?"

42. See the description of his own educational path as described in his autobiography. Sears, *What Is Your Life?*, 33–35.

he had no interest, indicating in biting terms his view that such efforts were insubstantial.

By contrast, his interest in English literature seems to have been grounded in deeply philosophical and theological impulses even though he was not very explicit about this. He sometimes talked fervently of the ways in which great literature could inspire students to ponder life's big questions from many different angles. At times, he also interpreted great literary works as if they were close kin to scripture. Given this deep interest in meaning making, it seems somewhat puzzling that nowhere in the letters (or in his autobiography) does there appear an expressed interest in specifically studying philosophy or theology. This lack of mention may have come about from Stone-Campbell influences that understood such disciplines as unnecessary for Christian living. Cline's lack of mention may also be evidence that he was simply doing what the NBST intended to accomplish. He was thinking about how his faith and Christian mission related to his academic pursuits and all other areas of life.[43]

Regarding organizational structure, the schools seem to have operated rather fluidly. The correspondence allows us to gain a sense of this as the authors discuss everyday administrative and managerial matters. Living and working within such a community of educators meant being linked in multiple ways, enacting many roles both formal and informal. But, conducting things this way also produced mixed reactions and results. Reports especially differ on Armstrong's personal approach to teaching and school administration.[44] Overall, he appears to have been a far better teacher than administrator. We can read, for example, Cline's repeated inquiries about the status of certain paperwork in Armstrong's hands and Woodson's admonition that he not offer too many scholarships in exchange for student work. But Armstrong was apparently not the only one exhibiting questionable work habits by today's standards. The letters reveal that Cline and Pataway

---

43. The NBST schools did not offer many courses specifically in philosophy or theology, seeming to prefer that such matters infuse all areas of learning. For example, the 1914–15 catalog for Cordell references the school's interest in preserving the body, mind, and conscience. Hard science offerings that year included physics, chemistry, physiology, geology, and astronomy while philosophical courses included only psychology, logic, and evidences of Christianity. There were no courses in theology. *Cordell Christian College Eighth Annual Announcement*, 8–9, 25.

44. Parks, *Cordell's Christian College*, 7–9, 11. Armstrong was generally thought to be a poor financial manager of the schools he administered. Hughes, *Reviving the Ancient Faith*, 154. This situation may have been exacerbated by the funding philosophies of these schools since there was typically an effort to keep tuition low so poor students could attend. See, e.g., a description of the financial workings of Western Bible and Literary College in Young, *History of Colleges*, 121.

discussed particulars of students' performances even though she was not their teacher. Cline also entrusted to her important faculty-related responsibilities such as grade recording and official correspondence even though she was a student herself.

Allegiance and Citizenship

As noted above, noninvolvement with government in the material world was a major tenet of the NBST. J. A. Harding so strongly opposed even the concept of civil governments—viewing them as seducing people away from God—that he advised Christians to live as if they were foreigners in the land.[45] They should try to coexist peacefully and respectfully by obeying laws and paying taxes. But they should avoid participating in any effort that would advance a worldly power's agenda.[46] Harding's aloof attitude originated, in part, from his experience as a Southerner living through the Civil War. Post-war talk that linked America's rising political power with Christianity may have further alienated him.[47] Harding's colleague and fellow Southerner, David Lipscomb, shared these sentiments. Equally and painfully affected by the Civil War, Lipscomb advocated passive rather than active engagement with political power structures.[48]

The NBST's negative regard for civil government ultimately influenced Pataway and Cline as their letters attest. But Cline, as neither a Southerner nor someone who had lived through the Civil War, may have had a less visceral reaction than did Harding and Lipscomb. Still, Cline had his own reasons for being wary of nationalism. His most extensive comments on the matter concern a display of patriotic fervor in 1916 when the United States was embroiled with Mexico. His observations were unambiguous then and are remarkably prescient now. Shorter commentaries in his 1920–21 letters address the ramifications of Christian noninvolvement in politics. At that time, Cline discussed the 1920 presidential contest; President Woodrow Wilson's record; and the League of Nations. He may have been a nonparticipant in political and military affairs, but he watched the goings on with keen

45. Hicks and Valentine, *Kingdom Come*, 28. Lipscomb was influenced in this by his mentor, Tolbert Fanning, who believed that even voting was "incompatible with the Christian profession." Hughes, *Reviving the Ancient Faith*, 119.

46. Hicks and Valentine, *Kingdom Come*, 28–30.

47. Ibid., 28.

48. Lipscomb's and Harding's own emphasis on education as a mission of God's kingdom was also probably influenced by their southern roots since schooling for the general public in that region did not begin until after the Civil War. Cremin, *Transformation of the School*, 13.

interest and a well-calibrated moral compass. Notably, none of his remarks express anything like the antagonism toward government that characterizes a considerable amount of current American public conversation on the matter. For Cline, being a Christian nonparticipant in government was qualitatively different from being a Christian opposed to government. Still, it is difficult to interpret the tentativeness with which he finally declared sympathies for one of this country's two major political parties. Perhaps he was merely musing casually about politics. Or perhaps he was genuinely uncertain about his stance. If the latter were the case we might wonder how the NBST's long practice of political disengagement affected adherents' analysis of power systems surrounding them.[49]

Cline's letters do recount one instance in which the NBST's non-involvement policy made a dramatic difference. The matter concerned Cordell Christian College's closing over Armstrong's pacifist policy during World War I. This story was long forgotten within the Churches of Christ, perhaps because many documents were not available to researchers until fairly recently. But a revival of scholarly interest in the incident over the last few decades prompts a brief summary here.[50]

Although Europe was already at war when Cline and Pataway started corresponding, American involvement began only in 1917. Believing that noninvolvement with military action was the proper Christian approach Armstrong advocated a pacifist policy for Cordell Christian College that differed from other Churches of Christ schools in the region.[51] College ad-

---

49. Parks contends that Armstrong's antigovernment stance impaired his ability to work with public officials and hampered students' education. Courses such as government, constitutional law, and civil rights, he says, were "barred from the curriculum." But, Parks also observes that no other Christian college at the time offered courses in government. Parks, *Cordell's Christian College*, 21. In fact, the best universities in the United States at the time—all located on the eastern seaboard—did not begin offering courses in political science, sociology, even much in the way of formal history training until the late 1800s. There was a considerable lag time for higher educational institutions out west following suit. Adams, *Epic of America*, 273.

50. Hughes asserts that official division into the Disciples of Christ and Churches of Christ left the Churches of Christ poor and of questionable social respectability. This eventually affected members' attitudes about World War I since many non-supporters of that popular war were ridiculed. Because the Churches of Christ's historically pacifist stance made its members vulnerable to additional scorn, many simply gave in and supported the effort. Hughes, *Reviving the Ancient Faith*, 145–46. This section of Hughes's book contains other noteworthy information on how the war affected the Churches of Christ. For more specifics on the situation in Cordell, see Sears, *What Is Your Life?* 68–85. The most comprehensive scholarly investigations into this matter to date are Casey, "Closing of Cordell," 20–37, and Casey, "From Religious Outsiders to Insiders," 455–75.

51. Sister school Abilene Christian College, for example, grew during the 1917–19

ministrators attempted to demonstrate support of the United States where appropriate by conducting activities such as Red Cross fundraisers, but they advised men subject to the draft to seek Conscientious Objector (CO) status.[52] Most of the school's eligible male students and faculty members took this route and, in fact, applications for CO status throughout the Churches of Christ were high.[53] But, Oklahoma was a region of particularly strong support for the war.[54] By the summer of 1918, outside opposition to the College's policy took such a volatile turn that agents from what is now the FBI came to investigate. Hearings before the Oklahoma State Supreme Court ensued and a collective decision was made that the school should not reopen that autumn.[55]

This was a costly, controversial action on many levels.[56] It put the Cordell faculty and administration out of work; left prospective and return-

---

academic years in part because of "its hearty cooperation with the government during the war. While Cordell Christian College was being closed for refusal to introduce military training, President Sewell agreed to establish a Students' Army Training Corps at Abilene." After the war ended, the city of Abilene gave the college $5,000 "in appreciation for the school's patriotic cooperation." Young, *History of Colleges*, 181.

52. This was standard practice in NBST schools. Lipscomb arrived at his support for conscientious objection after living through the Civil War. His publication, the *Gospel Advocate*, prominently supported the idea. Hooper, *Distinct People*, 109, 124–25. Lipscomb also felt that civil governments were naturally prone to force and violence while rich people's appetites for power and wealth forced poor people into battle on their behalf. Hicks and Valentine, *Kingdom Come*, 146. World War I was the first military conflict in which a universal draft was implemented. The draft encompassed all men between the ages of eighteen and forty-five who were considered fit for service—over twenty-four million in total. Adams, *Epic of America*, 384. There was also a strongly pacifist streak within general American society during the war. Ibid., 339–70.

53. Of approximately four thousand men who applied for noncombatant service during World War I, thirty-one claimed membership in the Churches of Christ. While COs from the Mennonites, Quakers, and Church of the Brethren outnumbered them, the Churches of Christ still represented the sixth-largest Christian tradition among the group. This is especially notable since, at that point, the entire membership of the Churches of Christ was only about two hundred thousand. Hooper, *Distinct People*, 112.

54. Washita County had a large number of German farmers at the time, many of whom were Lutherans or Mennonites who sometimes held worship services in their mother tongue. The German presence in the county also included a German language newspaper so, as national anti-German sentiment gained strength, the local government passed an ordinance that no German could be spoken or printed in the county. Information obtained from Washita County Museum director, 2013.

55. Casey, "Closing of Cordell," 27.

56. Parks claims that Armstrong and Cline misjudged the situation, perhaps because their historic lack of involvement with civil government made them ill-equipped to comprehend their circumstances. In his view, the College's closing was unnecessary and devastated the town. Parks, *Cordell's Christian College*, 21–25. Casey's examination of official state and federal records suggests that Armstrong and his colleagues knew

ing students without a clear route toward finishing their degrees; and shut down a vibrant community organization. But it also provided an example of the seriousness with which the letter writers took their educational mission.

Church Life and Worship

We have already noted the central place schools held in the letter writers' mission activities, but this does not mean that church life was a secondary concern. To the contrary, fostering Christian congregations was the reason the schools were so crucial. Schools fed the churches by providing them with inspired, well-prepared leaders.[57]

Such leaders, the letters suggest, were fashioned over time, not simply discovered as rough jewels needing a bit of polish. So, for example, the romanticism of Pataway's desire to run an orphanage rested on a foundational understanding that the best strategy for molding good leaders involved working with them from an early age. People who had lived within the community from early childhood; progressed through the Bible school; and then went on to nurture congregations in a variety of public and private ways would make the best Christian leaders. So, if this procedure were rigorously followed and replicated, what kind of church would emerge?

An imperfect analogy suggests the letter writers thought of the ideal church as being like a cultivated household. By this is meant that church members would be equipped to think well; to reason, to be aware of nuance and complexity; to have a solid sense of where they belonged; to whom they were responsible; where they had come from intellectually, spiritually, even materially; where they were going; and how they were to occupy themselves in the meanwhile.[58] This understanding rested on values that manifested

---

quite well the situation they faced. Casey, "Closing of Cordell," 25–35. Nonetheless, the dispute over the school's closing raises important questions for any community or movement that is as personality dependent as the NBST appears to have been. Such questions include: What is the relationship between the charismatic leader and the group? What happens to those in the external community when social movements change course? What might be Christians' responsibilities in such cases?

57. It appears that boundaries between these organizations could be fluid. Harding, for instance, considered the ideal church community one that involved worship; education through Sunday Schools; domestic and international outreach and service; and evangelism. Hicks and Valentine, *Kingdom Come*, 111–13.

58. In this we can detect Alexander Campbell's influence. A devoted student of John Locke's theory of knowledge, Campbell believed in the value of empirical evidence and reasoning over that of intuitive, emotional, and mystical knowledge. This made higher education critical because, in this view, Christian faith developed out of rationally discerning God's revelation in the Scriptures. Young, *History of Colleges*, 25–26.

themselves in people's everyday actions. Values such as duty, diligence, sacrifice, reverence, respect, commitment, and loyalty appear embedded in what the letter writers actually say. Also occasionally apparent are less noble ideals and actions inevitable in any household. Yet, the model church was expected to exhibit a unity of spirit even if friction and tension sometimes prevailed in the everyday.

While the letter writers did not speak of a *cultivated household* or overtly mention the values named above, they still held strong views on what constituted quality congregational life. For instance, Cline could be eloquent in linking good preacher training to inspiring congregants with passionate faith. He could also sarcastically condemn worship service and Sunday School content he disliked. While in Lawrence, for example, he seems to have feared that the rising popularity of jazz music might lure Churches of Christ toward more casual worship services. At the same time, he remained unimpressed with formalities observed during some ecumenical visits, particularly judging Roman Catholic practices pompous and silly.[59]

Rich descriptions in Pataway's letters also reveal some of her expectations for proper church life and worship. From her we gain an appreciation of how regular attendance at services was simply part of the rhythm of congregants' lives, providing social interactions as well as educational and devotional opportunities. That Pataway, as a woman, was not allowed to take a public leadership position in church did not appear to chafe her. Neither did it affect her ability to critique the work of male leaders. Here, her assessments were often as shrewd as they were humorous. Moreover, like her mother, Pataway appears to have been confident in her ability to understand and impart Christian teachings.

Gender Roles

Mention of these two women makes this a good point at which to discuss evidence in the letters about views on gender roles. The body of material by and about women in earlier eras of the Churches of Christ is slim,[60] mak-

---

59. Barton Stone had advocated simplicity and avoiding "ecclesiastical traditions of any kind" in church. Allen and Hughes, *Discovering our Roots*, 104. Cline's reaction to what he experienced in the Catholic service may be seen, however, as illustrating what such avoidance could yield over time. He evidently had no comprehension of the deeper meaning and potential value of liturgical forms of worship.

60. Fortunately, renewed interest in the Stone-Campbell Movement is changing this situation. Scholars such as Debra Hull, Loretta Long, and Mary Ellen Pereira are making major contributions to public knowledge about women in the tradition. See Williams et al., *Stone-Campbell Movement*, 6.

ing the women's words recorded here especially noteworthy. Although the women may have written largely to recount everyday news, we can learn much from their words. Woodson, who was only in her mid-thirties when she wrote the letters contained here, is the source of some of the best insights. Her own correspondence, along with Pataway's many mentions of her, corroborate outside accounts that she was a formidable, capable person. As a student, Woodson excelled in Latin, Greek, and Hebrew.[61] As a faculty member she taught classes; wrote, directed, and performed in campus theater productions while also overseeing the schools' residency and dining needs.[62] Moreover, she was sole parent to Pataway and J. D. during the many summer weeks Armstrong was away conducting meetings. All these responsibilities had to be fitted into or around laborious homemaking efforts generally considered women's work in that era.[63] So Woodson (and Pataway) canned hundreds of pounds of fruit, sewed, and performed household repairs. At the same time she exhibited a mature faith, clear comprehension of managerial matters, and astute awareness of politics in Stone-Campbell Movement institutions. In all, the letters reveal Woodson as a woman who understood herself to be a full, credible partner in the work that was her family's Christian mission.

Armstrong, too, seems to have grasped that Woodson was absolutely necessary to these endeavors and not just because she kept his house while he preached, wrote, and taught. Even though we have no direct correspondence from him to her, there is enough in the letters and supporting sources to suggest Armstrong had an appreciation for women's leadership abilities.[64]

---

61. Parks, *Cordell's Christian College*, 7.

62. She was apparently much handier than her husband. Ibid., 7.

63. Some current historical scholarship on the Stone-Campbell Movement identifies within it an affinity for what is called *the cult of true womanhood*, an attitude that dominated middle and upper class American society from the early 1800s until after the Civil War. This attitude prescribed ideals for women's lives that included such admonishments as making sure women were domestically adept and did not call attention to themselves. The stream of thought most closely associated with J. A. Harding exhibited a strong allegiance to the cult of true womanhood. Williams et al., *Stone-Campbell Movement*, 61–63, 92–93.

64. See, e.g., Armstrong's posthumous tribute to Ora Anne Bell, wife of Samuel Albert Bell. "Let it be enough to say here that the wives of the husbands of the Christian school faculties have carried the heaviest burdens, made the keenest sacrifices, and rendered the most heroic service. We husbands know who among us have carried the load; we know who have kept these schools running. We husbands have been loved and praised for our service to the Christian school effort and our names and pictures have become common in the homes of a great brotherhood, while our wives silently and unheard have been the greater servants. It is hardly fair. Do you think so? This is the reason we are making this issue of our paper a memorial issue for our faithful

One of the strongest inclinations in this direction comes from his observations about Pataway's eventually taking a major role in the work. In fact, her father's deepest concern about Pataway's early marriage to Cline was its potential to thwart her flourishing.

That Armstrong saw his wife and daughter as full, credible partners in the work is a point worth emphasizing in light of contested discussions over women's roles that have gone on for decades in the Churches of Christ. Often, the energy in those discussions has concentrated on whether or not women might assume public roles such as preaching or teaching with adult males present. But these letters can help us think about the issue from another perspective: one that considers not so much women's actions (what they can or cannot do) but the deeper matter of how they are regarded (where they fit relationally in the scheme of things). Armstrong's own words suggest his thinking had evolved somewhat from that of his influential father-in-law; Woodson's correspondence suggests she may have inspired her husband and daughter in this way as well.[65]

Although Pataway and Cline took it for granted that men should be responsible for the public leadership of Christian communities, neither one appears to have believed in what sociologists might call a structural-functional idea that God had endowed men with particular wisdom or skills inaccessible to women. Women might not engage in certain activities on particular occasions, but that was not the same as saying women were in essence genetically incapable of doing these things. In fact, the letters suggest that their authors were far less interested in allocating duties according to gender than they were in envisioning how to create the best overall environment for training Christian leaders. We might think of this distinction as a matter of focus on priorities. Two examples can help illustrate the difference. In their early correspondence, Cline's and Pataway's discussions of the envisioned orphanage contain at least as many thoughts on the size of the operation as they do on who should run it. Cline, in fact, was adamant that Pataway did not need him to oversee the orphanage. But he felt as she did that a small-sized organization was best. On another occasion, Pataway explained to Cline that she could not attend a church talk being given by a woman she knew because the

---

co-worker, Sister S. A. Bell." Armstrong, "Sad Loss," 787–88.

65. Woodson owed her strong character not simply to her father but to her mother as well. Knowing that Harding's first wife had been fragile and would cry when he left to conduct protracted meetings, Pattie Harding "always smiled and waved goodbye until he was out of sight, then hurried inside, fell across the bed, and cried her heart out." Harding, himself, recognized the major role that Pattie played in making their work possible (Sears, *Eyes of Jehovah*, 32) even if, perhaps, he could not envision a public leadership role for her.

event benefitted a mission society, something noted above as being counter to NBST values. Pataway gave no indication, though, that she was not permitted to go because a women was giving the lecture. In other words, the problem was not who was speaking but what the lecture was supporting.

The point here is not to say that the letter writers advocated full participation of women in church or society at a time when American women could not even vote. But it is to suggest that maintaining a hierarchical system in which women were subordinate to men was not of central interest to them. Second, while it may never have entered the letter writers' minds that women could take public leadership roles, their correspondence exhibits a sense of shared gender equality notable for that context.[66] This sense of equity also appears counter-cultural to the manner in which most Churches of Christ subsequently evolved.[67]

Beyond anything the letters might imply about how their authors viewed gender roles, the correspondence illustrates why hearing directly from women is so important. The women's letters generally focus on subjects different from the men's, so they expand the scope of what contemporary readers can learn. Many details of daily life from a century ago, for instance, come to us from the women's correspondence. The women's observations also nuance what is already known about certain historical figures and issues in the Churches of Christ. The most significant example of this is Pataway's description of a domestic violence incident perpetrated by a former Nashville Bible School associate. Whether or not this matter has been recorded elsewhere is unclear, but a couple of points about how Pataway and Cline discussed it are worth considering. The first point concerns Pataway's detailed recounting of it in contrast to Cline's brief response. While they agreed that the situation was bad, disparity in their discussion of the matter suggests they assigned different levels of importance to it. The second point is that both Cline and Pataway concluded the perpetrator was crazy rather than criminal. These points say a lot about how violence against women historically has been regarded and about how dominant societal attitudes can influence even those who have reason to think differently on the subject. Nonetheless, that Pataway documented the incident at all matters to the record.

66. Cultural historian Riane Eisler refers to these differing forms of relational organizing as the "dominator model" and the "partnership model." Eisler, *Chalice and the Blade*, 80–103.

67. It seems possible that the cult of true womanhood's power over Churches of Christ leadership in the late 1800s had begun to lessen a bit by the time Pataway and Cline were coming of age. Although they viewed themselves as set aside from society, they were not completely cut off from it either. Perhaps hearing public conversations about women, along with knowledge of their own capabilities, prompted them to shift their viewpoints somewhat.

Thus far, we have focused almost exclusively on gender roles in the letters as related to women, but a few points about the experienced reality of men's lives also deserve mention. Their positions in the schools, congregations, and society generally meant Armstrong and Cline enjoyed palpable benefits. For example, during his year at the University of Kansas Cline attended theatrical and musical performances and pondered theoretical subjects for his master's thesis. He did so while Pataway remained in Harper caring for their two children and working to help support Cline's studies.[68] Although Cline worked diligently and wanted Pataway to continue her own education, he did not at the time seem to appreciate fully the disparity in their circumstances.[69]

That there often was disparity in men's favor did not mean, however, that his or Armstrong's lives were carefree. In fact, the letters illustrate how unglamorous duties and keen worries counterbalanced the benefits of male privilege. Armstrong, like his father-in-law before him, maintained a schedule of itinerant meetings that sapped his energy and affected oversight of the schools he ran.[70] Both Armstrong and Cline also carried constant concerns about and responsibility for the comprehensive well-being of the schools and publications to which they devoted themselves. Moreover, neither one was averse to doing manual work when needed. Armstrong was known to have supported himself by physical labor[71] and Cline's correspondence contains numerous vignettes of his attempts at cooking, cleaning, and foraging for food by gardening, hunting, and fishing.

Stewarding the Household

This introduction might have begun internally with a discussion of the letter writers as a family and then moved outward to examine less personal issues. But there is a sense in which the authors' own attentions were more outwardly than inwardly focused. Awareness of their overarching mission and concerns larger than their own family pervades their writing. So this discussion of family matters is brief and comes at the point where it seems

---

68. She probably helped with Harper College's dining hall since many of her later years were spent managing these facilities at Harding College.

69. Later in life, he appears to have seen this situation differently. Sears, *What Is Your Life?*, 92.

70. For much of his career, Harding continuously led meetings lasting anywhere from ten days to seven weeks, preaching an average of ten sermons per week. Hicks and Valentine, *Kingdom Come*, 20. This kept him away from home quite a bit. Daggett, "Lord Will Provide," 38. Cline went on to work in a similar fashion. See references in Sears, *What Is Your Life?*, 132–34.

71. Sears, *For Freedom*, 92.

to fit best: embedded in the larger context. Moreover, *household*—the same term used above to describe the writers' conceptions of ideal church—seems appropriate here because of its broader connotations. In this regard, the correspondence illustrates how the letter writers maintained an array of interconnected relationships that both nurtured them and demanded care in return. The writers encouraged an extended family feeling, for example, by calling many fellow Christians "brother" and "sister" in a common Churches of Christ and Southern manner[72]

At a more intimate level, Pataway's and Cline's romance, as well as the obvious affection between her parents, prompted the writers to comment on marriage. Two notions seem apparent in these exchanges. The first is that they viewed love between spouses as central to a successful marriage; Christian duty did not extend so far as to suggest that marriage was simply a necessity to be endured. Nor did they embrace an idea occasionally put forward that any two people devoted to God should be able to marry happily. The second notion is that they desired equal respect and responsibility between partners. Pataway talked about this in terms of a *double possession* whereby each partner tried to devote her or his energy to pleasing the other. She may have been slightly melodramatic in declaring that failure to please should cause great distress and her own relationship with Cline followed a fairly traditional pattern. But the essence of her observation is still worth pondering. At a certain level, despite extensive personal doubts, Pataway understood the importance of equal regard between Christian husbands and wives and she did so in an environment where such equity was not at all assured. Cline seems also to have understood this about as well as the time and context allowed.

Since a significant portion of stewardship in any household goes to meals, the number of comments the letters contain about food is worth noting. In addition to describing menus and meals eaten, the letters invite contemporary readers to consider the accomplishment of preparing multiple cooked dishes often for large numbers of people but not always with running water or consistently heated stoves. We can also be reminded of the tremendous labor that went into food preservation and storage while only being able to guess at how much additional work went into food transport and meal clean up. Further, despite there being some monotony to diets comprised principally of sturdy starches, complaints about quantity or type of foods were rare. And the writers make no obvious associations between their fairly simple diets and poverty.[73] From our perspective, an opportune

---

72. This would not have been, however, a habit practiced exclusively by members of the Stone-Campbell Movement.

73. Pataway's description of a church member suffering from Pellagra comes close but, as the notes in that section indicate, there was typically a hesitation to see Pellagra

point for such a connection would be Cline's talk of eating crackers, peanut butter, and milk for daily breakfast and supper his first summer in Norman. Rather than lamenting this situation, however, he took pride in his frugality.

Indeed, the letter writers' general attitudes toward money and possessions demonstrate more a sense of thriftiness than an assumption of poorness. Granted, since most Americans of the time lived on about the same economic plane it was easier for them to view their lives as frugal instead of impoverished.[74] But the inspiration of Harding's trust theology might also have prompted them to view frugality and austerity as things to be desired rather than avoided. At the very least, lack of funds, possessions, and variety did not produce in the letter writers the sense that they had no power or lacked blessedness.

Race and Class Consciousness

The letter writers' economic status did not seem to elicit strong resentment toward more materially well-endowed classes; nor did there seem to be resentment toward other ethnicities even though several passages in the letters are racist in today's terms. These remarks, while derogatory, are not hate filled. They seem principally to reveal the authors' lack of awareness about their own lives and insensitivity to others' lives as well. We might think of such comments as illustrating how this country's social history of structural, or systemic, racism influenced the Stone-Campbell Movement and how it affected Pataway and Cline.[75]

Very likely they had not been previously tested on race consciousness. Since the NBST schools all began as segregated institutions,[76] Pataway, who grew up on such campuses, had few opportunities to meet non-whites on a peer-to-peer basis. The extent to which a youth spent in rural Indiana and Kansas allowed Cline to mix equally with non-whites is

---

as a dietary deficiency because that could connote poverty.

74. While the majority of early twentieth century Americans lived in less prosperous circumstances than do most Americans today, adherents to the NBST often lived in especially meager conditions. This was something they, in part, chose based on the influence of Barton Stone. Stone, who had grown up in poverty, led his followers to adopt a "strong bias against wealth." Hughes, *Reviving the Ancient Faith*, 131.

75. American Indians, for instance, were generally left out of Stone-Campbell Movement activities until at least the mid-1800s. While there was a somewhat better record of attention given to African-Americans, many black members of the tradition ultimately became discouraged with the overall lack of support for their leadership abilities. Williams et al., *Stone-Campbell Movement*, 39–40, 47.

76. Hicks and Valentine, *Kingdom Come*, 23–24. See also Williams et al., *Stone-Campbell Movement*, 47.

unclear but probably minimal. So, their written observations may record the points at which Pataway and Cline first had reason to think substantively about racial matters.[77]

While they appear to have endorsed their era's dominant views about the superiority of European-American ethnicity and culture, Cline's studies at integrated state universities seem to have challenged these assumptions. He expressed shock at easy cross-racial familiarity between students and was repulsed by some behaviors of non-whites. But he was also curious about others. In describing his visit to the Haskell Institute, for example, Cline did not comment on the significance of indigenous children being forced into Euro-American ways. Yet, his mentioning the episode at all suggests he pondered its meaning. Cline's letters further suggest that he understood Pataway to share his sentiments about non-whites, although he strongly countered her possibly subtle expression of racism in wishing for a light, rather than dark, complexion.

As alluded to above, economic disparities between the letter writers' settings and our own mean that they would have talked differently about matters of class than we do today. So a contemporary assessment of how Cline and Pataway, in particular, thought of class has to depend mostly on clues gathered from their comments and knowledge that class consciousness was hotly, publicly debated in the Churches of Christ at the time. In fact, various leaders Cline mentioned—Daniel Sommer perhaps being the most prominent—expressed almost rabid opposition to an educated pastorate and to gentrified elements of Southern culture.[78] Being a Northerner, Cline did not fully embrace habits of Southern gentility but his obvious distaste for Sommer and others who differed with the NBST may signal more than just a devotion to education. Letters written while on a visit back to his

---

77. Those who knew Pataway and Cline in their later years experienced them thinking differently on these matters. In fact, Harding College became racially integrated in 1963 and was the first private college in Arkansas to do so. White County Historical Society, "Harding Timeline." Even though this policy change came a few years after Cline had retired from the academic deanship, it appears that students on the whole, along with many faculty members, had been ready to make the transition for quite a while. Many financial supporters of the College, however, had not. Michael Brown, "Despite School Sentiment, Harding's Leader Said No to Integration," *Arkansas Times*, June 6, 2012.

78. Sommer had been openly opposing the Christian schools since the late 1880s. Hooper, *Distinct People*, 19; Richardson, "Models of Ministerial Preparation," 50. One of his main criticisms was that the schools produced preachers who would introduce "card-playing, theatre-going, pleasure-loving, higher-criticism, church-federations, [and] power-centralizing" in the churches. As quoted in Hooper, *Distinct People*, 20. Sommer also appears to have disliked Christian schools for the same reasons he disliked mission societies, namely that they tempted people toward desiring personal greatness, usurping God's greatness. Williams et al., *Stone-Campbell Movement*, 92.

family farm suggest Cline carried some shame at his own class background. Perhaps this shame contributed to his intensive pursuit of a cultivated mind and lifestyle. Perhaps it also gave him an ambivalent attitude about money since his letters sometimes vacillate between desire for obtaining higher status items and maintaining frugality on matters of personal comfort.

Pataway's correspondence reveals less on class matters than does Cline's, but she seems to have viewed the environment of her youth as having abundant intellectual, spiritual, and social riches. Any anxieties about what she lacked seem generally to have focused on personal aesthetics. Although she worried about clothing and body image she seems to have been less concerned about her standing in society perhaps for at least two reasons. For one, she may not have devoted much attention to class matters because growing up in a community of socio-economic equals prevented her from experiencing significant class difference. Another possibility is that Pataway had so thoroughly absorbed the trust theology views of her family that she had no reason to believe she was in any other situation than the best one.

Romanticism Encountering Modernity

Deep roots in the Enlightenment have influenced the Churches of Christ's dealings with modernity[79] and have done so at the expense of other things.[80]

79. For a good summary of Enlightenment-inspired qualities and their effects on Churches of Christ broadly, see Allen and Hughes, *Discovering Our Roots*, 75. See also the first chapter of Young, *History of Colleges*. Alexander Campbell's preaching particularly has been characterized as exhibiting a "cold-rationalism" that was a deliberate counter to some of the emotionalism present in pre-Civil War American revival meetings. Hooper, *Distinct People*, 10. Intriguingly, Adams cites the 1801 Cane Ridge Revival, a pivotal event in Stone-Campbell Movement history, as exemplifying "a natural outcome of the abnormal conditions in many sections of American life. Man craves an outlet for his emotions, and these had been completely starved in the monotonous, hard-working, lonely, drab existence of the outer settlements and frontier." Adams, *Epic of America*, 115–16. Hughes observes that, while Campbell's generally optimistic view saw Enlightenment-inspired reason and logic as representing necessary human progress, Stone's apocalyptic perspective was more pessimistic. Campbell's stance eventually prevailed throughout most Churches of Christ. Hughes, *Reviving the Ancient Faith*, 2, 122. The Churches of Christ also have been heavily influenced by Scottish common sense realism that "was the means of dealing rationally with both the supernatural and the natural." Hooper, *Distinct People*, 46. Yet, as has already been noted, Lipscomb and Harding were not completely enamored of modern thinking, being more sympathetic to Stone's general perspective than to Campbell's. They opposed, for example, the Enlightenment's Deistic influences on the Churches of Christ, insisting that God had a "personal and dynamic involvement" in Christians' lives. Hicks and Valentine, *Kingdom Come*, 16, 55.

80. See Hughes's argument to this effect throughout *Reviving the Ancient Faith* and in the foreword to this volume.

These letters indicate how tensions between perspectives affected their authors. For example, Cline's contemplations of values differences between country and city life are not simply random ruminations. They also describe country-wide dilemmas as industrialization created rural and urban divisions. Moreover, his accounts of handling ancient Middle Eastern artifacts or debating fellow students about evolution may record the first sustained exposure he had to scholarship inspired by modern techniques. His apparently mixed reactions to such scientifically based inquiries illustrate the NBST's influence and can leave contemporary readers wondering how his fellow university classmates and teachers perceived him.[81]

By contrast, there seems no doubt that he and Pataway were romantics, perhaps ill suited to the modern era.[82] Possessed of potent imaginations, prone to daydreaming, and beguiled by beauty they felt discomfort, even embarrassment, at such tendencies. Pataway, for instance, expressed delight at a pretty hat she bought, then checked herself, perhaps sensing the contrast between her pragmatic upbringing and her aesthetic urges. Cline dreamed about an idyllic future with Pataway running the orphanage, then quickly sublimated those dreams by recalling "the facts" of life as a summer school student on a hot day. Beyond inner tensions over being romantics, Cline and Pataway exhibited ambivalence about what romanticism itself constituted. Classical appeals to courtly love seemed attractive and worthy of emulation: Cline wrote an entire letter as if he were Sir Walter Raleigh while Pataway spent time reading *When Knighthood Was in Flower*. Yet, sensual, artistic expressions such as dance or popular music could elicit strong negative reactions especially from Cline.[83]

---

81. The stance Cline expressed in his letters bears Harding's influence. Daggett observes that J. A. Harding received his training at Bethany College just at the beginning of debates about the impact of scientific investigation and what we today call the historical-critical method of inquiry or higher criticism. Harding chose to reject Darwinism and higher criticism. Daggett, "Lord Will Provide," 32–33. The Churches of Christ apparently did little with higher criticism until the 1930s and Darwin's theories continued to be openly opposed many years after Cline's debate with his fellow student. See Hooper, *Distinct People*, 50–52. It bears noting that Cline, while opposed to Darwin's theories, did not seem to think a creationist stance—as it would be called today—would affect his scholarship. Nor was he opposed to science, as his letters make clear.

82. On this point, see Parks, *Cordell's Christian College*, 15.

83. We are certainly privy to some struggles of a young man in love but unable to fulfill his desires, so some of his remarks could be interpreted as attempts to tamp down his own impulses. Yet, the larger point here has to do with sensuality, not sexuality. While matters of sexuality are subjects of considerable contemporary Christian scholarship, less inquiry at least in the American Christian context, seems to be going toward the importance of sensuality, or what might also be thought of as involving intuitive, sensory knowledge and experience. This lack of attention bears on understanding the

Despite deprecating their imaginative impulses, Pataway and Cline managed to produce appealing letters that are interesting from literary, philosophical, and theological perspectives. They had, for example, a practice of writing to each other as if time and space barriers were irrelevant. So, they talked about handing items back and forth across the distance that separated them; looking at or hearing each other speak although being apart; simultaneously sharing experiences of beautiful moments; and invisibly helping when one or the other encountered a difficulty. They also ignored the time lag between sending and receiving their letters, talking in a conversational style as if on the telephone or face to face. At one point when Pataway had not heard from him for several days, she wrote, "Cline, what is the matter?" even though more days would elapse before she received an answer to her urgent question. Similarly, Cline punctuated his letters with small illustrations and remarks about his activities of the moment that created a sense of simultaneity even though his tasks would have been long finished by the time Pataway read about them.

On balance the letter writers' shared romanticism probably proved a boon to the schools they oversaw. The arts and humanities, especially under Woodson's direction, became legendary as did the relational teaching style practiced at NBST model schools.[84] The writers' romantic impulses may also have offered an important alternative to popular secular education efforts of the time since these were often enamored of modernism.[85] Moreover, their romanticism may have preserved a bit of J. A. Harding's desire that Christians have a spirit-filled (not simply intellectually based) experience of God.[86]

Churches of Christ since the tradition has been so significantly influenced by Alexander Campbell's preference for empiricism and rationalism and his distrust of emotion and mysticism.

84. Armstrong's educational philosophy emphasized mentoring that took into account individual students' differences and personal attention on the part of faculty members. "Each student was to be encouraged to go beyond the assignment and to demonstrate what he had learned. A warm and intimate relationship with the students would help teachers expand the frontiers of knowledge." Parks, *Cordell's Christian College*, 11.

85. Tyack and Cuban contend that modern educational theory of that era was demonstrating its own faith that "progress" could be achieved through "science, efficient management, and professionalism" applied to schooling. Tyack and Cuban, *Tinkering toward Utopia*, 17–18.

86. Harding saw the indwelling of the Holy Spirit as a "necessary supernatural power for living a holy life." Williams et al., *Stone-Campbell Movement*, 92.

Lessons for the Twenty-First Century

Thus far, we have principally focused on how the writers understood and carried out their Christian life purposes or missions within the past. We have pondered how this family, leading inheritors of the Nashville Bible School Tradition, saw themselves principally as educators, helping to bring about God's kingdom on earth through running a particular model of liberal arts school. We have also considered implications of this vision on practical existence, or everyday life, and have examined the meaning of all this for the legacy of the Churches of Christ. If we apply what we can learn from this correspondence to our own era, at least three lessons emerge.

First is the matter of Christian purpose. These letters contain valuable insights for understanding Christian mission now and in the future. Numerous present signs suggest that the modern era of progress and prosperity that seemed so good and inevitable when the letters were written has now over reached. In fact, most Americans later this century may live material lives more similar to those described by the letter writers than to lives considered normal today.

This matters a great deal to how Christians understand what it means to be human and, consequently, how to act in the world. In this regard, the most obvious lesson to derive from these letters involves the issue of pacifism, nonresistance, or—to use Cline's terms—nationalism and patriotism. Since, as noted above, various scholars currently are revisiting this strand of NBST thinking, it only bears saying here that the letter writers' avoidance of mixing Christianity with nationalism is perhaps more relevant in a globalized era of religious pluralism and intercontinental military reach than ever before.

A less obvious arena for deriving lessons on Christian purpose is the realm of everyday human existence in a world where conflicts will likely increase not just over fuel but over water; where food security will be a mounting concern; and with an ever-widening gap between rich and poor. Although it is hard to imagine concretely what such future days might entail, these letters offer hopeful clues as to the potential quality of such living.[87] The wit and generally good humor that pervade the correspondence, for instance, was managed in the midst of financial worries and multiple constraints. Hardships were sometimes more matters of interpretation than anything else. Group conveyance by mule and wagon surely had its discomforts, but it also afforded Pataway and her friends opportunities for

---

87. Hicks and Valentine assert that NBST teaching on spirituality is relevant for helping people deal with post-modernity's volatility. Hicks and Valentine, *Kingdom Come*, 16.

fellowship and fresh air. Summer Sunday afternoons spent locally playing tennis, singing, or eating ice cream with friends cost little but carried great value. Ownership of material goods might have been scant, but wholesome food abounded and workable living arrangements somehow developed as needed.[88] Without much access to cars or certainly air travel, people still managed some mobility and stayed in contact even at advanced ages over great distances. Communal interdependence undoubtedly created opportunities for gossip. But it also afforded the resourceful different ways of earning spending money and assured the vulnerable of help. Above all, a slower-paced life, disentangled from the overly material seems to have left more room for reflection and wonder, for awe of the transcendent and gratitude toward God.

The second lesson concerns learning itself. Various passages in the letters suggest some kinds of knowledge and skills that may be usefully revived in the decades ahead. Pataway and Cline appear to have been adept at identifying many plant and wildlife species. They also seemed quite cognizant of their physical places within the material world. Cline, for instance, understood how important the directional siting of his lodging rooms was to his comfort in cold winters and hot summers.[89] Pataway exhibited considerable resourcefulness in her abilities to cook and preserve food; to launder clothes with well water; to sew and do other handwork as well as to complete strenuous household chores. Today, the need for training, or reskilling, in these sorts of things is becoming apparent in various places despite technology's seductive promises about taking care of every life aspect. Since Christian mission work has historically mounted educational and practical skills building efforts mixed with reverence and faith in something bigger than ourselves, we could view this century as an exhilarating time for Christian education. What greater work in the world could there be than to help guide the making, or perhaps restoring, of connections between the spiritual and material worlds?

Finally and related to this second point, the letter writers evidenced a willingness to live counter culturally to dominant, or popular, influences. Whether this was in matters of personal and public power relations; matters of artistic and intellectual taste; or matters of theological and philosophical

---

88. Potter Bible College, for example, was organized as a co-operative. Teachers did not receive salaries but everyone shared the produce from the farm on which the school was situated. Male teachers received some cash for weekend preaching and song leading duties. Young, *History of Colleges*, 114.

89. Some of the letter writers' spatial adeptness may have come from living in the wide open, level terrain of Oklahoma and Kansas where directional orientation is easier than it is in mountainous or urban environments. But the point is still worth pondering.

import on a variety of planes; whether this came with an obvious or potential risk of losing face, even losing employment, the letter writers were willing to take an alternative approach. They did this imperfectly and sometimes with uncertainty. Yet they did it not just to be contrarian and surely not to be defeatist, but because they had a transcendent idea of the good that could result from God's generous reign. Having a transcendent vision of what can come out of this chaotic and uncertain century may inspire many Christians now to run counter-culturally as well. And perhaps the writers of these letters would find in that a promising prospect.

Editorial Rationale and Techniques

The primary editorial concern from a technical standpoint has been to balance ease of readership with fidelity to the texts. Consequently, I have not included words that the authors self-corrected by, for example, crossing things out, nor have I noted each point at which the writers inserted hyphens at line breaks. This level of detail seemed to add a cumbersome quality to the transcriptions. Obvious spelling errors and word omissions are noted by the use of "[sic]," but punctuation errors such as the use of commas instead of periods or the lack of periods altogether have not been noted. Again, doing so seemed to be more distracting than helpful. Places where the writers used lowercase letters when convention calls for the use of upper case (such as references to "mama" or "uncle") are noted only at the initial incident. Likewise, no effort has been made to change the styles in which the writers identify books, plays, or musical compositions, even though these usually do not conform to today's conventions.

Making clear the authors' intentions on other technical matters was most challenging when the writers wished to emphasize points. This they did principally by underlining various words and phrases throughout. Sometimes they double, triple, even quadruple underlined words. The published text faithfully reproduces in italics words that were underlined in the handwritten letters. But since there has been no clean way of rendering multiple underlines in printed form, a little of the letters' vibrancy has been lost. Enough remains, however, to communicate their points.

Where it has become necessary to clarify certain items, the practice has been to do so via a combination of brackets and footnotes. Brackets, for instance, contain the calendar dates of letters where their authors included only the days of the week or got the date wrong. Brackets also indicate words that can be deduced from the contexts when the paper on which the letters were written has deteriorated to such an extent that something is missing. In cases where too much paper is gone to allow for an educated guess, or where the authors' writing is illegible, brackets contain designations to this effect.

Readers may also be interested in the logic behind the letters' organization within this volume and criteria for parts left out. As to organization, every attempt has been made to keep the flow of the authors' correspondence in the alternating sequence in which Cline left the envelopes in their boxes. The lag time between when each received the other's letters means that responses one day may reference something written two or even three letters prior. So it may be necessary to flip back and forth a little in order to follow some of the exchanges.

About one-third to one-half of the extant correspondence appears in this volume. The primary questions posed before any excision was made centered on whether the material would be interesting and useful to those beyond the writers' descendants and/or whether it would be repetitious and tedious. The repetitious-and-tedious criterion most often applied to Cline and Pataway's repeated assertions of love for each other. Sufficient numbers of these assertions have, however, been left in to document their mutually held ardor. Other sections that were deemed unnecessary included Cline's lengthy descriptions of homework or artistic events and talk about daily life that carried no obvious, broadly historical value.

A final editorial remark concerns identifying information about the numerous people mentioned throughout the letters. The clearest way to keep track of individuals seemed to be via an index rather than footnotes. So, an annotated index at the back of this volume contains the names of anyone whose identity is not made clear in the letters themselves. Biographical details and corroboration of information contained in the letters have been obtained from a variety of sources. Principal among these have been federal and state census records and other primary documents available through Ancestry.com. Relevant facts have also been gleaned from conversations with experts in the history of the Stone-Campbell Movement; descendants of some individuals mentioned in the letters; extensive online searches; and by consulting the archives, catalogues, and other records of Harding University, Oklahoma Christian University, the Universities of Oklahoma and Kansas, and the Washita County Museum, Cordell. Various scholarly books and other publications referenced in the bibliography have been critical to the entire editorial process. Any mistakes of transcription, identification, or interpretation are my own.

Elizabeth Cline Parsons

I

Summer 1915

The year that Cline turned twenty, he enrolled in summer school at the University of Oklahoma, Norman. The impetus for this came from J. N. (Jack) Armstrong who asked Cline to teach a couple of English courses at Cordell during the 1915–16 academic year. Since Cline was still pursuing his own college degree he had to take some additional classes at the university before joining the faculty.[1]

Before leaving for Norman, he had been staying in the dormitory that also housed the Armstrongs' apartment. Woodson and Pataway were there, too, but Jack was away conducting meetings and other students had gone home for the summer. Pataway unexpectedly contracted diphtheria and Cline found himself quarantined in the building with the Armstrong women. He helped with Pataway's care and she subsequently sometimes referred to him as *doctor*.[2] When the danger of contagion passed, Cline left for school and his correspondence with Pataway began en route to the university.

In their letters, Cline and Pataway continued a tradition of calling each other by the names of characters they had played in a school theater production. Pataway had been cast in the part of a young woman named Jean while Cline had the part of her older brother, David. After the production closed they also continued casually referring to each other as *sister* and *brother*.[3] Woodson Armstrong wrote many of the plays at the schools

---

1. Sears, *What Is Your Life?*, 50.
2. Ibid., 52–53.
3. Ibid.

where the Armstrongs served and a surviving script fragment entitled "The MacDonalds of Kentucky" is almost assuredly a version of the production in which Cline and Pataway acted.[4]

Oklahoma City,[5]

Monday Night.
[June 15, 1915]

Dear Jean,

My own little Sister! I wonder how you are to-night, and if you are as lonesome as I am. But of course not, how could you be when you are safe at home and I am in a large city all by myself.

But I am not only lonesome, I am heart-sick with pity for the poor fallen and ruined girls of this city. I never before in all my life realized so fully the immeasurable value of a pure life. Pataway, *nothing on earth* ought to take yours from you. You are as white as the snow. You have never even seen any evil. I have been at Cordell for five years, and all summer and winter I have been with you, but I didn't value you in all that time half as much as I do to-night. You must always see the darkness before you can appreciate the light. But when you have stepped out of the darkness into the light again, what seemed to be bright before now dazzles you. I have had my first glimpse at *the other side of life*! I didn't dream that it could be so black!

---

4. The extant fragment, in possession of the editor, was written for the Harding College Campus Players and so dates from at least 1924. But the reasons for linking this play and the one in which Cline and Pataway were cast about a decade before are threefold. First, the Harding production contains characters by the same names, although David is a member of the MacDonald family and Jean a member of the Buchanan family. Second, in a late July 1915 letter to Cline, Woodson references an exchange between a Mrs. MacDonald and Mrs. Buchanan. Given the nature of that exchange and the context of Woodson's remarks, she was likely recalling the play. Third, Cline mentions this play by name in his August 28, 1915 letter to Pataway. Whether Woodson changed the characters' relationships in the 1920s when Pataway and Cline were already married or whether Cline's autobiographical depiction of the characters as siblings was a slip of memory will remain a small mystery.

5. Cline's autobiography contains a poignant explanation for this letter. "I had never been to the City and knew nothing about the hotels; so I got a room in the first place near the depot labeled 'Hotel.' I was just undressing for bed when a knock came at the door. I opened it and a girl stood there. 'Wouldn't you like for me to spend the night with you?' she asked, trying at the same time to crowd through the door. 'No,' I said. 'I don't want any one,' and shut the door and locked it. But it shook me through and through. I was twenty years old and knew prostitution existed, but I had never come face to face with a prostitute." Sears, *What Is Your Life?*, 53.

I knew that girls had fallen, and that in every city some could be *found*, but I never dreamed that any could sink so low as to try to gain admittance to a gentleman's room at night without his request. May the Lord be as merciful to them as possible! I am sorry for them from the bottom of my heart. I wish I could help every one of them to a clean life. I wish I could have talked to the girl who came to my door—maybe I could have helped her.

Jean, you cannot know how I feel about it. It is now about one o'clock, but I cannot sleep. Just think of the thousands of boys in a city like this, who are submitted to such temptations every-day. It is no wonder to me that there are so many crimes committed, so many asylums, so many prisons and reformatories....

Now, little Sis, since I have told you everything, I think I can sleep. May God send his angels to watch over you and keep you *pure*! Good-night!

Cline.

229 West Symmes Street

Norman, Oklahoma
[June 16, 1915]

Dear Jean,

I have just been studying your picture, and I have come to the conclusion that pictures belong in purgatory.[6] I realize that this is a strange conclusion, but I think after a little reflection you will agree with me. When I look at your picture for a long time, I forget that it is a picture—you yourself seem to be present; but when I start to speak to you, the spell is broken, and I feel your absence ten times more—you are gone again and the picture is all I have left. Then it becomes a torment, and torments belong to the far-away country they call purgatory—I think Catholics say.

But when I think again, I am almost willing to change my mind. For if I did not have your picture, perhaps you would not come at all; this would be much worse. So after all I am not quite willing to condemn it to the flames.

(Of course, I am not in earnest about its belonging to purgatory. I think it would [sic] much nicer just standing on my dresser as it is)....

I met my first class this morning. The teacher, Mr. Ramey, is a nice looking man, but I am afraid that is about all. Anyway I have a desire to be a better teacher, and if I cannot I will not be fit for our college twenty years from now. This recitation, however, may have been accidentally bad; for when he tried

---

6. Cline took a photograph of Pataway with him. Ibid., 60–61. The one he had is almost assuredly the formal portrait of Pataway reproduced in this volume.

to open his desk drawer it would not open. Of course he did not say so, but I strongly suspect his notes were locked up in it.

After he had tried for about fifteen minutes to pull it open, he assigned a lesson for to-morrow, and then took up a book and began to read the author's treatment of business letters, and discussed them a while, and dismissed us. To-morrow I shall have my lessons under Mr. Scott too. I think he will be better....

Your big brother, Cline.

Cordell, Okla.,

June 17, 1915.

Dear brother [sic] Cline,

I am anxious to know just what standing you succeeded in getting at the University. Papa wanted to know before he left but, of course, that was impossible for he left this evening. He took the jitney to Clinton and from there he goes to Memphis. He reaches uncle [sic] Leon's home some time Saturday.

We are no longer in jail. Dr. Kirley came up this morning and took our red card down.[7] He fumigated the three front rooms but we are not satisfied with that, so we are going to fumigate the rest of the house.

If you will believe me, Dr. Kirley told papa [sic] this morning that while I was so sick he thought it more than likely that my whole throat would "fall in." I don't know just what he meant by this, but he mentioned the loss of the uvula. Is that the way to spell it? My dictionary, or rather sister Smith's, is being fumigated. Any way, if I had lost the uvula I couldn't talk. Wouldn't that have been a terrible misfortune to befall a girl?...

Tuesday evening I went with papa to get the cows. That was the first time I had put my feet on the ground since I got sick. We went close to where the Home[8] will be built, then we came back and went to see the pigs....

Yes, brother Cline, I thank God that it has been my happy fortune to have known no real evil. If a girl born and reared in a Bible School is not a pure, clean girl, where will we go to find one? I have never heard anything in my life but pure thoughts expressed in pure speech. Your experience was horrible, but I have confidence enough in my brother, to feel sure that he will

---

7. It was common public health practice at the time to put a red card in the window or on the door of houses where communicable diseases were found.

8. Pataway was planning to build an orphan's home. In this she was probably inspired by the work of George Müller, a theologian from the Plymouth Brethren who was influential on J. A. Harding's thinking. See the names index for more information.

withstand any temptation that may come to him. Will he not? I should be very unhappy if I did not believe this. These poor, *poor* girls of the city have not heard *one* of the lessons that I have heard every day of my life....

As soon as I am able a crowd of us are going out to Ella Gentry's some evening. Won't you go with us in spirit? Maybe things won't be so bad when I can go places. I hope not. I am lonesome.

Jean.

229 West Symmes Street,

Norman, Oklahoma.
June 17, 1915.

Dear Little Sis:

... This morning I had my first lesson under Professor Scott, and I have to admit that he redeems the school, to some degree, for me. He is a fine teacher, but very, *very* rigid and strict.

He asked one of the boys a question, and he answered it correctly except he did not make a complete sentence. Scott looked at him for a full minute; then in a rough voice said, "That is a poor way to answer my question. What is it?"

One must say things exactly right. He said if he found a student in the ninth grade using incorrect language, he would stop him at once and never let him begin Rhetoric until he could speak every sentence correctly.

He didn't call on me to recite this morning. I don't know what I shall do when he does—perhaps stammer and sit down. No, I will not do that bad, but it will be hard until I get to where I do not make any mistakes in English....

... Did you ever think just what would be the lonesomest place in all the world to you? I think it must be among the great crowds of people whom you meet and talk to, but among whom you have not a single *friend*. I am finding it so.

Lovingly your Brother,

229 West Symmes Street,

Norman, Oklahoma,
June 19, 1915.

Dear Jean,

...Jean, I am now forever and eternally, even unto the end of the world, amen, opposed to a *large* school at Cordell. I don't want a school with six or seven hundred students in it. It is impossible with such a large number of students to do the real heart training that we have to do in a Christian College. I am opposed, too, to raising our college to the rank of a university, unless it can be demonstrated in the years to come that we can do university work and not lose our spirituality. This will first have to be shown to me.

I have never dreamed of a school with a thousand students at Cordell, but I have planned for at least five hundred. I am afraid now that we cannot have that many. I am almost of the opinion that two hundred and fifty are all we need or can take care of.

You know in the country, life is simple, and people are unassuming, unaffected, friendly, and sociable. The reasons for this are plain—at least, some reasons, for we may not know all. Country people, however, usually live some distance from each other, and do not have as much intercourse as those who live in town. This fact, connected with the natural longing of the human heart for companionship, leads them to desire friendships and makes them sociable and amiable. In town, on the other hand, men see men at every turn, on ever [sic] street and corner, until they are tired of the sight. Out of the whole multitude there is not one they care to make a friend. It is not uncommon for a man not to know his next-door neighbor, even in a town no larger than this, and in large cities it is unusual if he knows who lives in the flat below him. Such conditions make close friendships hard to form.

In the country, too, all a man has to do is to farm his land and enjoy his family and his friends. He is free and without worry; when the man in town is continually bothered with light bills, water bills, and much more by the competition of other firms and business houses. As competition increases, complications become greater. Thus in every large city we find the most complex business and social conditions, while in the country and small towns everything is simple. (Don't think I am writing a text-book on Sociology)[9]

In our school we allow the students to write their names on paper and hand them to the President or Secretary. Here you must go first to a room of admission, next to the registry, then to Professor Phelan, and then to the treasurer. They have a very complex system of enrollment, and just as complex

---

9. This parenthetical remark is inserted in the text as if written after Cline reread his letter.

system of classes. I have one pamphlet to tell me what courses the school offers, a second one to tell me where the classes meet and at what hours, and a third to tell me what books I am to read in my different classes. [I] have just three classes, but I have not yet learned the periods in which they meet, without consulting my pamphlet.

Of course, all this is necessary in a large university—and this one has only about five hundred students—but such complexity and formality really kills all chance to come in close touch with the student. In one of my classes I have just five or six classmates and we are getting acquainted pretty well. In both my others, I have fully fifty, and if it were not summer there would be a hundred or more. In these classes, I don't know the name of a single student. Even Dr. Scott has to keep a list at hand from which to ask questions. Certainly he can't have the influence with those students he could have if he knew each one of them, and did not have to look down at his list every time he called a name.

Where there are so many students it is impossible to do the work we must do. So we must expect to have a small school always. And, Jean, to tell the truth I like [word missing] so much better. There every one knew every one else, and all had an interest in each other. Here it would take you a year to learn a man's name. I have tried it to see. Whoever I ask doesn't know anything about him. They are perfect strangers, and so is every one else. Of course, we all talk with one another, go to school with one another, and eat together, but that is as far as it goes. I don't know the name of the boy who eats by me—on [word missing] side—I know the one on the north, for I saw his name printed on his clothes pin (they use clothes pins for napkin rings).

In conditions as they are here, and such as they must be in every large school, it would be impossible to have any Christian influence over the students....

Cline

Saturday, June 19, 1915.

Dear brother Cline,

Do you want to know what I am doing this hot afternoon? I am cleaning house—not right now, of course, for I am writing to you, but I have been all day. You may thank your lucky stars that you are not here, for if you were, we would put you to work. We have been at it for two days now and the worst part about it is, we are not through yet. We have cleaned out every box, drawer, and pigeonhole on the place. Monday we'll wash windows and picture glasses. Then we'll be through....

Bro. Valentine came over this morning and fixed our screens for us and now I am going to fight flies until we won't have any when you come home. Flies are a disgrace to people and we have two billion. I am going to get rid of them in a little while though....

Bro. Homer has just been in and brought us a wild grape pie. He said I might have it if Dr. Sears would let me eat it. I told him Dr. Sears was not here and I could do as I wanted to, so I will have grape pie for supper....

Jean

Norman, Oklahoma,

June 20, 1915.

Dear little Sister,

I too am *glad* and *very, very* thankful that your throat did not decay as Dr. Kirley feared. God has been so good to us that we can never begin to repay him. Jean, it would have been terrible if you could never have talked again! I *love* to hear you talk, and if that had happened—I don't know what all of us would have done.

But still that would have been better than for you to have died—*much* better. If you couldn't talk, you would still be here, and that is *everything*. Maybe I am selfish, Sis, but honestly I don't see how I could give up my *very best* sister. I wouldn't care any more about the Orphan's Home; for it is *yours*, and it would be rank sacrilege for another to run it. And besides there would be no other fit to run it. I think the whole dream would vanish.... I would much rather die myself than that you should die; for I really believe you can do far more good in the world than I can ever do. Your influence in the Orphan's Home will make more than fifty preachers, whereas I would be only one,—and a rather poor one at that....

I went out walking yesterday afternoon and evening with myself. I had never been on the other side of the University buildings and I wanted to see what was there.

The campus is about one hundred and twenty acres, covered with trees and grass. Around the buildings the grass is kept trimmed into a beautiful level lawn, but out farther back of the buildings they have allowed the trees and grass to grow almost naturally, and the place has a wildness that is fascinating. Men may cut their lawns and trim their trees if they wish (and no yard would be pretty without it), but the place which has the greatest charm for me is the wild woodland, tall grass, tangled underbrush, twilight and the mourning dove. (Poetic, isn't it?)....

There are ... times ... when one ... is away off among strangers, that the whole world seems empty; then some silent, secluded place is more welcome than a carnival. Our carnival has been in town a whole week now. I think it came in the same day I came, and hasn't left yet. The preacher lectured the congregation this morning for going to see it.

I met Brother Fleming last week and he told me where the church house is. I went this morning, and it was like going home again. Jean, there is no place in the world as home-like as among Christians. I felt perfectly at home as soon as I came inside; I was no longer a stranger—I was at home and they were my brothers and sisters. It is pleasant to feel so close to people whom you have never seen before, and only Christ himself could have made such a perfect fellowship. He has blessed us abundantly. I can see it more and more every day. I think being among people who have never thought of him once in their lives, makes me think more....

Cline.

Monday, June 21, 1915

Dear brother Cline,

... Mama, J. D., and I went over to Beulah's yesterday for dinner. We had a nice time, of course. We always do when we go over there. Agnes, old Bro. and sister [sic] Wright, and Bro. and sister Clarence Wright were there too. The Wright women are good people and I love them. After dinner Mae, Beulah, Agnes, and I went upstairs in the south room, pulled up the windows so we could get the breeze, then we lay down on the bed and sang, (till I was hoarse) talked and laughed when any one was pushed off of the bed.... When it got cool we went out to the tennis courts and they played tennis until nearly time for church. I think I would have tried to have played some if I had not promised to wait until next Sunday....

We had quit [sic] a scare here last night. We started to church and as we came up to the house here Mama and Mae saw a light in the middle north room on the second floor. No one had been here all day so they didn't understand it. Mama said she would go see about it, but by the time she got around to the steps the light was out. She went on up the stairs and into the room, but the light bulb was cold. Then she came into the hall and felt of the one there and it burned her fingers. She knew then none but human fingers could have turned it off and that it had been on. It frightened her a little so she hurried down stairs confident some one was in the house. She didn't want to wear her hat, so she turned to take it off and the light flickered twice and Mae saw it. They got out as quickly as possible and came on to church. When they told J. D. and Raymond about it they said they heard some one walking up there when they came over to milk the cow. After church Mama had Bro. Vaughn and Bro. Geo. O'Neal come and go through every room and look in every closet on the place and Bro. Stafford and Bro. Homer Utley came by. They knew about it so they stopped and help look, but "Evenso" could not be found. The light in the hall would not come on, so we judged that Saturday night when we went to bed we left that light burning. Sunday morning the lights don't come on[10] and so it did not come on until about six yesterday evening and that it burned out from the time they saw it until we got around to the steps. It was a little singular but I think that is the way it was. I am glad there will be a man on the place tonight....

...I am of the opinion you are about our Bible School in the future. We don't *want* a very large one, but I tell you, we will never *have* a large school if we *wanted* it, because the Book is hated too much for many people to send to our school. In all the history of the school work the schools have been small. The Nashville Bible School is larger to day than it ever has been, but it is losing its spirituality—and we must not do that. The Orphan's Home must not be large for the same reason. If the Home is crowded I can not have the influence over the children I must have to do what I believe the Lord would want me to do. It would be impossible for me to know each child's disposition and to know what traits should be encouraged and what traits should be fought and mastered, and, too, I want them to know and love me, but they can not do it if I have too many....

We are going to have ice cream for supper. Won't you come out and have some?

Jean

---

10. Cordell's first power plant began operation in 1909, distributing electricity produced with diesel fuel. At that time, power was mostly used for lighting and was on only during the hours of greatest need—generally weekday evenings—hence Pataway's observation that there were no lights on Sunday morning. When the company prepared to shut power down for the night, customers would have received a flashing signal about ten minutes prior, hence the various notations in this correspondence about lights flashing when the authors were writing late in the evening. Information obtained from Washita County Museum director, 2013.

Norman, Oklahoma,

June 21, 1915.

Dear Jean,

... In my last letter (I mean out of my last letter) I left something out. I meant to tell you just how much I appreciated your confidence in me; but since I have begun, I don't know how to do it. I can't think of how to express it; so you must just *try* to understand. But I do value your confidence, Jean, more than any boy ever before valued the confidence of his sister, and I promise you, for your sake and *because it is right*, that I *will never again* consciously do *anything* that will bring reproach upon myself or any one else. All of my life hasn't been like that, and it is the bitterest thing that I shall ever have to bear; but I *can* make the rest of it clean, and perhaps some time I may not feel the shame of the past so sharply, though I hardly think that time will ever come.

Are you not glad Dr. Sears was not there to keep you from eating that pie? But really I think that is just what you need now. (Doctors are eccentric!)....

... [B]y the time these miserable fifty-six days (seems like fifty-six months) are past you will be able to go anywhere. We will go see our Orphan's Home again. I think we can buy the piece of ground by the last of next summer. We will lay a plan for the grounds, so that we shall know where to plant the trees. Then when we get the place, we'll put out our trees and flowers, and sow the lawn in grass, and have things pretty when we build the house. It isn't ages before we begin to build, you know.

These are dreams yet, are they not? The real facts are that it is as "hot as blazes" here and I have to read about one hundred and fifty pages of a certain history this afternoon....

Cline.

Tuesday afternoon,

[June 22, 1915]

Dear little Sis,

... I have just got back from the University. It is five or six blocks away but seems much farther, especially when the thermometer registers one hundred and fifty. (I'm merely guessing at the temperature to-day).

We have been studying Shakespeare in our class in literary criticism... [he] was a wonderful man, and he grows greater and greater the more one studies him. Yet Shakespeare's greatest lessons are the ones taught in the

Bible. He clothed the simple and direct teaching of Christ in a garb of fancy and poetry, and we cannot say that they always gained by such a change. But his greatness in the eyes of the world, and his "littleness" in comparison with Christ from whom he borrowed his thoughts, only serve to exalt Christ the more....

Last evening I took another long walk. I like to go away off where there are no strangers and no hard books. I can think of you and Sister Armstrong and all the rest at home, and wonder what you are doing, and plan what we will do when these eight weeks are gone.

As I was walking down the boulevard I saw the hose wagon of the fire department pass. The two large gray horses were covered with sweat and pulling at the bits till the driver could hardly hold them.

I came to a yard further on covered with a coat of beautiful grass, with beds of cannas, petunias, verbenas, coxcomb, larkspur, trumpet vines, and hollyhock, all in bloom. An old gentleman was mowing the lawn, and as I passed he stopped and began talking to me. He showed me everything he had and finally told me that he came from Indiana. Of course, we were friends at once, for I am a friend of any friendly northerner—and *southerner, too*. He was almost too old to push the mower, and as he was a pleasant old gentleman and especially since he came from my home state, I offered to come over every afternoon when I could and help him mow it. So now I have turned florist as well as doctor. I shall take strict care that I do not mow all his hollyhocks down when I am cutting the grass....

Sincerely, Cline.

Cordell, Oklahoma,

June 23, 1915.

Dear House-doctor,

This is to certify that crusade against flies has begun. We now have only a quarter of a billion. One sensible fly, after drinking the poison prepared for him, betook himself to the middle of my bed and there gave up the ghost.

... Thank you for permission to eat the pie. The deed was done before your letter came.

Last night was one night! We went to bed early, but about two o'clock we awoke to find the lighing [sic] flashing and the wind blowing harder than it has blown this spring. We called J. D. and Mr. Colson, and after much fumbling about in the dark got our clothes on and started for the storm house. When we got out side we saw lights all about but none at sister Short's. The storm house here is so bad—and then we thought they should be up too—that we decided to go down there. By the flashes of lighting [sic] we could see Mr. Colson hobbling along to the side walk. In the rush he failed to get his shoes and the cinders hurt his feet, but we didn't stop to smile. We stayed in the dugout about an hour and a half, but as nothing happened but wind and rain we came out and went to bed. Last night was the first time I have been really frightened this spring, but the wind came in puffs and the clouds were broken. Scary times!

And the dream would have vanished had I died! No! No!! No!!! surely you would never have allowed that to happen. There are enough of you with out me to carry on the work as it should be. I know the Home is mine now, but by the time the dream becomes a reality, we may find some one with more wisdom than I (and do you know it will take a great deal of wisdom) some one who will be far better fitted to run it than I can ever be. If so I will be content in being her "right hand man" I am determined to stay in the Home and I won't be driven out even if I can't be "boss" there.

You speak foolishly some times. I hope to be able to help make fifty preachers out of orphan boys, but what about the influence of the president of Cordell Christian College over these same boys, as well as over the many other boys in the school. Added to all this is the wonderful good you can do yourself as a preacher. I can't preach (Except privately, you know.) Our dream must *never* vanish no matter what happens....

After you have read all the terrible books your teachers have assigned you, your brain will be too tired for George Müller, won't it?...

An Obedient Patient.

Norman, Oklahoma,

Thursday, 24. [1915]

Dear Jean,

...I just came back a moment ago from the university. I took that list of credits up. I don't yet know what standing they will give me, but I will know in a day or two. I think they will give me even better than I thought. You know I am the first student from our school and that will count some, for the standing they give me may encourage others to come. We are affiliated with the university for only twenty units. If they give me full credit for all my work, they will have to give me more than twenty. They counted most of the things I had taken in high school and gave me fourteen units for them; so I lack only one unit having a full high school course. This I will make up in physics and plane geometry. I'll tell you just what standing I get as soon as I find out.

When I was talking to Professor Williams about it, he almost made me angry by seeming to doubt the quality of work we do. He spoke of our letter head where it mentions university affiliation of twenty units, as an *advertising scheme*. I came very near telling him that our English work was far better than their same work, but I remembered that "a soft answer turneth away wrath, but grievous words stir up anger,"[11] and since I wanted just as much credit as I could get, I made *no* answer. I did tell him, however, to see Professor Parsons, who examined the work in our school, and learn what quality of work we did. I am to see the Greek teacher to-morrow and see whether I can get thirty-two or only sixteen hours credit for my four years in Greek.

I didn't know till a few days ago how bad a beginning our country had. In the early colonizing days $40,000 was raised by lottery by the London Company to settle Virginia. Some grocers ventured £62.15s, and won a silver dish and cover valued at £13,10s. This is almost a stain on Virginia—I am glad it was not Indiana or Tennessee, aren't you?

There was one good thing about Virginia, though. . . . The laws absolutely forbade flirting. . . . Honestly, I don't think—I *know*—that I was not born fickle; but the things I did, I did because I wanted to be a man and I thought nothing else was manly. Of course, deep down in my heart, I knew that it was wrong, but there are times when, if a boy gets in the wrong company, he disregards right and wrong. At one time I thought it was not manly to *feel* any kind of emotion; and even with girls, not to love anyone, till I knew she loved me. The result you can easily understand. I really think I hurt a few girls in that way. I found out too late that I could never on earth be more than a friend to them. From all this experience (which I wish could be blotted out!) I have, at least, *learned well* one lesson, that I will never again try to make any girl love me till I *am sure* that I could not live without her. . . .

Cline.

Norman, Oklahoma,

June 25, 1915.

Dear little Sister,

Will you be very, *very* offended if I should tell you that you are the *most sensible* girl of sixteen I ever saw? I realize that girls of sixteen are "crazy," or perhaps only foolish, and I could mention some around Cordell that tend

---

11. Proverbs 15:1 (KJV).

that way; but you are the *only* exception I have ever seen.... [T]here are no girls who understand so well the needs of our school, or who have such noble purposes. Some of this may have been gained from being in the school as you have been.

I have seen several brilliant girls here. They can interpret the deepest literature with seeming ease, and give logical and psychological reasons for their judgments; they can quote Shakespere [sic] and Milton, and have read Euripedes [sic] and Horace, but few, if any, have found the real purpose in life. I had rather be ignorant and know my true relation to the world than to have all the degrees of scholarship and be without this fundamental knowledge.

I came back a few minutes ago from an interview with Professor Paxton, the teacher of Greek. I told him the work I had done, and he said it "looked like a pretty solid piece of work" and that I ought to get good credit for it. He told me to write to Brother Armstrong and get my grades and a statement of the quality of work I did. I am enclosing a note to him, and you can send it in the next letter to him. I don't know his address for certain....

Your Doctor.

Friday, June 25, 1915.

Dear ever-present brother,

My! didn't we enjoy our day at sister Rutherford's yesterday? Wasn't that dinner good! I know I ate more beans, peas, potatoes, cucumbers, beets, corn, fried ham, corn bread, grape pie and egg custard than you did. And you wouldn't help me drink the butter milk at all. It was great fun knowing you were right there and eating that dinner and no one could see you but me.

Then I wasn't a bit afraid perched on top of the very highest shock of wheat in Bro. Stafford's big wagon, 'cause I knew you wouldn't let me fall.

But, oh! dear me, we could not wade in the creek, could we? for fear my throat would get sore again and you would have to wear your knees out doctoring it. All we could do was watch sister Stafford and Amanda enjoy that beautiful water.

And *did* you hear that impertinent question Amanda asked me? She wanted to know how often I hear from you. I saw you grin at my predicament, for you know how hard it is for me to evade a plain question. You laughed out right when I told her for all she knew I didn't hear more than once in two weeks. She almost heard you that time for she looked very suspicious as she said, "Agnes says she knows you hear from him twice a week any how," and I replied, "Agnes doesn't know any more about it than you do." Her final decision, "Well, he hasn't been gone but two weeks and I know you have heard from him twice," made us look at each other and giggle, didn't it?

What a foolish girl you'll think I am. I'll be sensible now. But, really, you are a great deal of company, for I always had a vivid imagination....

I don't like your Professor Williams. Of course, we use our university affiliation as an "advertising scheme." When you get a chance ask what else it is good for.

I like Virginia's law on flirting, but I wonder just how they went about carrying it out.

You must have had a queer idea of girls, for no well *taught* girl will allow herself to care *too* much for a man until she knows he wants her to. Suppose you found that girl whom you could not live with out, then couldn't make her love you, what would you do?...

Cordell is turning to tramps, I think. The sheriff was in this neighborhood last night looking for one and this morning the passenger stopped and the brakeman put a tramp off! Beulah said this evening they had had more beggars come to their house this summer than ever before, but a great big consolation is, if they get us they'll turn us loose by day light.

I have three days work in one to do to-morrow. I have to wash and iron and put up dew berries, besides what cooking it will take to run this ranch....

Bro Tenny is still afraid of me. He will not come in the house. Well, they did get him to breakfast, no, it was dinner. But he won't stay at night. He goes down to sister Short's. Last night the roof of his mouth was a little sore and he wanted to know if that could be Diphtheria. Now did you ever!...

Jean.

Norman, Oklahoma,

Saturday Afternoon.
[June 26, 1915]

Dear Jean,

...I have finished one of my books, and am beginning the comedy "The Rivals," by Richard Sheridan. I have heard Sister Armstrong speak of it till I have decided to read it instead of those "Iphegenia in Taurises"[12] and other unheard of plays.

I have also about half finished one of those books on teaching English. Two others follow! We are also reading a volume of Stevenson's letters, essays, and stories. Also numerous selections from Keats, Tennyson, Wordsworth,

---

12. A reference to Euripides's play "Iphigenia in Tauris" he had been assigned.

Shakspere [sic], Coleridge, Gray, Browning, Shelley, Cowper—and others too numerous to mention. By the time I finish all these my eyes will be ready for a complete rest of three weeks. And I'll take it, too.

... They are having the Southwestern Tennis Meet at Oklahoma City now. The university here has been victorious thus far. The universities of Kansas and Missouri are represented, and all the higher state schools I suppose.

This is a foolish thing to do. Several of the university boys have been away all week in the games. Of course, they will get no work done, but the teachers give them their grades. We'll have none of this in our school, will we Jean? I tell you what I think. I think our College is the *best school in the world,* and I *love every brick in the building and every scar on the walls.* Now, don't you? ...

Your brother.

Sunday, June 27 [1915]

Dear Jean,
... This morning I was studying my Sunday school lesson, and it got so dark all at once that I could not see to read. I went to the window and the whole sky was covered by heavy clouds, and the wind was whipping the great limbs of the trees outside till the roar was terrific, while the whole house trembled at every fresh gust. But in a few minutes the wind had passed and a heavy downpour of rain began. It was almost ten o'clock; so I got ready, took my rain coat and set out for church. The church house is over a half mile away, and I got soaked before I had gone half way.

When I reached the house, the door was locked. But as the rain came from the northeast, I crept back under the eaves in an angle of the house on the southwest side. Here the water from above poured down over my head and fell on the platform at my feet, and by standing close I kept comparatively dry.

I stood there for fully a half hour; till at last the rain slackened and almost stopped. Then one of the brethren came and unlocked the door and we went in. By eleven o'clock there were ten of us present.

The rain had stopped now; so we waited till almost eleven-thirty for others to come, but as no one showed up we had meeting by ourselves. There was no song leader and I was forced to do the leading. But we got through fairly well; if I made a mistake I was sure they could have done no better, and tried the harder the next time.

There is something exasperating, however, in trying to do something for someone and make [sic] a failure of it. One old brother (indeed, there were only three of us *old* brothers there; the rest were children and one lady)—one brother who sang bass asked me to lead a certain song. It had pretty good bass, and I am sure that is the reason he wanted it. But when I started it, I got it so low that he could not possibly reach the notes; however I didn't take the time to change it—the rest of them were singing and I didn't want to get behind.

Jean, you really cannot appreciate our school and church. You have always been in such a place, and have never seen the poorer churches—not poorer in money but in spirituality. Everyone goes to church at Cordell whether it rains or snows, but this short rain this morning kept nearly everybody away here.

It is surprising to me how untaught the people of the country generally are. They have learned a few of the very first principles of Christianity and are blinded to all the rest. This condition is the result of the preaching of such men as A. J. McCarty, Charlie Nichol and their scores of followers. They drive at baptism, faith (one part of it), a form of repentance, and confession, and never touch on the very most vital of all Christ's lessons. No wonder the churches are not strong.

And so bad is this condition that it will be impossible to change it in one or two generations. The people are not willing to receive the great lessons which they ought to have. I have spoken to a few of them about the Gospel Herald and wanted them to take it. Mr. Fleming said he took it for a while when it first started but that he was not taking any paper at present. He thought there were too many papers in the brotherhood as it was—and left the impression on me that he did not propose to help any of them by even one year's subscription. I may have been mistaken, and I hope I was.

Another brother said he took it for a time, but he didn't care for it any longer. It was a very good little *local* paper, but he was taking the Firm Foundation, and—. They do not value the lessons our paper has as highly as they value the docrinal [sic] matter of the Foundation and its wrangles and strife. This same man said he used to take the Gospel Advocate, and liked it pretty well, but—. And I understood that he regarded it somewhat as he does ours.

Preaching to these brethren might lift them up in two or three generations, but the trouble will be in getting a preacher. All the preachers they would have are the kind which would only emphasize the same condition, and make them worse instead of better. They need someone who can *teach* to live among them and work and make everyone else work. This can only be done by men trained from their boyhood. And I know of no better place to give boys this training than in a Bible school. We are engaged in the greatest work in the world, and it *must go on*. Even if you should die the work would *have* to continue, and I should do my best to carry it on. And I know if I should die you would keep it going; there would still be sufficient—more than sufficient—friends to make it go. And I hope to see it turn out hundreds of preachers, boys and girls, who will make a reformation throughout this whole country....

Jean, did you know that there are two of you? I got acquainted with one half of you last winter and this spring, and now I am becoming a friend to your other half. I suppose you are having the same experience. I mean one of you is yourself and the other is your letters—they are not exactly alike. But I am delighted with your letters. They do not yet express *yourself*, neither do mine, nor did Browning's writings express himself, but they have enough of yourself to make them seem like you, and with the help of your pictures when I read them I can almost imagine I am at home for a moment. (But of course it isn't half as good as being there)....

Cline.

[June 27 or 28, 1915][13]

Cordell Christian College
Notes.

Editor of the Norman Daily,
Norman, Oklahoma.
Sir,

On Saturday August 7, 1915, just 967 hours from the writing of these notes, Dr. Sears of the University of Norman Oklahoma will be in Cordell for a three weeks [sic] vacation before he begins his strenuous work as teacher of English in Cordell Christian College.

Former students of Cordell Christian College are swelling the matrimonial list immensely.

Leo Duncan has recently married a California girl. His mother and wife are to be in Cordell in a few days. Leo's whereabouts unknown.

---

13. This letter is undated. The envelope is postmarked June 30, 1915 and Pataway's mathematical calculation in the letter means that it would have been written on either the twenty-seventh or twenty-eighth.

The announcement of the marriage of Mr. John Tomlinson to Miss Willie Albert has just been received.

On June 28 Miss Edna Hatchet [sic] of Foss Oklahoma was married to Mr. Oscar Smith of Cordell at the home of the brides [sic] cousin in the north part of Cordell. Miss Hatchet is not a Christian.

The rumor is that Mr Cleburne McCaleb, age 22, of Bankston Alabama and Miss Eula Jaquess, age 20, of Boswell Oklahoma are to be married this fall.

The writer of these notes sends hearty congratulations to the eight young people. May the remainder of their three score and ten years be the happiest part of their lives.

O. D. Bixler, we are told, sends semi-weekly letters to Cordell addressed to "My dearest Alice." It is not known just what this indicates.

Messers Colson, Short, Armstrong, and Rutherford and Misses O'Neal, Short, Bills, Armstrong and Rutherford spent the day Sunday at the home of the Misses Symcox. Tennis was the game of the evening.

Miss Rutherford and Master Armstrong played against Mr. Rutherford and Miss Armstrong. Only two sets were played. The first set Miss Rutherford and Master Armstrong were victorious with a record of six to two, but the next set Mr. Rutherford and Miss Armstrong regained their playing ability and they were victorious with a record of six to one.

The crowd was then called into the house and the Misses Symcox served delicious ice cream. Every one had an exceptionally good time.

Mr. Colson had the pleasure of going to church with Miss Mae Symcox Sunday night, Mr. Short with Miss Beulah Symcox, Mr. Symcox with Miss Bills (Glory be!) and Mr Rutherford with Miss Armstrong.

Mr. W. W. Freeman returning from the Baptist Seminary of Louisville Kentucky Saturday night preached for the Church of Christ at Cordell Sunday and Sunday night. Mr. Freeman's "front hair" roaches as nicely as ever.[14]

Mr. Freeman conducted singing at the Church of Christ Sunday evening. The Symcox home being so far from the church, the young people there had just a family singing, Miss Short being the conductor.

Miss Aline Ledbetter of Columbia Tennessee, an old student of Potter Bible College,[15] and a very dear friend of Mr W. W. Freeman is in town to

---

14. An undated photograph of W. W. Freeman that makes Pataway's remark clear is available from the West Texas Digital Archives. See http://wtda.alc.org.

15. Potter Bible College was what nowadays would be considered a spin-off from the Nashville Bible School. J. A. Harding left Nashville in 1901 to establish the college in Bowling Green, Kentucky, and it ran until 1913. Potter Bible College was located on a farm two miles from town on land that belonged to the Potter family. Like Bethany College (where Harding had done his studies) and the Nashville Bible School, Potter

spend a few days with the Freemans before she returns home from the San Francisco exposition.

Last Sunday evening Mr. Rutherford suggested that the young people write Cline Sears a letter, each one writing one line, but they decided not to do this for fear Pataway Armstrong would write more than the assigned amount.

The young people of Cordell Christian College are much concerned about Pataway and her brother at Norman.

Next Sunday afternoon July 4 a crowd from Cordell Christian College intend to go to Dougford school house to Bro. Vaughn's meeting which begins that day. An enjoyable time is expected since the conveyance will be a farm wagon drawn by a pair of mules.

Saturday of this week several families in the Church of Christ intend to go fishing. Please, come go.

Since Bro. A. E. Freeman can not hold the meeting for the Church of Christ; they have employed Bro Crumley ("Don't that beat the band?" Mrs. Forrester.) It is said the meeting is to be held in the Harrell [sic] building begining [sic] the third Sunday in July. It can not be ascertained just *who* is *responsible* for Bro. Crumley's coming.

Bro. Rice was in Cordell Sunday night and has made arrangements to conduct a singing school, making preparation for the meeting which is to follow.

Wednesday of this week a young man about two miles north west of town lost everything he had by fire. The family was in the field hoeing cotton, and as it happened they had the two little girls in the field with them. The mother was left with nothing except the dress which she had on—not even any shoes. The children and father had nothing except what they had on. They had one dollar bill and that was burned up in the house. Isn't that terrible? The Church of Christ is helping them. They have given them a stove, some groceries, clothes, and chairs.

The Armstrong household washed a two weeks washing to-day!

Continued prosperity to the Norman Daily. It is the most interesting paper read in these parts.

Contributor.

Bible College offered daily Bible study. Young, *History of Colleges*, 111–14.

Monday, June 28, [1915]

J. A. D.

Dear Jean,

...Jean, you asked me a hard question in this letter, and yet it is simple, because there is only one answer to it. If I should love a girl until I could not live without her, and find at last that she could not love me, the very most sensible thing for me to do would be to die, I think, don't you?

And you still scare Arthur! I didn't know my sister was such a scarecrow. Put some rice flour on your nose and some red ink on your cheeks and I venture he will be all right. Tell him the doctor says you are not dangerous, and to send a few samples of the paper over here. I'll try soliciting.

I finished reading Byron's "The Corsair" this morning, and I had a nervous depression for two hours. It is a catalog of murders, homicides, and horrors. I don't see why a poet would select a subject like that. I'd much rather have written Shelley's "Ode to a Skylark," or Browning's "Rabbi Ben Ezra." You can read them sometime and see if I am not right. However, you will require a "sight" of endurance to plough through one of Browning's poems. Each stanza is as bad as an algebra problem, but when you do finally get the meaning it is wonderful. I wish he were less obscure.

Well, Sis, I almost got you into bad trouble, didn't I? But really it was just so funny I had to laugh. And the way you answered her! When are you going to change places with Solomon? To tell the truth, it would be a little embarrassing to you if people knew just how often I write. They cannot understand that I sometimes get lonesome over here by myself, and that you are the only sister I have who will write to me. If the other girls would write, I might adopt them for sisters, too. Though please don't ask them this summer! I really haven't time!...

Cline.

229 West Symmes Street,

Norman, Oklahoma,
Tuesday, 29, 1915

Dear little Sis,

...I got a letter from Mother this morning.[16] She said a cyclone destroyed part of a small neighboring town, and was coming in a straight course

---

16. Cline's mother was widowed by the time of his writing. She and some of his siblings still lived on the family farm in Kiowa, Kansas, just north of the Oklahoma

toward our house, but when it came within about a mile and a half it rose and disappeared. That was a close escape, wasn't it? Now after all danger is past, I'm writing her to be *careful*. Another one may come, though.

I am almost afraid I shall be too tired for George Müller after I get back. I think I shall want to rest for a while. Maybe I shall change my mind when I get there....

How is cooking, Jean? Can you make pies and fry chicken and whip cream, and bake light bread? I am anxious to be a judge of some of your work. By the time I get home you will know how to do everything....

Sister Armstrong said the first Sunday after I came home would be *my* day and asked me what I wanted to do. This is what I want to do, I want to spend that first Sunday with my little sister if she will allow me. What shall we do, Jean? Shall we stay at home, go kodaking,[17] take a long walk, or what? I shall be satisfied with anything or anywhere, just to be with my sister again. What do you want to do? I just have one reservation: I do *not* want the *whole town*. If you want Beulah and Agnes and a few others—all right. That will suit me—only I don't want to entertain them.

Cline.

Tuesday, 29, 1915

Dear brother Cline,

... And so you think there are two of me? I warned you that I couldn't write letters. If you had not been such a dear, *good* brother and such a *faithful, conscientious* house-doctor (but only a "university man") I should have refused absolutely to write to you this summer. Even now I think I should back out if it were not for getting your letters, because I never wrote a letter in my life of which I was not ashamed. But never you mind, some day I am going to write as sensible, interesting letters as Miss Mary. The handwriting won't be so good. How could it be with my ancestry?

But, I hope my letters are not exactly like me. I hope *way deep down* inside of me I am better and more intelligent than anything I am able to put on paper would indicate.

No, no! I am not so good in *many* ways as Miss Mary, but I am trying, and I feel like that in years I can be her equal in some ways and perhaps her superior in a *few* others. She loves all humanity, and she just makes every one love her. If you name the good traits of the people round about, then

---

border. Sears, *What Is Your Life?*, 19.

17. This expression was popular at the time and referred to taking pictures.

look at Miss Mary, she has every one of them. and, too, she has this love and consideration for all people which makes her *shoulders* and *head* above every one around her.

I think you are wrong again because you think I am the most sensible girl of sixteen you ever saw. You have never *before* been looking for the *sensible* side of girls.

I know *brothers* are better than *some* lovers, but whether lovers letter's [sic] are more interesting I can not say, for I have had *no experience* with letters from lovers!...

Do you know I'm a funny child. When I see married people I wonder if they really love each other and it worries me if I think may be they don't. I am so relieved because I found out that Bro. Stafford idolizes his wife. They were married so young I was afraid that he didn't. It frightens me to think how lightly people consider marrying....

I think you will be here one week of Bro. Crumley's meeting and I know it will be a feast to hear him preach....

Jean

229 West Symmes Street,

Norman, Oklahoma,
Wednesday. [June 30, 1915]

Dear Jean,

...I went to a lecture last night by David Starr Jordan, Chancellor of the University of California, and one of the foremost advocates of peace. He was in Germany a while before the war broke out lecturing in the German language, and while on that trip he found out the feelings of the Prussians toward France. At the invasion of Belgium by the Germans the minister of the Belgium [sic] government fled to England and took refuge with Jordon [sic] in the house which he was renting in London.

He gave a short history of the war and told the real reason for its outbreak. He said that in the battle of Ypres more men fell in one day than were killed in the Southern army during our whole Civil war. There have already been six million men killed and wounded, and five hundred ships sunk. Forty billions of dollars have already been spent—enough money to buy every farm in the United States; or enough to buy all of Russia, ice, plains, steppes, mountains, rivers, cities, and czars; or enough to pave every railroad in the United States and the great Trans-Siberian Railroad with twenty-dollar gold pieces and then have enough to buy all of Turkey; more money than all the commerce of all the nations will be worth for the next hundred and fifty years.

If we had the very least part of this—just the price of Turkey—we could build our Orphan's Home easily, couldn't we? This is a great waste. But it will have to stop soon, for they will run out of money. None of the New York banks will lend them any more money, and so they are left to their own resources. The great debt they already have will never be paid. France had a debt of several billions of dollars before this war began, which she had left from the Franco-Prussian war, and on which she had barely been able to pay the interest—sometimes not even able to meet it.

The worst thing about the war will come after peace has been made. It is only the finest of the young men who are allowed to go to war. Those from the slums or those who are not perfect physically and mentally are excluded. Thus in London all the available young men, the students of Oxford and all the other schools—athletes, teachers, writers, poets, and musicians—have been called to the army, and one fifth of this number have already been killed. The loss has been even heavier in the other countries. So the only class left is the class in the slums—degenerate, deformed, and mentally unbalanced. This is the class which will be left, after the war is over, to be the fathers of the next generation. This will be the worst result of the war. It will take more than a century to outgrow the evil effect....

I wrote to Miss Gussie a few days ago and told her all about my school. I like it better all the time (except Mr. Ramey's classes—they are just the same), but it can never be what our college is. It has too many students, and none of them is like our students. Most care nothing for church at all. I heard some of them talking about playing pitch all Sunday morning. Of course, that has been done in our school too—the boy who came from Alabama with Cleburn [sic] and Joe McCaleb played all one morning with some other college boys,—but that is not a common thing, and it rather shocked me when I heard these boys talking.

Yesterday I got into an argument with one of the boys about evolution. He seemed to take it for granted that evolution had been proven and that everyone believed it who was not a "back number." I couldn't bear that; so I calmly informed him that I differed from him and that I thought evolution had been sufficiently "exploded" and that the leading scientists were now adopting other theories. More than twelve months ago one of the leading scientists of Europe in a lecture in Melbourne, Australia, tore the philosophy of Darwin to pieces and constructed another theory of his own. Then we charged, and for a time the battle was hot...

Cline.

Thursday 30, 1915.

Dear big brother,

I have a feeling in my bones that you had to pay extra postage on that candy the other day. If it were any one else the feeling would be dreadfully humiliating, but as it's only my brother I don't care *very much*. The window was closed when I got to town and it seemed to be closed for the night, therefore I could not have the candy weighed. I put as many stamps on it as I thought it would take and mailed it, but the more I think about it the more afraid I become that I did not put enough stamps on it....

Just what does J. A. D. mean? Inform an ignorant little sister....

I read a story the other day that was more consolation to me than anything I ever read. It described the heroine as having large hands and feet, brown hair and gray eyes—besides being *dark*. If a girl in a story *could* be like this maybe it is not the *most terrible* thing that could happen to a girl in real life.

No, I don't think the most sensible thing for you to do would be to die. Would you just give up and *die* because some little girl, maybe not half good enough for you, would not marry you? There are so many people in the world who need to be taught and so much good that you can do that I believe you would be more sensible, at least, if you were not I would be ashamed of my brother.

The first Sunday you are at home, if we invite one there are about ten we will have to invite—or so it seems to me—no, eight, not counting home folks. Mae, Ernest, Beulah, Agnes, Sybil, Bro Short, Amanda, and Bro Homer. The way invitations have gone this summer I see no way to invite one without inviting all ...

Jean.

Norman,

North America
July 1, 1915.[18]

To Her Majesty Queene Elizabeth, Regent of England, Scotland, Ireland, Wales, Normandy, and France, and of the countrie of America, greeting.

---

18. Cline quotes extensively from this letter in his autobiography. He places his own use of the letter within a discussion of human imagination which, for him "was as natural as breathing." Sears, *What Is Your Life?*, 57–58.

The interest of my Queene in this new discovered countrie doth justify by me a short detail of all the interesting parts which I have yet found out and laid claim thereto for Her Majesty, as well as a proper account of my sundrie happenings and adventures since I left the shores of England to come to this countrie for my Queene; whatsoever I have not previously reported to thee, I herewith give account. And I shall send by your Majestie's Captain Conductor, of the Royal Navy of Great Britain, whom I am dispatching to you quickly this same evening to bring supplies from your Majesty to her subjects at this place. For, verily, without aid from thee, our Queene, we should all very like die of disheartenment even before food gave out. But thy graciousness doth constantly strengthen us to endure new dangers for thy Majesty.

Firstly, I shall venture a briefe description of this straynge land, which is wilder than the furthest portion of Westmoreland about the Lake District. It is bountifully covered by large trees of many kinds, so that one can walk for long distances without sunning himself ever so much as to make the complexion red or brown, and withal the land is very healthfull and salubrious, abounding much in dryness of climate, though of late we have experienced a few severe rains.

This countrie bears testimonie to have been at one time void of trees and other vegetation which might afford a shade to the inhabitants; for all the people whom I have been privileged to meet of the natives are burned to an ugly copper color or to a black complexion somewhat resembling to the natives of Africa though with sundrie different features.

Two of these uncomely creatures, maidens of a nearby tribe (who call themselves by a name of peculiar sound when they grow older, being of the sound in Indian of "squah" with a broad accent of the latter syllable)—two of these straynge creatures, one as buxom a lass as ever one sees in England, weighing probably nigh two hundred pounds avoirdupoise, [sic] the other equally as high but lacking somewhat in natural heft, weighing more nearly one hundred pounds by your Majestie's standards, stalked boldly into our eating room and took seats at a table opposite my own. Being much interested how they should manage the knife and fork and other instruments of eating, I did watch them closely, but to my surprise, I must confess, they seemed well practiced to them, eating easily and voraciously....

These are the extent of my late battles. Two other campaigns, by your leave, I project—the one against Hamlet, the prince of Denmark, whom I wish to conquer completely, and the other against Lord Maeterlinck of Germany, who has been guilty of making several attempts against my interests in these parts. Him would I conquer before I come again to England....

Thy most obedient servant,
Sir Walter Raleigh.

Norman, Oklahoma,

July 2, 1915.

Dear Jean,

...I... have often wondered if married people [word missing] loved each other. So many of them act as if they do not, and I half believe that many of them, if they would talk, have the same ideas which Mrs. Wilson advocates. It would be worse than death to be married without love. But I suppose *most Christians* who marry really do love, although they often treat their wives in such a "cold Northern fashion." It is just the way of my countrymen. You must overlook that, Jean...

Cline.

Saturday, 3rd, 1915.

Dear brother Cline,

... Let me tell you something. Sir Walter Raleigh is in this part of the country! I *know* because I got a letter from him addressed to *me* but written to Queen Elizabeth. I felt quite honored to get a letter written to a *real Queen*. He must be close to Norman for he secured an envelope that you had addressed to me. It was a very interesting letter and I shall always keep it. I shall show it to the little orphan boys to inspire them to treat all ladies as queens and to the little girls in order that they may make themselves worthy of such service. Before you come home I wish you would inquire for him and bring him home with you. I am sure it will be very interesting to hear him talk. I shall have the boys and girls assembled to hear him deliver a lecture on old English.

Delia wrote brother George that at the normal they wouldn't give her credit for the work she has done but did give a Thorp Springs' student credit.[19] I don't understand it exactly, but I know it will be a drawing card in

---

19. Thorp Springs, Texas had a succession of Stone-Campbell Movement schools that opened, closed, or moved elsewhere. In 1910, members of a Church of Christ purchased the physical plant a few miles from the town and established Thorp Springs Christian College. (Both college and town are rendered variously as "Thorp Springs" and "Thorp Spring.") The college had a normal school training department and followed the curricular example of Bethany College and the Nashville Bible School especially in that the Bible was taught daily. For a brief time (1915–16) the Thorp Springs Christian College functioned as a four-year institution rather than a junior college. When C. R. Nichol became board chairman in 1916, much effort went into improving the physical plant and academic standards. Young, *History of Colleges*, 72–75, 77. Several faculty members and students from Cordell moved back and forth between the

drawing the O'Neals and Bro. Bixler away from here to Thorp Springs next year, and it may be best, too, for I doubt whether Alice will be happy here any more. I think she has something on her conscience that she should tell.

I think sister Holland was sick when you left. Well, she has lost her mind and is getting weak rapidly. This is the last stage of the disease. I hope she will not live long, for it is so hard on brother Holland. He is there most of the time, by himself. Even her sisters are afraid to come and, of course, other people are, and there he is with a dying wife and no one to comfort him. The loneliness must be terrible. We should be ashamed to complain of being lonesome when we see things worse at our very door. Dr. Freeman said Wednesday night that Pellagra[20] is nearly four hundred years old but that the medical profession knows less about it than about any other disease that the human race has. But they do know it is not contagious in the sense we speak of things being contagious, and he advised the people to go and visit them. But I am afraid for mama [sic] to go. I guess that is selfish, but I can't keep from being a little selfish some times.

The day Oscar Smith married, he won for himself a secure place in my heart. Mama and I were coming from town and when we reached Stella Hamic's (the old Carter house at the top of the hill) Nina, Stella, Bro. Oscar and his wife were sitting on the front porch. We stopped to congratulate the birde [sic] and groom (another hard thing for me to do) when Nina began laughing and said she knew something funny. She said "you should hear old Mrs. Freeman tell how Cline Sears looked and did when he came for doctor [sic] Freeman when you were sick."[21] Then she went into detail and told what sister Freeman said you said. "Oh doctor, doctor, Miss Pataway is about to die, come quick!" Then she laughed and laughed but Bro. Oscar spoke up and said, "I venture it was not a funny thing to sister Armstrong, Miss Pataway and those who had the care of her." Nina laughed some more and said "I guess not but it sure was funny the way Mrs. Freeman told it, and she said no body *need tell her* that Cline Sears was not"—Oh well, I won't tell you what she (sister F) did say, but she attributed it all to sentimental reasons. Here Bro. Oscar spoke again, "Well, Nina, any gentleman would have done as Cline

---

two institutions and the letters make clear that some level of competition was felt at least on the part of those at Cordell. It also appears that Thorp Springs was on the more theologically and doctrinally conservative end of the spectrum.

20. Pellagra is a vitamin deficiency disease that reached epidemic proportions in the American South during the early 1900s. The general public and politicians preferred to think of it as an infectious disease rather than one of malnutrition because of the general social embarrassment associated with poverty. Bollet, "Politics and Pellagra," 211–21.

21. See a description of this incident in Sears, *What Is Your Life?*, 53.

did." Isn't old Sister Freeman in big business? Bro. Tenny [sic] told us that Eunice was creating a good deal of fun at Sentinal [sic] over the same little matter. Of course, they exaggerate beyond measure, but I am glad you were scared a little when I was so sick. You wouldn't have been a brother worth having if you had not been. But I'm afraid I am a selfish girl after all, for since the smiles had to come, I'm glad you (and not I) are getting them. You are a boy, you see, and so it doesn't really matter, does it? Suppose you were a girl and were being accused of trying to catch a man who wouldn't be caught. Oh, Big Brother, you'll never be able to realize how some of the things I had to bear *stung*.

I don't think any one will criticize us for the house-doctor services because they know how sick I was and they know, too, they left us alone. But they hide behind the fact that we were quarantined. Mama has heard so many say "Oh no one was allowed to go in, you know. They were quarantined." We won't *tell* them, but we didn't *need* them, did we? a mother and a good big brothers [sic] are "a plenty" to care for *one* girl, especially when one of them is better than a trained nurse....

Jean.

Sunday Afternoon,

July 4, 1915.

Dear Jean,

...I am *very, very sorry*. Whatever I can do to help my little sister I shall certainly do it. I would not have thought it of him,[22] would you? I didn't think he could be so "fickle"! But never mind, you can forget about it in the years to come.... But how did you learn that he and Miss Eula are to be married? I, too, am much concerned in this, for I shall have to begin to forget Miss Eula—and it will be a terribly pleasant task. We will have to help one another bear it.

And I am much afraid that I shall have some more forgetting to do soon. "My dearest Alice" sounds like it, does it not? But just wait till school begins—unless they both go to Thorp Springs I shall murder him in a premeditated accident and kidnap "my dearest Alice" and then see where his plans will go. However, for the present I hope he can keep her "crazy" over him. If she is perfectly satisfied she may not talk any more.[23] Both these couples have my

22. The reference is to the notice of Cleburne McCaleb's engagement.
23. The letters suggest that references to Alice O'Neal and gossip aimed at Cline and Pataway probably pertain to an incident recounted in Cline's autobiography. He had

"heart-felt" congratulations and my entire friendship and good-will. I really love them all, especially, I must confess, the *boys*. . . .

We had a larger number out at church this morning. There were fifty or more with the children, I suppose. I had to lead the singing again. I wonder what they would do if I were not here. They all say they cannot sing, but I notice that when I start the songs they always carry them on. We really do have pretty good singing—much better for the size of the crowd than we have in the summer at home. If I keep on practicing, I shall be a good leader when Sister Symcox comes. And really I like to be able to do anything when I have to, even lead singing.

Then when the classes took their places, there was no teacher for the young folk's class and I got to teach that. I think I shall get it the rest of the time I am here. I hope so, for it is a pretty good class and they have not been very well taught. Maybe I can give them a few of the lessons we get at Cordell. I gave out some sample copies of the "Herald" but I don't know whether I shall get any subscribers or not. They seem to like the "Firm Foundation" more.

Every time I go to church, Jean, I get homesick. Things are so different here; and then I think about all of my friends there, and especially of my little sister, and I really feel lonesome. I would give anything just to be there on Sundays. But I know I can do much more good here, if I can do any good at all. For they do not need me there, and the church does need some one here.

I am going to change my boarding place. I am going to stay with Brother Henton, a widower who lives alone and, like me, sometimes gets lonesome. His wife died a little more than a year ago and he is too old to forget her—about fifty years old, I think—and so he likes to have someone around to keep him company. He asked me to stay all night with him last Sunday night, but I couldn't . . . This will be a much better place for me, because he is a Christian and because he will not charge me any board except part of the light bill if I sit up and study late and half of the coal and food if we decide to get our breakfasts and suppers. I shall eat dinner at some boarding house, but we could easily get our own breakfasts. An egg, some oatmeal, and bread and butter would be all I should want. That is all I get at the house where I now stay, and I know I can cook eggs as well as anyone. . . .

The university is going to adjourn, or abscond, or whatever you want to call it, to a place between here and Oklahoma City. They intended to go to the Belle Isle Park at Oklahoma City,[24] but something changed their minds.

---

been dating another Cordell student (not Alice) and, when they broke up, he "incurred the condemnation of a good many students, for she was a very popular girl." Sears, *What Is Your Life?*, 51–52.

24. Belle Isle Park was owned by the Oklahoma Railway Company. The Company's

I don't suppose I shall hear Scott if he speaks up there, for I'm not going. I'm going to stay here and get your letter when the postman comes, and study. I have to read "All's Well that Ends Well" to-day and to-morrow . . .

Last night I took a walk. It was about ten o'clock, and not many people were on the streets out this far from town. I never saw a more beautiful night . . . The air was cool and still and silent. The buzzing of automobiles on the boulevard not far away, with the noise of fire-crackers down in the town—and the occasional laugh of a passerby, was all that I could hear. There was no moon, but the sky was studded with billions of stars. One large one, brighter than the north star, stood directly above our home. If stars are angels who are set to guard us here, this must have been your guardian angel, Jean. For it was the brightest and prettiest star among them all; and I think of all the stars, God would give the best and most perfect one to be my sister's.

Cline.

July 5, 1915.

Dear Jean,

Didn't my "ignorant little sister" really know what "J. A. D." meant? But of course she didn't—no one would, unless it was explained to him. I should have written it out. It was "Just After Dinner"—and a very good dinner it was too. We had chicken, creamed potatoes, salad of a rare sort, dressing, and all the other things that go with such a dinner, and pineapple pie with pineapple ice cream to eat with it. Doesn't that [word missing] good? We never have such dinners except on Sunday. All the rest of the time they leave off ice cream and substitute pork or veal loaf or beef roast. Meat seems to be their principal beverage and dessert, and I would give it all for a dish of ice cream such as we had at home. I might not be getting so—I detest "fat," but I suppose that's what I'm getting. You will hardly know your brother when he comes back. I must weigh something between [one] hundred and twenty-five and two hundred right now; what will I be in five weeks more?

I do believe you have a big imagination, Jean. Why, you had enough stamps on that box of candy to send it to Philadelphia and back. No, hardly that many, perhaps; but enough to send it safely this far. I didn't pay a single cent on it. Now, will you rest easy? . . .

I know the first girl a boy ever really *loves* doesn't go out of his memory half as quickly as the second, nor the second as quickly as the third. But when

---

street cars carried people to the Park and its lakes for swimming, boating, and other amusements. The site of the Park is now a shopping mall. Griffith, *Oklahoma City*, 45.

several girls have come and gone and been forgotten, a boy grows callous to love and may become incapable of loving at all. Instead of love he has a sentimental *fancy*, which disappears like a mist before a sun when the object of his fancy is no longer near....

When a boy who has had good training loves for the first time, he is generally as pure in his love as any one can be. But the very first time he is allowed a privilege which does not belong to him, he has fallen. If after that he continues as he is he will never really *love* any girl. I do not think that *love can* be *impure*. Lasting love must be made of better stuff; it must be as pure as the snow and as high and holy as God himself. If this is true, it is impossible for a boy who goes with a girl for the privileges she may give him, ever really to love her. But boys do go with girls for this very reason. Every boy does who has received one privilege; he is poisoned, and, like the mad dog, tries to spread his own madness. Perhaps I should not say every boy, but the exceptions are indeed scarce. But when a boy does go with girls for this purpose it is no wonder that he forgets them in three weeks. It is the only natural thing for him to do. He does, however, remember longest those girls who do not allow such privileges, but even they are forgotten while he is in this condition....

... The basis for a pure, lasting love can never be a desire for privileges, but it must be a deep spiritual connection—a likeness of dispositions, or more properly, of tastes. There must be something more than mere beauty. So much, however for this. I see I have written quite a long "dissertation" when it was perfectly useless, for you know all this already....

Jean, I wish you would promise me one thing. Will you? You must promise before I tell you what it is. Now, will you promise? Then it is this: Promise me never again to make any more reflections on your hands and feet and eyes and complexion. Why, if I had known how you despise them, I should not have tried to save them for you at all when you were sick. If you had died you would have been very white. Would that have suited you better? You must like your complexion and hands and feet and eyes because your brother does. I like dark people much better than fair ones, and your eyes are more beautiful than anything else on earth and even the stars in heaven, and your feet and hands are not nearly as large as mine. So please hereafter make no no [sic] reflections on my sister.

If you want to invite the whole crowd, Jean, let's go out on the creek right after dinner. Which would you rather do, invite them and go on a picnic or spend our day at home? Or could we take a walk just by ourselves—out by the Orphan's Home and down on the creek, or up north toward Gentry's or wherever you want to go? I want to do anything you wish. I shall be too happy, for one time, to be *stubborn* ...

Cline.

Tuesday, 6th 1915

Dear brother Cline,

... We had a splendid trip to Dougford. The drive coming home was more pleasant than the drive going for we had to go six miles with the sun in our faces. The beautiful lane we reached at the end of the six miles made us forget how hot we had been. I wish you could have been here and gone down the lane with us. That pretty place had a different effect on me from the rest. It gave me the blues and finally I *cried. I just couldn't help it!* ...

Our wonderful singing school started last night and of all the ridiculous things any one ever saw and heard we saw and heard them last night. We are not going every night because we need to sleep more than we need to hear ridiculous things. Here I am criticizing....

Don't feed too much on "air" or *you* might come to the same sad fate as the Prince of Denmark (I've never read Hamlet, but I'm told it's a "dying" play.) I prefer that you should eat candy. Notify me when you are out. I just helped make this. I'll make the next by myself. Certainly, I am learning to fry chicken. You should have eaten a wing of one I fried for dinner to-day....

I am afraid Bro. Homer is not making much out of his garden because there is no market. He is not content farming. He wants to be preaching or going to school.

I don't need your sympathy, Sir! How can I forget what I have never remembered? But my! what a list you have had to forget. Your heart must be *full* of cracks.... Does the old pain grow easier with time or do you still feel that you will never find a girl whom you can love so much? To go back to Mr. McCaleb and Eula—The information concerning their approaching wedding came through Oneida.

I am glad you are being pushed forward in the church work there because the experience will be worth a world to you. I hope you can keep the class of young people just *four Sundays longer.*

I am glad you are going to change your boarding place. A lonely old widower and a lonely young bachelor will be very congenial together. If it were not too hot I would send you a sample of fried chicken for one of those breakfasts ...

Do you know I like the guardian Angel thought. I hope God will let uncle Paul be my guardian Angel to watch and guide me. I am sure his star would be brighter than the north star. Since this beautiful star was directly over your home, may be God has lent him to you during your sojourn among evolutionists. May he guard and keep you....

I had a long newsy letter from grannie [sic] Pattie the other day and she actually asked me if I had a sweetheart. I guess she though [sic] I was getting to the age when most girls find it necessary to fall in love. She doesn't know that Cordell Christian College boys and girls have decided to be brothers and sisters until time proves unmistakably to them that they must be more. I shall write her about my brothers....

Jean.

Tuesday 6, 1915.

Dear Jean,

... I am a little surprised that the normal would not [word(s) missing] [our] work since the university does. And yet I am not very much surprised; because the state schools will not give us any more credit than they have to. I suspect Miss Delia approached them in the wrong manner or failed to dema[nd] proper credit as a right and not a favor. The schools are not especially fond of granting favors....

I suppose I was a little scared when I got to Freeman's, and I was out of breath too, but I didn't speak as if you were dying, for I knew you would last long enough [for] Dr. Freeman to get to you. But let Nina laugh; she [word(s) missing] at my expense before when I did what I thought was right, and so I have got used to it....

Cline.

July 7, 1915.

Dear Jean,

I had the rare *pleasure* a few days ago of eating with the same two Indian girls Raleigh described to you. The slender girl's eyes are black and they always glance restlessly around and are never still. The other one is one of those fat, broad-faced, high-cheeked, girls who finally become the ordinary black, greasy Indian squaws we see around town....

The time *is* passing, isn't it? In just thirty more days I can come home again. I have been comforting myself with the thought that *all* things have an end except heaven, and that this summer will some time pass; but that means, too, that my stay at home will have an end, and I cannot think of that just now. I am just going to think about coming home, and dream about it, and wish for it till I do come....

Cline.

Friday, July 9, 1915.

Dear brother Cline,

Queen Elizabeth kept me so busy picking out nuts for Sir. Walter's cake, I have only time to write you a little note. Be on the look out for that cake for I'm afraid it won't be good if it's left in the Post office over Sunday. If secured at the proper time it will do very well for a Sunday night supper in the bachelor quarters.

Bro. Rice is also an Expression teacher. He has those who lead paint the picture before his audience with the waving of the hands and the silly little smile he persuades them to get—I wish you were here to lead so you could get some Expression this summer.

Mama is so afraid I'll miss the train that I must stop.

Jean.

University City,

July 10, 1915.

Dear Jean,

... You cannot conceive of the difference between Bible school girls and common town girls. I passed the Y. W. C. A. house, where a number of the girls stay, a few nights ago, coming home from a lecture. They had the tables pushed back in the long dining room, and one was playing while others were dancing. There is a dance somewhere every week—three to-night. One of the young men who stays here was invited but he isn't going because he doesn't approve of dances, especially as they are carried on here. They are worse here because of the boys, and most of the girls, who attend have no sense of morality...

I had my eyes tested to-day by the best optometrist in the United States, Mr. Taylor. He is an old man of about seventy years, I think, with gray hair and a fine high forehead. He makes me think of Brother Harding. He has a deep low voice and is as gentle and kind as can be....

I wish you could go with me to Belle Isle to-morrow. We would stay till the moon came up, and get us a real boat and row all over the lake; with the moon and the stars above, a soft breeze on the water, and the slow music of an orchestra on the shore ...

Cline.

Saturday, July 10, 1915

Dear big brother,

...I think you have found the cause of fickleness in most men. But the girls, poor little simpletons, won't believe it. Many of them are not taught and most of those who are, will listen to the voice of some man much loved rather than the voice of a mother....

Oh! dear me, what a "taste" you used to have when it came to girls... I wonder how much your taste has improved. Write me a *full description* of the girl you are to go boating with to-morrow. I wonder if you'll tell her that you have a *real true* sister *already* and the fairies won't allow a boy but *one*.... I am glad you are to have this nice outing. I hope you'll have the nice time that your days of hard study deserve. There will be the boat, the man, and the girl. Will there be the moon and who will sing the song?...

The "world wags on" and the singing school "wags" with it.... While you are in a boat with the wind in your hair to-morrow afternoon, I'll be hearing Bro. Rice say, "Turn to number thirty seven, please—'There Is Sunlight'—This is a very beautiful selection." Oh dear me!...

Jean.

July 11, 1915.

Dear Jean,

...We started this morning on the nine o'clock car, three boys and three girls. I rode to the city with a Miss Elizabeth (not my Queen Elizabeth, for I should have been infinitely happy if it had been)—Miss Elizabeth Hamilton. She is about sixteen, I think...

When we arrived in the City we went to church at the county court house. They have a larger church at Oklahoma City than I thought they had. Brother Milholland, in a meeting there this summer, united the two bodies, who had separated about some preacher and made the church as large as it is.

After church we took a car to Belle Isle Park. We ate our dinner as soon as we found a tree with sufficient shade; for I am sorry to say the trees in Belle Isle are very small. After dinner we explored.

There are two main lakes. One of these is only a small one and is not more than five feet deep. This is the one used for swimming, and they have spring boards, a shower bath, two diving chutes, and dressing rooms.

I watched the swimmers a little while to see whether I wanted to join them, but I was soon convinced that it was no place for a Christian. Girls and boys were swimming together, and, as is only natural when girls put themselves on an equality with boys, they were subjected to the worst indignities I ever saw offered to girls. Of course, this was no place for a Christian, and we went over to the other lake....

After watching them for a while I suggested that we all go boat riding. Miss Hamilton agreed at once, but the others thought the sun was too hot yet. So Miss Hamilton and I went alone. We got (see this big ink blot just below? I great big, buzzing bug lit on my neck, and in my effort to dislodge him I spilled this blot.)—well, we got a nice little boat with the oars fastened on, so that, if I got excited and let one loose, we would not loose [sic] it; also to make it easier to row—and we started out.

Rowing was new to me. I had not been in a boat for three or four years and had not rowed any for seven or eight. However, after some difficulty I succeeded in getting out of the dock. Then to make rowing easier I went with the wind, which was pretty strong and made the waves large....

We were on the water fully two hours and must have rowed almost ten miles. My hands feel as if it were at least that far, for I have four large blisters in the palms. My boat ride was very pleasant, because it was new to me, but the rest of the trip was not so good although I had a "nice" time.

I was glad I had a chance to see some more of Oklahoma City's morals. It has none! To give you a good example of them, I saw a boy lying with his head in his sweetheart's lap in one of the most public places in the park about six o'clock in the afternoon. This was *one* of the worst things I saw. And when we passed he didn't condescend to change his position! From all I saw, I would not allow my sister to go there *at all* without a good chaperon, [sic] or someone to protect her against the indignities of a class of boys who frequent the place....

Your sailor brother.

Monday, July 12, 1915.

Dear brother Cline,

... Well they had a regiment at Agnes' yesterday—ten girls and five boys. We had the finest dinner, well prepared. The chicken was especially good because *I fried it.* See? After dinner we went to the creek to take some pictures and after we had taken several pictures Ernest and Agnes, Bro Short and Beulah, and I ran off from the crowd to gather some plums we saw on the creek bank.... Then we came back to the bridge to wait till the rest came but the *rest didn't come,* so we went on to the house thinking maybe they were there. They were not! We stayed at the house until seven and still they didn't come. We had some cream we wanted to eat and it looked as if they were never coming, so the only thing left for us to do was to go find them. I didn't want to go much because it stuck my pride for I knew they were only staying down there to get the best of us. We finally went, found them, brought them home and ate the cream. When we finished our cream it was time to go for your letter. Beulah, Mama, and I went before the rest to the office.

The fairies were abroad last night making the world beautiful with a million tiny torches. Just before church time I went to the post office just as I told you. The office was empty, so I stood by the window and read your letter in the twilight. I came up the street wishing I could be in a boat on the lake with you when I glanced up and almost caught my breath at the beauty of the scene. Under the trees and among the flowers in Mr. Lee's yard were hundreds and hundreds of fireflies. I think I have never seen anything more beautiful. The whole world seemed filled with these tiny fairy lanterns. This time I didn't cry at a beautiful scene. You enjoyed it quite as much as I did. There is quite an advantage in being together though separated, isn't there? You enjoyed my fireflies among the trees and I enjoyed the wind in my face as you sailed across the lake. Isn't there a lot of nonsense in the world? Sometimes I think our imagination makes us very nonsensical, but when nonsense comforts and cheers the lonely, I say "Hurrah! for nonsense"...

Jean.

421 North Stewart Aven[ue]

July 12, 1915.

My dear little Sis,

... Jean, I am getting more acquainted with Professor Sco[tt.] He knows me when he sees me, if he doesn't know my name; for last night I passed him at the interurban station and he recognized me and spoke before I saw him. Then I met him this afternoon on the street and he recognized me again. I hope I can make him remember me in some way, for it will be of value to me. He will take a greater interest in my work and give me more opportunities to let the student[ts] and the teachers see what kind of work we do at Cordell, if I am a fit representative of it. He might then ask me to make a talk at the Story Teller's League[25] or at some of the Literary Conferences, as he does

---

25. A number of conferences on important educational issues were held at the University of Oklahoma during the summer of 1915. One conference involved the Oklahoma Story Teller's League. *University of Oklahoma General Catalog* 1914–1915, 338.

some of his old students. I suspect I shall not have this opportunity till next year, however, if then...

I spoke to Dr. Scroggs, the professor of psychology, about going out to the asylum with his class if he went. He had not decided to go this summer, but he said he would consider it and if he could arrange for his class to make the trip he [would let me] know. He is a good old man of about sixty- or sixty five, slightly bald, but with kind, clear eyes, and a preacher. Last year he taught a class in social morality, as he called it.

This makes me think of your singing school. I am truly thankful I am not there if they sing number thirty-seven. "It is the limit!"—and Brother Rice teaches expression! Now I wish I were [word(s) missing] I believe I could do him some good—I certainly should try. I would, like Priscilla and Aquila, draw him aside and teach him the way more perfectly.[26] If he wouldn't listen, then I wouldn't lead. Certainly I should not make myself a *fool*.

I saw a girl yesterday who knew Brother Rice and who told me he was holding a singing school over at Cordell (as if I didn't know it already)....

Cline.

441 N. Stewart Ave.,

July 13, 1915.

Dear Jean,

...I went again to see Professor Williams about my credits this afternoon, and he told me how much they had decided to give me. In my high-school work, I lack two units of having the required amount. Physics and plane geometry *have* to be taken in high school and I have never had them. But he told me how to keep from taking physics if I wished. I think, however, I shall take it. Then above the high school work he gave me fifty hours in the university. (I wanted forty!). My eight hours for this summer's work makes me fifty-eight, almost half of the A.B. degree.

This is pretty good, don't you think? I did not expect so much. He told me, however, "not to go back to Cordell and tell them that the university credits the College with fifty units." He explained that this was a personal matter; that he would not give every student we sent him so much credit; and that if he had not liked my looks and thought that I could do the work, he would have given me about twenty-five hours! Of course, I thanked him—and went away. Before I left he explained fully their credit system, so that we can give our students just what they need to enter the university. Then he showed

---

26. A reference to Acts 18:26.

me what course I could take if I wished to specialize in English, what work I had to have, and what work I could elect. Altogether we had a pleasant talk. However, I still dislike being favored; I like to earn what I get! I know I have earned all he gave me, but *he* doesn't seem to think so, or, at least, he seemed to think that he might have given me too much credit. I don't blame him, though, for thinking no other school can do work like the university; I think the same thing of our College in some things, yet there are, no doubt, plenty of schools that can surpass us. But I wouldn't have much respect for any man who would spend his life in any work which he considered inferior to some other...

Cline.

Cordell Oklahoma,

July 14, 1915.

Dear brother Cline,

...I canned some beets yesterday and they looked as pretty as mama's. Oh! I'm getting to be a cook right but I haven't tackled light bread yet. I don't know whether I will till next summer. I doubt it...

A man came around a while ago with some apricots and mama wasn't her [sic]... and I couldn't get her over the telephone. I knew she wanted some more and that they were about gone, so I got some. The only trouble is I paid about twice too much for them and I have ordered a bushel more. I don't know what mama will do with me but if she does any thing *terrible* I'll write you the results....

Mama is going to Clinton to-morrow to meet Papa. They spend the day there to-gether and then come down on the evening train. Papa leaves then Friday evening for a meeting in Texas.

Jean.

July 14, 1915.

Dear Jean,

I have things in pretty good shape at the Bachelor's Hall now. I take breakfast and supper at home but eat dinner at a boarding house closer to the university. It is too far to walk home; it takes me thirty minutes walking as fast as I can to get here, so the distance must be about two miles. I am experimenting to see just how cheap one can live comfortably. Homer ought to be with me, since he wants to try the same experiment.

I attended a conference on libraries this afternoon, and I think I shall have some books selected for ours. At least I shall talk to Brother Armstrong about it. I am also examining the magazines of the library and some of them we ought to have. I am trying to get all the good things I can find for our school...

Cline.

Norman, Oklahoma,

July 15, 1915.

Dear Jean,

I have just finished supper and washed the dishes. You can never guess what I had to eat! A pint of milk with crackers and peanut butter. I am going to get a quart of milk hereafter. This afternoon is the first time I have got any, and the lady from whom I got it didn't have but this much left. This is my supper, varied sometimes by substitutions for peanut butter. My breakfasts are the same without the milk; but my dinners include everything—chicken or other meats, potatoes, cabbage and other vegetables, pie, cake, etc.

... I had my eyes tested for the glasses this afternoon. Dr. Taylor did the testing, but he doesn't sell glasses; so I got them from Dr. Campbell, the leading optometrist of the state. He has to order the glasses ground at Omaha, Nebraska; so I shall not get them for about a week. Won't I look funny with glasses? I shall be old indeed then—gray hair and spectacles! I shall be quite a dignified man!...

Cline.

Cordell, Oklahoma,

July 16, 1915.

Dear brother Cline,

The catalogues are out and they are little beauties. I am so pleased with them. We are sending you several this evening and if you give Miss Petty one maybe she will come to school next fall. I think I did a good deed in burning the old catalogue. The new one is much better. I don't think I shall be guilty of such a thing again, however....[27]

27. In the biography of J. N. Armstrong Cline wrote that Mrs. Armstrong

It is so very hot! Mama didn't get after me for getting those apricots. She only made me can them....

Grannie Pattie and Grandpa will be out here next winter if the Lord wills. They have never wanted to come before but Grannie Pattie's last letters have been filled with the idea of their coming. We want to have them out here by Thanksgiving any how. I hope when they come that Grandpa will be satisfied and I feel that he will be satisfied here if he will be any where because we are in a work here that he loves. If I can learn to wait on him like Aunt Sue does that will make him more satisfied than anything and I am going to try hard.

I am so anxious for you to know Grannie Pattie. *I* think she is one of the finest old ladies on earth ...

Papa leaves this evening for Kirkland Texas. He won't be home any more till school opens. He has been at home now for three days ...[28]

I shall feel very small and timid when I face my grey haired, spectacled Professor of English in September! I "hate like pizen" for you to have to wear glasses, yet, I would not have you do anything else since your eyes need them. You'll take them off on our Sunday, won't you?

Jean.

July 16, 1915.

Dear little Sis,

... You are learning how to care for the orphan babies, are you?[29] It is time to learn, because it won't be many years till our dreams must come true. When I think of *that*, I feel like "jumping up and shouting" although it would be a very undignified thing for a "University man" to do ...

I have a "whole lot" to write to you but I cannot this afternoon. It is time for me to go to another lecture.... I will try to answer Sister Armstrong's letter to-morrow. The work is crowding me more now ...

Thy brother.

"accidentally burned" the catalogue manuscript just before it was ready for printing. Sears, *For Freedom*, 147. Here, however, Pataway takes responsibility for the mishap.

28. Armstrong's brief trip home was to deal with the loss of the college catalogue. Ibid.

29. Ora Anne and S. A. Bell had a child that summer. The delivery had been difficult, so Woodson periodically went to help care for the baby.

Norman, Oklahoma[30]

July 18, 1915.

Dear Sister Armstrong,

This letter must be *strictly private*; it is for *you alone*.

I received your letter yester[day], and it was just filled full of good things. But I am more sorry than I call tell about Homer. I was afraid he did not care for Miss Mary, but yet I tried to hope he did. I love him as I love my own brother and I wish he would not be jealous. Still I cannot blame him, for I was jealous of him *one* time. It was the night you and Miss Healy gave that rec[ital] at the college. All day I [had] looked forward to this time, for I wanted to talk to Jean; but to my surprise, when the crowd came, Homer took my place and kept it the whole evening. I was not expecting this and was unprepared. Had I expected it in the least I could have controlled myself; but it took me a week to feel exactly [rig]ht toward him.[31] Since then [I] have had many things as bad to happen, but I have always been ready, and have never felt the least bit jealous.

Now would be the time to hold to my old ideas of friendship; but friendship is *not* stronger than love. It would be worse than death to me to sacrifice my love for Jean on the ground of friendship, noble as such a sacrifice might [be,] I cannot do it.

Before I left home I [said] I would not tell her of my love for a year at least, and I have tried to keep my word, but it has been impossible. Every letter, every line, and every word are full of it. I write and clip and rewrite, sometimes throwing away whole pages, but still it creeps in. I have tried to appear a brother, but no brother writes as I do. This [word missing] what I said you might not [word(s) missing] but refused to tell you. I thought I should wait until I came home, but I studied about it afterward and finally decided to write.

This is what I want to do. On the first Sunday I am at home, our Dream Day, I want to tell Pataway of my love for her and ask her love in return. *For I do love her with my whole soul.* One reas[on I] want to tell her now is [word(s) missing] I am afraid to wait much longer. I have so many hard things to tell her, so many things she does not know, that she may be unable to overlook them. If these things must forever separate us, the sooner each of us knows it the better.

---

30. This is a separate letter, addressed to "Mrs. J. N. Armstrong, Cordell, Oklahoma." It is postmarked the same day as it was written and is now in very poor condition.

31. Cline refers to this incident in his autobiography without naming names. Sears, *What Is Your Life?*, 51.

But I know I am the least able to decide about this. I would speak to her at once [word missing] it may not be best. I have thought much about it and have prayed every day, but I have finally decided to leave it to God and you. Whatever you say, I shall do. If you had rather I should wait another year, I can do so. But please think about it and tell me, either in a letter or when I come home. I think you need have no fear of my love for her; I have sounded my [heart] to the bottom. So many [word(s) missing] have happened that we [word(s) missing] each other now as few people do before they are married, I think.

My only regret is that I am utterly unworthy of her love, if she choose to give it to me. But if a life of devotion can atone for this, I will gladly give it. I am writing this to you because I believe [you] would want me to (I know [I] would if I were in your place) and because you have been a real mother to me and I love you next to Pataway and my own mother. . . .

I almost wish I could attend the singing school. I would try to teach Rice a lesson he would not forget. . . .

The dinner you have planned is as good as I could select. It will be a feast to me after the hurried lunches of my bachelor days. A man can live very well on milk and crackers twice a day with a good dinner, or even without such a good dinner. If you do not have them already you need not get the beets [word(s) missing] like them only moderately.

Jean has told you, of course, what I want to do on the first Sunday. Now we have our day and our dinner planned, I can hardly wait to come. Nineteen more days! Watch for me!

Cline.

July 18, 1915.

Dear little Jean,

. . . This morning, besides teaching my class, I read a chapter and made a talk. I think I spoke about thirty-five minutes, but intended to talk only about twenty. It is such a joy, however, to give people teaching that they have never heard that the time flies past. I am going to conduct their prayer meeting next Thursday night. I asked one of the boys of about my own age to read the lesson and make a talk and three of the older brethren to follow him, and I shall close the meeting. I think this is new to them.[32] They have been

---

32. Cline here describes what J. A. Harding and his followers termed "mutual edification" by which the responsibilities of conducting a worship service were shared among several men in the congregation. Hicks and Valentine, *Kingdom Come*, 111–13.

taking some subject and reading chapters and verses on it, but have not been speaking. And they have not been trying to get the boys (there are only two of them now) to take part. I have never been to their prayer meetings yet, because of the amount of work I had to do. I wanted to go last Thursday, but when I looked at my books I remembered another lesson I had to get for the next morning. I had to read over a hundred pages of a certain book. I don't know whether I was right or not, but I thought a good record for our college would be worth as much to the Lord in the years to come than my attendance at the meeting. But I am going every time I possibly can. The church needs encouragement, and I can give them some. Next year my work will not be so heavy because I will not take three English courses, and I can help them more than ever. Three courses in English are about as heavy work as one can do. There is so much reading and writing to do....

Cline.

Monday, July 19, 1915,

My dear old bachelor brother,

. . . Bro. Crumly [sic] is here. He began his meeting here yesterday. I hope the meeting will be good and he will not cause trouble. Hope is not the right word. I wish it but I do not expect it. He already has many of the faction coming out and has preached both times on unity. . . .

We are still hard at work preserving fruit. We have seventy five gallons in the cellar and three bushels of plums to be canned to-day. We'll get some thing like fifteen or sixteen gallons out of that.

Eula Tomlinson is in town now. She gave a program at the Baptist church last Friday night. I wanted to go so much but the money received went toward helping the Ladies aid and, of course, we couldn't go. Sister Foster, Ella Gentry's mother, went and she told mama that there was just a little handful there. She said Eula did a fine job. Eula is very talented and she has been away two years, both summer and winter, studing [sic] Expression and English, so she should be good . . .

Your "only" sister.

Cline's comment indicates that mutual edification was not a practice common to all Churches of Christ.

July 19, 1915.

Dear Jean,

... From my observations of life women are hard to possess. Even Caesar's wife told the great Caesar that he *should not* go out of his house. 'It is a wonder she didn't say "my house,"' says Dr. Scott. It is very often the case that a woman possesses her husband, or a sweetheart her lover. If you wish to see two kinds of women—one the possessing kind, the other the kind that is *possessed*, but by her womanliness is really the ruler, the Queen, of the home—read the parts of Calpurnia and Portia in "Julius Caesar." Calpurnia can command the omnipotent Caesar and fail in her desires; Portia pleads with Brutus and wins his full confidence, till he imparts to her all the secrets of his heart. Two common and distinct types of women.

I have examined the catalogs. They *are* beauties. I think it one of the best catalogs the school has ever had. I am going to change some things in the English course next year. It sounds too hard as it is. I can clip some of the unnecessary parts and make it much better. In the last course in the college work I shall put Essenwein's [sic] book on short-story writing in,[33] unless I can find a better one. I wonder who will teach our college work next year. We haven't found a teacher yet, have we? ...

I am indeed glad that Brother and Sister Harding will be with us next year. I *love* Brother Harding though I never talked to him but twice. One time he walked with me from your home, where the boys now stay, to the college. He came to our debating society and I had to debate before him. I was glad our side won the debate, though of course he forgot it at once.[34] Another time he ate dinner at Brother Bill's when I was there and I talked with him some.

I would like to see Sister Harding too, because I have heard you talk so much about her that I almost know her. You must tell her about your brother so that we may be good friends, for I should hate to get one of her sharp speeches. I think some one told me her tongue was sharp sometimes. But I expect to love her as much as my own grandma if she will let me.

Of course, Brother Harding will like to be here. How could he help himself when he has my little sister to wait on him and take care of him. He ought to think himself in paradise! ...

---

33. Joseph Berg Esenwein's *Writing the Short-Story* was published by Hinds, Noble, & Eldredge in 1909.

34. This is probably a reference to the dementia that overtook Harding late in life. He had begun suffering from periodic blackouts and was forced to resign the presidency of Potter Bible College. Young, *History of Colleges*, 115; Hicks and Valentine, *Kingdom Come*, 21.

As I was coming home from singing last night (we have a "singing school" every Sunday night here; but it is not a *"fake"*) I heard some one playing "Il Trovatore." It sounded so beautiful on the still night air and brought back so forcibly the memory of that night last spring when I gave "Aux Italiens"[35] and you gave "After the Wedding" and "Vanesse,"[36] that I had to stop and listen. I could see you as you looked that night with your angel wings and your "full, soft hair" falling down over your shoulders, and I would have given a year of my life to have seen you again and have lived anew that night. But it is gone! No, we have it yet, and can never lose it. It is still ours!

Cline.

July 20, 1915.

Dear Jean,

... Tell Sister Armstrong if she hasn't sent my grades yet to be sure to do it; because I promised Professor Paxton I would have them sent to him. Of course, they will not change my credit now, for it has already been determined.

Ben Fleming, Mark Fleming's brother, made the remark at the table Sunday that he believed the church ought to build dormitories at the different universities instead of building Bible schools. But most of us at the table hardly agreed with him. A Christian dormitory at a place like this, if it were regulated as our Bible schools are, would soon lack boarders. I don't think Ben Fleming has ever been to a Bible school either. All who have been must disagree with his statement. It was surprising to me to see how the people here regard Bible colleges. Almost every one of the students I have talked to admit that small colleges like ours do better work than the university. Some of them have been to different denominational schools, and they say the schools which teach the Bible and moral living are almost without exception the best schools in literary work.... I have found numbers of students who have heard of our college and they ask about our work. They all understand that we do work far above the average. I didn't know we did have such a wide reputation before. Several times I have had students, when I told them I was from Cordell, to ask me "if that is not where the Christian College is; that

---

35. "Aux Italiens" is a poem by Victorian-era author Edward Robert Bulwer-Lytton.

36. These two references are unclear. The first is possibly to a chapter entitled "After the Wedding" in *Dr. Dumany's Wife* by Hungarian author Maurus Jókai, published in English in 1891. The second may allude to Jonathan Swift's poem "Cadenus and Vanessa."

they have heard about it, and guess they do fine work; that they have heard it was much better than any of the high schools."

Of course our school is not known to every one all over the state but it is known pretty well to the students from all the surrounding counties.

I saw a bulletin to-day from Vanderbilt University. Vanderbilt stresses the Bible and their "School of Religion." They can afford to do so, for it is the greatest book in the world. I have been reading some views on its authenticity by Ruskin, and I don't like them at all. He believes it is not inspired but was the work of great men who were trying to fathom the spiritual world and find its relation to the natural. He admits a kind of Divinity and a kind of spirit, but he borders dangerously on absolute infidelity. *He* puts his position next to what he calls the rankest kind of infidelity. He is entertaining but not convincing in anything he writes.

I also saw an Indian second reader[37] a few days ago. Sequoyah invented the alphabet and established the first Indian school or printing press, I am not sure which, it has been six years since I read about it . . .

Cline.

Thursday, July 22, 1915.

Dear brother Cline,

You are a *bad, bad* boy writing mama letters that I can't read. . . .

We lack one pint having ninety gallons of fruit, pickles and a few beans in the cellar. We have plums and grapes enough in the house to be put up to day to swell the gallons to one hundred. It won't seem to take us half as long to preserve the last hundred gallons as it has the first. . . .

There is a negro minstrel in town. I don't know how good it is nor how long it's going to stay, but I do know one thing and that is that every one will go from the best families in town to those who can't buy clothes nice enough to come to church in. I say this because there hasn't been a show in town for a good while so people will go crazy over this one.

I couldn't be hired to go. I went to one show once in my life and I said right then I'd never go in another one. I was never in a place in my life where I felt so much out of *place* as I did under that tent.

We have our services on the south side of the house now. The brethren put a platform, seats, and lights out there. We have had three meetings out side, I think.

---

37. Most likely a book in an educational series similar to McGuffey's primers, first, and second readers.

You are right about the matter of possession. Few men possess their wives nor do many women possess their husbands. From my observation men are about as hard to possess as women.

I wonder some times if my idea of married life is impossible of fulfillment. I believe there should be a double possession. Each should want to please the other and be miserably unhappy when they failed to do so. But from my observation most women and men go on their way doing as they please regardless of the desires and tastes of their husbands and wives . . .

Jean.

July 22, 1915.

Dear Jean,

. . . To-day I heard a man speak on "Law." That is, I was in the room, for it was chapel, but I studied Tennyson all through it. Only the noise of his bluster reached me faintly, and now and then I recognized an unusually loud word, which just would push into consciousness in spite of all my efforts. . . .

To-day we were discussing the European war in the class, and I told them I was opposed to war and believed that all killing was murder. Ramey said he thought the bond of patriotism and national honor was stronger than the bond of religion or any brotherhood movement. I told him it might be for many, or most, people, but that it was not for all and should not be for any. After many other views had been expressed, he told us we could develop our theories in our short-stories, and I have chosen this for my theme. I shall have to invent my plot and incidents now. . . .

Cline

Friday, July 23, 1915.

Dear little Mother,[38]

This letter too must be *private*, mustn't it? It's a pity too, since Pataway doesn't like private letters. However, she may see them some time with my full permission.

I should like to tell you just how happy I am, I can never, never do it. My heart is too full. Though I cannot know the *full* meaning of the duties and obligations I accept when I ask Pataway to be my wife, yet I do understand

---

38. This letter is addressed to "Mrs. J. N. Armstrong, Cordell, Oklahoma."

something of the great responsibility I take, and it tinges my joy with soberness and makes it deeper and more abiding than I had ever dreamed that joy could be.

And no little part of it comes from your confidence in me. If gratitude ever inspires men to live more nobly and honorably, I shall never disappoint you in the least act of life. I wish Brother Armstrong could trust me as perfectly, but since he cannot yet, I shall live all the more carefully to gain his confidence. I love and revere him as I did my own father.

I promise you willingly never to influence Pataway to keep anything from you. She shall be at perfect liberty to tell you anything she desires, for I think nothing else would be right. You will still be her mother and will have a perfect right to know all her secrets.

But I am writing as if I had already gained her promise to be my wife. That must come yet, and I am in suspense till then; for she will have so much to overlook in me, and I am so unworthy of the least of her love that I can only wait with some degree of anxiety.

I must be sincere with Homer. I received a letter from him a few days ago in which he confessed that he had been jealous of some of his best friends and was just now getting over it, and said that he had never loved me so much before in his life. I hope I shall not lose his friendship. I must treat him in such a way that I will not.

I must write some now to Jean, and then study. My work is now coming in waves; as soon as I breast one, another comes.

Lovingly,
Your son.

July 24, 1915.

Dear little Jean,

You are a very, very cruel sister! I had to wait twenty-four hours, *long long* hours, for your letter—just because I write a private letter! Then I had to write another; what *will* you do this time?

I am sorry you cannot read them, but there are some things a brother cannot tell even his best and only little sister. But I haven't done anything to be put in prison for—not murdered anyone nor stolen the United States—in fact nothing very bad. Please do not use any further punishment; I am in sack cloth and ashes till I receive again the favor of my little sister Queen.

Jean, will you tell Carl and Brother Short to write to the Book Supply Company at Chicago and have them get the "Cambridge Edition" of

"Tennyson's Poetical Works" for me? I have to read all of Tennyson's "Idylls of the King" before I teach any of them.

Then tell them to write to Allyn and Bacon and ask them to send me a copy each of "Im Vaterland" and "Immensee."[39] Tell them to sign my name to the letter and explain that I teach German—that is, write the letter as if he were the teacher of German in our school. Teachers get books for nothing if they are thinking of using them for their class. Then tell them to find out who publishes "Andersen's 'Märchen'" (Fairy Stories) and ask them to send that to me, using my name as in the other letter.

Then have them write to Scott Foresman, & Co., and ask them to send me "Marsh's Manual for Teaching English Classics." Have them write this letter in the first person and sign my name as teacher of English. They will also send this book without charge.

Have them next to write to Ginn and Company and ask them to send me "English Classics" by Trent, using my name as before. And also tell them to find who publishes Essenwein's text on Short-story Writing. I don't know the exact title of the book but Essenwein is the author. I think Hinds, Noble and Eldredge are the publishers. I think this book will make a good text for the last course in the college English. It is used by many of the large colleges and universities. They ought to get this book also without charge to teachers. Have all of them come there, for I shall be at home before they could get here. This is all I shall need at present. They will have to pay for only the poetical works of Tennyson.

Now I am making my little sister work for making me wait! ...

I think too that not many married people are a "double possession." They are not unhappy when they cannot please one another; and a few, perhaps, even glory in being obstinate and stubborn. I was reading of the domestic life of the Spanish yesterday and I was surprised at what I learned. Most of the Spanish families show a tenderer love and a stronger union, and are happier and more contented than the average American family. But there are some where the extreme opposite of this exists. The husband and wife have a quarrel, and though one word would make things right, they are both too proud to say it. And so they never speak to each other on the street; one comes in at the front door, the other at the back; if they should chance to meet at the stairway, neither recognizes the other. Thus they continue to live, year after year, without speaking, in separate parts of the house, while one word would set things right. They cannot get divorces for the church will not permit it,

---

39. Paul Valentine Bacon wrote *Im Vaterland* in 1910. It is an introductory German text book emphasizing understanding the language through conversation, song, and acquisition of cultural knowledge. Popular German author Theodor Storm published his novella *Immensee* in 1849.

and they are unwilling to endure the shame of a public separation. This would be worse than all the tortures of purgatory!

I do not think your ideal of married life is impossible of fulfillment if people could really see the nobleness and greatness of it and strive to attain it. It may be too high for many; their foreheads are too narrow. But it is without doubt the only way for married people to be the very happiest and most contented. Perhaps, low ideals are not the only thing which keep people from such a life. For we must admit that it would not be *easy* to live perfectly all the time, and the life you have as an ideal is almost perfect. . . .

My glasses haven't come yet, and I do need them badly! Why, I studied your picture . . . for an hour, perhaps more, before I began this letter. Don't you think I shall ruin my eyes? But, you see, I am just that proud of my little sister, for she is the *only sister* I have.

Lovingly,
Her brother.

Saturday, July 24, 1915.

My dear big brother,

I am sorry my last letter had to be such a little thing—but I could not help it. As it was I had to run to the train with it. Before I got to the top of the hill the train whistled and by the time I reached Dr. Freeman's it was at the station. I felt sure I had missed it but I hurried on. When I got in sight of the power house the train started off but as it happened it had to stop to hitch on the show car. I ran and got there just in time to pitch my letter in at the car door. I don't know whether you'll get it or not because the mail clerk didn't see me throw it in. I suppose he'll find it. It was in plain sight on the floor. It's a wonder that I didn't miss the door when I threw it and I [sus]pect I would if the train had not been running. I threw it at one side of the door and it went in on the other side.

. . . We were in fruit Thursday "up to our chins" and Mama was not well and when we got through I was too tired to think or write. I tried to get up early yesterday morning to finish but didn't give myself time. . . .

. . . You'll have to love Grannie Pattie when you know her. She may scold you if she thinks you are doing wrong—I think mama has done that a few times, hasn't she? and I believe you love her—but if you are sick or in need she "sticketh closer than a brother."[40] She is a great old lady and you must love her because I do. She may look at you rather sharply when I tell her you are

---

40. Proverbs 18:24 (KJV).

my big brother because she loves me and will want my brother to be a *very nice man*. But I am not afraid of her judgment of you. Just smile at her and ask her to let you be her boy and you will capture her soul and body. She is very tender hearted in spite of her occasional sharpness.

Of course everybody loves Grandpa. He is easier to learn but not one bit better than Grannie Pattie. I'm not sure that the stars won't be more beautiful in her crown than in his . . .

Mr. Fleming doesn't know anything about a Bible School. They didn't have one when his "brethren" were here. I'm glad you are finding our school so well known. Faithful work always wins in the end . . .

The faction is coming to church now and several of them have made public confessions. We are all going to meet and worship together tomorrow. Usually when they say they want to come back it is on the condition that Papa not be allowed to preach. This time they don't come that way. I feel more hopeful than I ever have that they really want to do what's right. I do hope they will.

Sister Holland is up and comes to the meeting some. I thought that woman would be dead in a few days when I wrote you about her. She may get well after all and live to be an old, old woman. It would be a pity for her her [sic] to die now because her children are both small. I am speaking from a human standpoint. If she should die we would know that for some reason the Lord saw it was best. . . .

Jean.

July 25, 1915.

Dear little Jean,

. . . I'm afraid I made a great big mistake this morning. I made another talk at church and gave some teaching on prayer. I forgot that the people might not believe as we do at Cordell. Of course I knew that some of them would disagree with me but I didn't know the whole church would. My talk was too strong for them; I could tell it before I got through. It will be harder now to teach the lessons on prayer that they need, for they will be more prejudiced.

I ate dinner at Brother Petty's and we had the discussion there. He said he could not agree with me in what I taught at church and began to explain why. I listened patiently and spoke when I could. There were four men arguing against me, so I had a hard time. I think, however, that I "converted" Miss Mary Petty, for before we quit talking she helped me against all the rest of them. It is hard to remember, when you are talking, just what to say; and it is hard to know just how strong to make a speech. I think I have learned a lesson, though....

Jean, have they tried any more to get another English teacher? I wish Miss Wells could come. Unless Sister Armstrong is going to take the College English we really need some one for it, don't you think? I was talking to Mr. Ramey yesterday about teaching English in the high school, but I don't like his ideas as well as I do Professors Scott's. He doesn't seem to care for interest in a class; he wants work, and doesn't care if the students detest it. I don't like that idea of teaching. I think a teacher ought to try to create an interest in his classes *first*, then give the work and he will get much better results. Scott said no teacher ought to teach a single classic which he did not like and have an enthusiasm for. Scott himself practices this and you cannot go to sleep in his classes, but I have longed for a bed in Ramey's!...

Cline.

Cordell, Okla., Monday, [July 26,] 1915[41]

My dear Son,

Your letter came Saturday and I appreciate it more than I can tell you. I want to thank you from my heart for your promise not to teach my girl to hide from her mother. Not many men are so kind. This seems to be the effort of most men from the very first—to put a wedge between the girl they love and her mother. It is strange, isn't it? but I have seen it over and over again. I have always said that I would be a miserable woman if I could not love with all of my heart the man Pataway chooses and if he could not love me.

Do you know I despise the very term "in law" I wish it could be banished from the dictionary. My mother, my son, my daughter or my sister sounds so much sweeter and happier than my mother-in-law my son-in-law etc. I never want to be a mother-in-law and I never on earth want a son-in-law. I am glad that I have known and loved you since you were a child. I am glad that you loved me before you loved Pataway. She is my life, Cline, and anything that would separate us would kill me. I know you realize this to the full.

---

41. This letter appears on Cordell College letterhead that reads down the left hand side, "J. N. Armstrong, Pres. High School Affiliation. Accredited by university for 20 Units. Therefore sufficient entrance credit for sophomore standing in university. Senior standing in all state normals." On the right side of the letterhead appear the following items of information: "Founded in 1907. Our students are from twelve states. Bible taught daily to every student. Complete catalog sent for the asking. Board and tuition very moderate."

In less than two weeks now you will be home. We had planned to have all of the young people here the night you come home but present prospects seem to indicate that the meeting will still be in progress at that time so we may have to change our plan but your "Dream Day" shall be saved for you if it be possible. If not there is another day.

Pataway has already received several invitations for that day but has quietly answered that she has an engagement for the day. Homer heard her tell Alice this yesterday and asked afterward what special plan (meaning you & she) had.

She told him nothing special and he asked no more. I am sorry for him from my heart.

The meeting seems to be doing much good. I believe the faction is coming back to do right. This will be a glorious thing. Brother Crumley is a better man than we had thought. I am sure of this. Pataway wants the pen—we've only one decent one in the place—I gave her both of your letters to me and told her that they contained your secrets and you alone could give her permission to read them but that she could keep them until you were willing for her to read them. She put them with your letters to her in a box that is now quite [full].

Lovingly,
Your Mother.

Monday, July 26, 1915.

Dear brother Cline,

...Alice told me yesterday that she and Bro. George and Miss Maud are going to Thorp Springs next year. I had heard it before but I thought it was just talk. I suppose it isn't though because Alice told me with her own lips. I think it will be better for all of us....

Clyde Utley and his wife were here the other night. Bro. Clyde told mama that Ira is working for him. He said that Ira is as faithful and steady as an old work horse, that he'd trust him with anything he has. I am so glad that he has turned out that way because I think a great deal of Ira. I know he can make some thing if he will only try. He is as bright as a new dollar. He is thinking a little of coming to school next fall but I hardly think he will.

Sister Smith and Ola are back now.[42] They came Friday. Sister Smith didn't get to go to church a single time while she was in O'Keene. I can't see how she could stay in a place like that over Sunday. She stayed because she

---

42. Mrs. Smith had gone to O'Keene to work as a hotel cook for a few weeks.

wanted the money Why she told me the other day she would not be satisfied until she made a fortune. That she didn't want Ola to have the hard time she has had. I am afraid that woman is going to let money send her and Ola both to perdition. She asked me the other day if I didn't want to travel for a book company or a condensed milk company. She said she was just crazy to travel for some kind of company. That she believed she could make a lot of money that way.

Mama and I both have talked to her and told her she was stepping on dangerous ground, but she don't [sic] think so and won't listen to us....

Bro. Rice left this morning to rest his voice for a week before he goes with Bro. D. Bills in a meeting. His voice has just given out and must have a rest.

I am sorry he had to go because he *can* get more singing out of this congregation than any body nearly in spite of his disagreeable expression.

Bro. George O'Neal is going to lead from now on. He is the best we have.

Bro. Crumley has been preaching on people talking about one another. Last night Old Sister Treece came up to me and she said, "Honey, if I have ever said anything to hurt your feelings I want you to for give me, for I never done any thing to injure you in my life. If I said any thing it was because I was ignorant and not because I willfully done it. If there is a pure girl in the world I believe it is little Pataway." Now did you *ever*! I suppose the things she has said she said, Sir, because she thought they were *true*!...

Delia will be at home Sunday. Alice is going to take a crowd of us out home with her then. She wanted us to go the second Sunday but I told her I couldn't come then for I had an engagement for that Sunday. And a *very* important one it is too. *Too important to break.*

Jean.

Tuesday,

July 27, 1915.

My dear little Sister,

At last your letter has come and I am happy again...

I, too, am "sorry" that you had to run so hard to catch the train. Never do it again! Didn't you know over-exertion in such hot weather was dangerous? I should be an unnatural brother to want my little sister to kill herself merely to mail a letter on time! So when you just cannot send a letter on time, send it the next day, and I shall get it just the same and perhaps enjoy it more for the wait....

Of course, Jean, I shall love Sister Harding and I shall do my best to get her to love me; and I suppose, if I am just myself, that she will like me as much as the rest of you do, that is, after she has known me as long. It sometimes takes a long while for people to know each other. Why, my sister used to hate me! (If she could ever hate anyone) No, hate is not the right word, for you didn't know enough about me to hate me. You merely had an extreme abhorrence!...

Cline.

Wednesday, July 28, 1915.

Dear brother Cline,

... Mama and I, together with sister Short, Sybil, Amanda and Bro. Crumley were invited over to sister Wilson's yesterday for dinner. We all had a *nice* visit.

Do you know I feel so sorry for sister Wilson and sister Short. The subject came up about girl's marrying. Sister Wilson began! She said a girl should stay single *as long as she could and have a good time*. She would not have one *after* she was married. She said *she* lived a *miserable* life and only married for a home, and, of course, she loved Bro. Wilson, too. She talked like this *all the after-noon* and said other things that I can't think of now. Sister Short said she knew Mr. Short loved another woman better than he loves her; that he went with this girl befor [sic] he married his wife, and would have married her but she *went back on her promise*. Now isn't that terrible? Amanda told me after we left that such things as that made her feel as if she *never wanted* to marry.

I don't believe a man has a right to marry one person loving another one better. It isn't treating the girl he marries right. Should I ever get into anything like that, I'd never let my neighbors know it....

Bro. Crumley's wife and three children are here to-day. This morning he had the baby up on the stand with him while he made his last remarks. I tried to imagine papa doing a thing like that, but I could not ...

I have more hope of the church's being united again than I ever have had. Every time before they have said, "we'll come back if Armstrong won't preach." This time they seem to be willing to do any thing that's right. Many of them, both women and men, have made public confessions.

I am sorry, but I have misjudged Bro. Crumley. He is a good deal better man than I thought he was. I think the debating he has done causes him to have the manner he has....

Jean.

July 28, 1915.

Dear little Jean,

    ... I am sorry George and the others are going to Thorp Springs next year, but perhaps it is best. I do not like for students to leave the school dissatisfied; they are dangerous influences....

    I should like for Ira to be in school next year too, if he has changed as you say. If he would try, he could do almost anything he wished, for he is far more brilliant than most people. Does my little sister still think she could love him as she once did?

    Brother Crumley does seem to be doing the church some good. Perhaps those confessions to you were really from the heart. I hope they were and that they will never talk again. Sister Treece still has a talk laid away for me, I guess. She told me she had one this spring and started to deliver it one day, but didn't have time. I hope she has forgotten it....

Your "big brother."

July 29, 1915.

Dear little Jean,

    ... I have just come back from a little fire. The third house south was set on fire by one of the children. I think she built a stove under it and wanted to burn some things. When I got there the fire was out and the fire wagon was ready to go back.

"Moral is,"

we must have no places under the Orphan's Home where the children can build furnaces, and we must have the building of brick and made fireproof. I should not like to get a sudden report that you and about thirty children had been burned alive! Also we must have a good big cellar with three or four rooms, lighted by electricity, and furnished with beds, chairs, a table, etc. So that when cyclones come you can go below and let the children sleep there. The table and book case in your room will furnish you amusement as long as you want to watch the storm. Wouldn't this be nice? I am planning all the time ...

Cline.

Friday Afternoon.

[July 30, 1915]

Dear Jean,

... I don't believe Sister Wilson knows what love is. She may think she loves her husband, but I seriously doubt it. Or if she does love him, he must be a dull clod of a man if he cannot make her happy. Of course, things will come up in the happiest families to mar their happiness for a time—we will all have to be perfect before we can prevent it—but where there is *real love* and mutual understanding between a man and his wife, I believe *that* must be the *very happiest* life on earth. But I should think married life without love would be one of the unhappiest on earth. It would be like Sister Wilson's. She may marry for a home and a living, but if she does she may expect nothing but unhappiness. I rather think, however, that Brother Wilson is such a man as could not make any woman *supremely* happy. He always appeared to me to be dull, uncommunicative, self-contained, gruff and coarse, and not tender and affectionate and sympathetic, as a man ought to be.

I have always felt sorry for Sister Short. I didn't know Brother Short loved another woman, but I was sure he did not love Sister Short as he ought to or he could not stay away from home so much. He is away all the time and only comes back for a visit a few times each year. I don't think any man with a family of children has a right to be away all the time. He is putting all of the greatest, noblest, and most difficult work that men have in this life upon the shoulders of his wife. Of course, the mother naturally has the greater influence on the lives of her children, but I am sorry for the child, especially for the boy, who has never known a father's love and advice. The influence of the father and the mother are needed alike.

But if Brother Short does not love her, he is doing the best he can; for it is better to live apart than to be unhappy all the time as Sister Wilson is. They are both to be pitied. ...

Cline.

Saturday, July 31, 1915.

Dear brother Cline,

... Papa came home yesterday on the morning train and stayed until evening. Mama went to Hobart to stay over night with him.

His visit home was short but I believe it was a profitable one. Bro Crumley came up and talked a good while and Bro. John Harrel came and confessed some things and told him he wanted the past completely blotted out and start anew. Sister Harrel invited Mama and me out to see them. We intend to go next week.

Only seven more long old days to wait and then my brother will be home.

Mama had a letter from Bro. Terry last night and he said, "Only six more weeks till school opens and what a meeting that will be."

Our students don't have to be here long before they learn to love this old place and are anxious to get back...

Next Saturday Ringland [sic] Brothers Circus is to be in Clinton. Bro. Homer, Bro. Short, Bro. Colson, Ernest, Mae, Beulah, Agnes, Sybil and I are going not to the show but to Clinton. If you come through there Saturday we'll meet you there and if you come Friday so much the better. You can go back with us. We intend to take our dinner and go to the park and stay until the evening train...

Sallie Ellis is here now visiting Mae and Beulah. I don't know whether she will stay until next Sat. or not but we want her to and go to Clinton with us....

Jean.

July 31, 1915.

The very last day!!!

Dear little Jean,

... I have finished my thesis for Scott, have it copied, bound, and ready to hand in. I thought he had to have it to-day, but when I came to the class this morning he said he would want them next Wednesday. This was in our class in Literary Criticism. We had our last recitation this morning in it. We meet next Wednesday at our regular class period for a short examination. He said it was only a mere formality, for we did not need an examination, but that it was required by the faculty and so he must give it. He is going to make it easy, though, and hold us only one hour instead of two....

Your big brother.

Home Saturday

[July 31, 1915]

My dear Son,

I am sending you a check for ten dollars. If this is not enough to get you through write me at once.

A week from today at the latest you will be home. We will all be glad as can be, but I think one little lady is counting the hours. You are very much in her thoughts this summer. I hear old Mrs. McDonald cry "what will the end be" and lis[ten] for Mrs. Buchanan's reply, "Happiness for all of us I hope."[43]

Mr. A. came home for a few hours yesterday and I went with him to Hobart last night and spent the night. He will not be home till school time. By the way, that time will soon come. We are getting lots of catalog calls. We must pray for a good school.

Mr. A. talked to George about his going to Thorpe [sic] Springs and he said he was going because he thought the change would be fine for him *not* because he is in any way at outs with us. I was glad to hear that and am rejoicing in my soul that they are going. He would *always* be jealous of you. With George, Delia & Alice and Bixler away the chief jealousy of you as a teacher will vanish. I feel sure of this—Bixler would be so jealous as a cat of you. Of course, it "sticks" us a little that students would leave us for another school but I have a joy so abiding in the matter that it overshadows this pride—perhaps false pride. If they are against us, they could do us *far* more damage among us than away....

I only meant to write a note and here I am writing a great long letter. I promised Pataway I'd finish a dress for her to wear tomorrow but if I don't [illegible] I'll not be able to keep my promise. It is nearly finished. It just has to be hemmed and the waist and skirt put together and some sort of fasteners put on. It's just a little old pink gingham but she wants it to wear out to brother [sic] O'Neal's tomorrow. A white dress would look too dowdy for church tomorrow night.

I must tell you one thing more. Yesterday afternoon brother John Harrel and brother Freeman came up and brother Harrel told Mr. A. that he wanted to ask his forgiveness for every injury he has ever done him. Said he brought brother Freeman along because he wanted him to hear the confession. Things are going better than they have ever gone. Our God is so good we should be ashamed *ever* to doubt him. Things are in better condition here than they have been for ages. My! how this church has been "lambasted" for *talking too much*. I think we shall have some peace of our lives for a while, at

---

43. See the introductory material to this chapter regarding this reference.

least. Maybe it will help to break the blow of your going with Pataway. Really, I think it will. People make many things their business that in no wise concern them but I am sure it is God's blessing to us that this upheaval came when it did. They *cannot* be so bad as they would have been. They've m[ade] too many confessions, promises and "such like."

Sallie Ellis came today to visit the Symcox girls. Pataway is over there with them today. Sallie Ellis seems *delighted* to get back to Cordell. She'll be better too, I am *sure*—I tell you boy, God is good. We can't do half enough for him.

Last night Jack said to me "I hope you'll advise Pataway to quit referring to Cline as a brother. Those children will make themselves utterly ridiculous by any such pretentions. Why, don't they know everybody can see better than that!" He is gradually getting used to the idea of his little girl's caring more for another man than for her father. It has come hard to him and I have been as sorry for him as I *have been* for myself.

He is everlasting proud of you. You must not disapp[oint] him in any way. You should see his eyes twinkle and shine when we tell him of some particular success you have had in your work.

Dear me, here I am still writing! I am in a talkative mood this afternoon and am here at home by my lone self. Come and keep me company.

Mother.

August 1, 1915.

This is your longed-for month—and mine!

Dear Jean,

I suppose you are out at O'Neals having a glorious time to-day. At least, if you *are* there I hope you are not as lonesome as I am this afternoon. You were never away from home much, were you? Just wait till you go to the university and I "have to stay at home." You may think it will be fun, but I suspect you will change your mind before eight tremendously long weeks crawl past. Then I should be at home having the "glorious time" and you would be here wondering if summer schools ever really end.

But I doubt if that time ever comes. I don't know whether I shall let my little sister go to the university or not. I would if there were some one to go with you, but I don't think you ought to go alone, unless you can stay in some Christian home. I should not want you to stay in a common boarding house, because you would be miserable there. You are so different from these girls here and have such different ideals that you could not be happy with them.

And if my little sister were not completely happy, I should be miserable too. So to spare both of us, you must stay with Christians. That's settled! ...

At church this morning I taught my class again and made another talk. This is three talks, (Brother Fleming calls them sermons) I have had to make in succession. This time I was careful not to say things too hard for them.

It is strange, isn't it? But we are made so that we can see only a very little at a time. In teaching any strong lesson one must lead up to it by easier things or no one will believe it. At the table the other day we were talking about the way one of the boys treated a fellow who copied from him on examination. This boy went to Norman to school and his friend from whom he had copied was already there and had already received his standing. So when the new boy enrolled, he went to the dean and told him of this boy's copying, and caused him to lose a half year's work. Of course it was what he deserved, but the boy who reported him did it because he copied and he wanted to "get even with him," he said.

Well, when we were talking about it one of the boys said this fellow did wrong in reporting him, because God had said, "Vengeance belongeth to me."[44] This little lesson was easy for him to see, but if I had spoken just then and taught a lesson on civil governments, he would not have believed a word of it, because he is studying law at the university now.

I read a short play last night dealing with the problem of war. The hero was a young lawyer but was firmly opposed to war because it was murder! You could never on earth have convinced the author of the play that law was equally murder. We are all a strange, blunted, bigoted set. We are so prejudiced against every thing we have not always known that many of us think there really is nothing else to know worth knowing. ...

Cline.

August 2, 1915.

Dear Jean,

... Professor Scroggs is to take his psychology class through the asylum this afternoon. I am going over and go through with them. I shall tell you about the trip when I get home, for it will be too much to tell in a letter.

I got a card from Brother Armstrong this morning. Some of us were talking of going down to Lexington Thursday night, but I don't expect we shall. Then I got a letter from Homer. He began it on Monday and finished it on Thursday. I have some good long talks for him when I get back. ...

44. Deuteronomy 32:35 (KJV).

It is time for me to go to the asylum now. Please do not be uneasy till I get back, for there's not a trace of insanity in my ancestry, even if your unfortunate brother does show signs of it. I am sure they will not detain me.

Thine own brother!
Lloyd Cline Sears.

Tuesday Afternoon.

[August 3, 1915]

Dear Jean,

... I am glad you have planned that trip to Clinton. I shall be at the train waiting for you Saturday morning....

But really, Jean, if you are just coming to meet me and keep me from getting lonesome while I wait there, you didn't need to plan the trip. For I intended all the time to walk from Clinton home Friday night. I could walk that far in three or four hours and it would have been much easier than waiting all night and all the next day. For what boy could have waited when home and his little sister were just eighteen miles away? He would have to be void of feeling.

But I am glad all of you are coming, for it will save me this walk and I shall see you almost as soon. Please make the time hurry up!

Tell Sister Armstrong I received her letter to-day and would like better than *almost* anything to be there and keep her company while you have run away on a visit. If I were she, I think I should let you finish your own dresses and put on the fastners! [sic] Perhaps you would learn then not to be such a "gad-about," and would stay at home more. (This is not serious).

Also I received the money. It is more than necessary, I think.

I visited the asylum as I said I was going to do. It is *horrible! horrible!* I saw so many crazy people that every one I saw looked crazy when I came back to town. I was overjoyed to get back among people whom I *knew* were sane. I actually believe the nurses and doctors are influenced by being among them. They lose their facial expression and look as blank as a wall. The doctor who guided us looked almost as crazy as many of his patients. I think I should be influenced so far that I should *go* crazy, if I had to stay out there very long. It is a strain on sensative [sic] nerves...

Cline.

August 4, 1915.

Dear Jean,

...I have had two of my examinations already. They were not very hard and I think I passed in both. This finishes my work under Scott....

I also had my last class under Ramey to-day. He kept us only about half a period and then had conferences on themes some of us had written. The rest of us were "turned loose."...

I got A's on all three of the papers I handed to Scott. On one he put also "Excellent." I think most of the class made A's, although some fell to A−'s....

Sister Armstrong wrote that you were getting a great many calls for catalogs. I hope we shall have a good school next year. I expect a larger enrollment than usual. And our catalog will help bring some, for it is unusually good this year. The Beacon did a good job of printing.

One good thing—I think our troubles are about ended, Jean. If several leave school who say they are, and if people profit by the teaching of Brother Crumley, we shall have no more trouble. We can do just as other people do without hearing a continual whisper about it...

Cline.

Wednesday, August [11, 1915][45]

My dear papa,

I'm going to tell you some thing that I both rejoice and hesitate to tell. You know that I love you and mama more than I can express and that I have the purest and best fath[er] any girl ever had. But I realize now that I love Bro. Cline even more [word(s) missing] I love you [and] [word(s) missing] with all of my [word(s) missing]. Last Sunday evening he asked me to some time in the future become his wife, and I told him I would. We don't mean to and won't marry for eight or nine years yet—not until I finish high school and

---

45. The following three letters are contained in one envelope dated August 12, 1915, and addressed to "Mr. J. N. Armstrong, Lexington, Oklahoma." The gap in time between these and Cline's previous letter is due to his return to Cordell. At that point he had proposed to Pataway. Sears, *What Is Your Life?*, 64. The three letters to Armstrong are in unusually poor condition compared to the rest of the collection with much, especially of Cline's letter, simply missing. Cline quoted from these letters in his autobiography. Discontinuities between his quotations and the primary material suggest that the letters had already begun to deteriorate as he was writing his autobiography. Nonetheless the transcriptions contained here rely on the version contained in ibid., 64–65, to fill in some gaps.

my college work. Of course, we will guard ourselves against doing anything that will bring a reproach upon you, ourselves or the school.

[word(s) missing] know I'm very, very [word(s) missing] love him with my *whole soul* [word(s) missing] just sixteen, but I fe[el] that I know my heart [and] that I am doing the right thing. You must never think for one minute that you have lost a daughter. You must remember you have gained the dearest and best son on earth.

I love you dearly and wouldn't do anything in the world to displease you. I am happy an[d] [word(s) missing] [contented] now but I [word(s) missing] so much [word(s) missing] find out that you [word(s) missing] care in the least [word(s) missing] t[old] mama about it and I wanted to tell you myself too.

The meeting is still running. We have pretty good crowds every night. This morning Ammon Wright and the little Holland boy were baptized.

Did Mama tell you that [word(s) missing] Johnie [sic] Hudson will be [in] [school] next year? Now [word(s) missing] not surprised?

[word(s) missing] much.
Pataway.

Augu[st 11, 1915]

Dear Brother Arm[strong]:

From what Sister Armstrong told me you [word(s) missing] some knowledge of my love for Pataway [word(s) missing] sure this will not [word(s) missing] complete surprise [word(s) missing.] Last Sunday I [word(s) missing] [l]ove and gained her promise to be my wife. Of course there must be years before we can be married, but we shall be careful in the meantime.

I shall never ask Pataway for a single privilege which I could not take before you or her mother. Nothing else is [word(s) missing] we are both determined to [word(s) missing] else. And I am [word(s) missing] [de]termined, and I have also promised never to influence her to keep anything from you and Sis[ter] Armstrong. I [word(s) missing] able to prove to [word(s) missing] through the [rest] [word(s) missing] life that the [word(s) missing] and that [word(s) missing] [perfect] as it is pos[sible] [word(s) missing] me to make it. [word(s) missing] already have [word(s) missing] Armstrong's consent, [word(s) missing] all we lack is your [word(s) missing] [app]roval. I want always to be like a son to you, and to fill the place in your heart a son would fill. I shall always strive to be worthy of your confidence [word(s) missing] [a]nd your love.

[Sinc]erely yours,
Cline Sears

Cordell [word(s) missing]

Wednesday [August 11, 1915]

My own dear Sweetheart,

Pataway and Cline [have] just finished their letters to you. Of course, we both realized this was coming but hoped with our souls it could be postponed a while. Sunday afternoon Cline and Pataway came to me and Cline told me that he had asked Pataway to marry him and she had prom[ised] that she would and they wan[ted] my approval and blessi[ng.] Cline said he wanted to [word(s) missing] me two or three prom[ises] that they would not [word(s) missing] till Pataway is [word(s) missing] would never ask to [word(s) missing] privilege with her [word(s) missing] would not take in [my] presence and third, that he would never try to influence her to hide from us. They did not want me to write to you about it till they did. Pataway was sick Monday and Tuesday so today is the first chance they have had. Or rather, that [she] has had, and they wanted [word(s) missing] [se]nd their letters together. [word(s) missing] [to]ld Cline that he was [word(s) missing] for the dearest thing [word(s) missing] and we will [word(s) missing] [exe]mplary life in him. I appre[ciate] [word(s) missing] much his coming to [word(s) missing] he has done. Few bo[ys] [word(s) missing] Why, sister Symcox told m[e] once that she'd appreciate it if I could find out for her whether Mae and Elmer Taylor were going to marry. I think I'd be miserable under such circumstances. I told Cline that you and I had sen[sed] this coming for some time but hoped it could be postpo[ned] for a while. . . . I love you [word(s) missing] and I love our baby. [word(s) missing] she loves Cline [bet]ter than she does us (I have just read her letter. She had never told me that) but she doesn't yet. Of course, she will if her life is to be happy and we must love each other all the better. I don't believe she will love us less because of her love for him but we must [word(s) missing] him know that we [word(s) missing] him as a son if [word(s) missing] her love as completely [word(s) missing] want it. I'll never [word(s) missing] [su]ffering it caused me that you[r] [word(s) missing] [word(s) missing] was so opposed to me. I think I have never [loved] my mother quite so well because I felt that she did not make you quite as much of a son in deed and in truth as I thought she should. Of course we will have to be *very* careful in the school but we must *not* make the mistakes our parents made. We love Pataway too much for [word(s) missing] I'd die if I lost [word missing] of her love. Cline [word(s) missing] good [word(s) missing] make him clean and [word missing] in every way. He said that he had told her the very worst things in his past life and she told me that he told her of nothing worse than hugging and kissing several girls. I believe he told her all. He said he did. I am thank[ful] of this from my heart. I am sorry for Homer but [I] know no way to help it. [word(s) missing] so glad you wrote [word(s) missing] [Ma]mma and Papa. I had [word(s) missing] from Mamma last [word(s) missing] they appreciated [word(s) missing]. We must try to [word(s) missing] winter a very happy [word(s) missing] I hope we can. Mam[ma] didn't say when she thought they'd come. I wrote her today that the turmoil of the opening might be unpleasant for them and if they thought best they could wait two or three weeks.

The meeting continu[es] [word(s) missing] He preached a serm[on] [word(s) missing] this morning that [word(s) missing] don't believe. Part [word(s) missing] was good but [word(s) missing] was [word(s) missing] teaching, if I un[der]stand him, that people have no right to have special friends—that they are not true Christians unless they love every Christian alike. He has bored heavily on this several times. I think [he] is giving it to us ['c]ollege folk' especially. [word(s) missing] are said to be a very [word(s) missing] set." We may be but [word(s) missing] quite believe it....

Don't promise too many boys work. Don't forget in answering Dell's letter that those two rooms are *no* job at all. I know we are being criticized for [ha]ving "so much help." ... Bro Kieffer wrote [word(s) missing] about work in the [word(s) missing] but I understood [word(s) missing] back is not dependent upon [word(s) missing.] We won't need every [word(s) missing] in the office. Kieffer and [word(s) missing] do this business work for you if brother Blansett doesn't. We must watch expenses both as to collections and expenditures. We now have in the boys home Mr. Colson, Homer, Cline, Keershal Smith, Mr. Dasher, James Sheppard, and perhaps Dell, Hubert, Edwin and J. D. and perhaps [word(s) missing] brother Randolph.... This le[word(s) missing] for about five mor[e] [word(s) missing] house [word(s) missing] same boys dorm [word(s) missing] in the basement and Mary, Miss Hells, the three Jayne girls (if they come) Fannie, Sallie Ellis and, I think, Bessie and Eula. Your girl from Texas, sister Smith and Ola and you and me. This leaves room on the third floor for six girls. I pray that we may have [th]em.

[I] love you
Woodson.

Lexington, Oklahoma

Aug. 13, 1915.

My dear Pataway:

I have but one desire for you, and that is that you may be happy—always happy. I have always tried to be ready and willing to make any sacrifice for your highest and best good. So I am ready now to sacrifice my judgment in this matter for your happiness, and am willing to give you and Cline my blessing. I have but one baby in the world and it breaks my heart to give her up, even in promise. It was sweet in you to tell me, but it all but breaks my heart. I am to blame but I can't help it. You are *so* young, *too* young to make so important a promise as you have made. Maybe God will shield you from any harm therefrom. I shall always pray him to. Human experience and history prove that *long* engagements are unwise and many times serve to break hearts. I know you think you know your heart and so does brother Cline think he knows his, but in eight or nine years you may find you did not. But should time reveal to either of you that your promise to each other was made hastily, I beg of you now a promise; namely, be frank with each other and repent of the promise. It is far the better.

As to Brother Sears, there has never been another young man in our school whom I should prefer before him, and to whom I should so soon you would make such a promise. It is not he, but you, my child, that breaks my heart. I read your letter just before I had to preach to-day, and I felt that I could not preach. You must not forget that you are my only one, and you *so* young to take such a step. I would spare you.

No doubt at any age I should have grieved to give my approval to a promise like this. I am sure I never could think of giving you up without grief, but your age thribbles the sorrow it causes. But while I *feel* volumes this afternoon, I have written enough. I give you my blessing in the promise and shall be ever ready to help you out of any trouble your hastiness may bring into your life. So I "sorter" consent, but it is a case of "sour grapes."

Now you have told me, and your mother of your promise. This is enough. Tell no other friend howsoever good he may be. Your father with all my heart,

J. N. A.

Lexington, Okla., Aug. 16, 1915

My dear Cline:—I didn't mean to be this long in answering your letter to me, but am so pressed these days that I have been hindered till now.

As I wrote pataway [sic] it breaks my heart about it, when I think she has promised herself away. For she is *but* a *child*. She is *too* young for so grave a step, far more grave than either of you think, or can think today. Her age is the chief burden in the case. Had it come four years later it would not have grieved me so. I had great plans laid out for her and they are now somewhat shattered. Of course, my plans may have not been what the Lord wanted and I submit. But Pataway is very capable, as I judge things, and I think can easily be the greatest woman of her state for the Lord, but she needs time to do it. While I have not given up my plans, they will doubtless have to be greatly modified by the years to come. Should it be the Lord's will for her not to marry for eight years, my plans don't have to be modified a great deal. So I shall hope and pray for the best.

In a letter to her that doubtless you have seen, I promise you my blessing and I repeat as much here to you.

For a year nearly it has been in my plans to have you take the responsibilities of dean of our school just as fast as your age would admit. I am tired of these duties besides being unfit for them. I have a future picture of our school and you have filled an important place in this picture. While this picture was all made independent of your present relation to pataway and without a thought of this ever being your relation, I shall never get credit for it. My plan did not leave pataway out, of course, and so these plans need no change, nor is the picture marred.

But it does mean we must be very wise as we proceed to develop, or execute our plans. Severe will be the criticisms in spite of our wisdom. I am sure you realize to some degree the need of wisdom here and I ask that you be very discrete and prudent in your association with pataway.

I have always wanted a son that would or could approximate my ideal of a son, and while I love J. D. and hope to help him to be a good man, I can't hope in him for my ideal, and maybe the Lord means for you to fill this place in my life. If this be his ordering, I cheerfully submit. I could but love the man that Pataway learns to love, but I loved you before she did.

No difference whether Pataway's foolish and childish promise to you ever means more than a promise, I want you to be a full partner with me in my work in the school and on the Herald. This has been my plan. Now nobody should know our plans but you, Pataway, and her mother that we may the more effectively execute them for the Lord.

All this if God will.

Homer has also had an important part in my plans. I love him as I do you and regard him useful, very useful to the Lord and to us. I hope you and he may be brothers in the work.

With love I am your brother,

J. N. Armstrong.

Kiowa, Kansas,[46]

August 26, 1915.

My own Jean,

I am at home at last. I didn't have to wait at Enid but about two hours. The train should have left just as mine came in but had to wait on a car from Guthrie, and so I caught it in time to come home. It was an early train, however, and I got home about three hours earlier than I should have otherwise.... I came in at six and Mother expected me at nine. I had to walk home—about six miles—with the exception of a ride or two from people going my way. When I got within half a mile of home Mother and Ruby met me in a buggy.

Mother has just a few gray hairs and is forty-nine, a little older than I thought. Ruby is just fourteen, almost as tall as you, and a good deal fatter. I think she weighs one hundred and twenty-three. Now don't talk any more about being too fat!

I told Mother and Ruby and Opal about you last night, and gave Mother your gift. She told me to tell you that she "thought it was mighty sweet of you to think about sending it. And that she knew she would love you because I do and because you look so sweet and pure and innocent in your picture." I told her all I could remember of what you asked me to say, but afterward I told her just what *I* thought. She much preferred accepting my word to yours. Just like a mother, isn't it? Now, Jean, I have done it. What are you going to do with me? I have told her all about you and she too has given us her "blessing," but not a "sorter" one; so you ought to be satisfied even if she does think you are prettier than you think you are...

Cline.

---

46. After spending a few days back in Cordell, Cline went to visit his mother and siblings.

Saturday, August 28. [1915]

My dear Cline,

... I'm so glad your mother (Or would it be allright [sic] for me to say our mother?) gave us her blessing. I knew she would though. It would be impossible for her to do anything but pronounce a blessing upon you, the dearest, best boy on earth. I know she is proud to be the mother of such a son. I'm the proudest girl you ever saw to be loved by you but she is even more honored than I because she is your mother.

Yesterday evening I tried to varnish the stairway. I got it nearly all finished and got up early this morning to finish it before breakfast but when mama came in she made me take a pan of coal oil and rub it all off. I didn't know any thing about painting so I put it on too thick and it looked terrible. It took me almost as long to take the paint off as to put it on. Its [sic] needless to say that I *cried*! I suppose you would too if you had tried as hard as I did and then had it look so bad....

Sister Smith told me to tell you she is glad you are gone. They can get more work out of me when you are not here. I believe they are trying to kill me before you get back.

I haven't got a scratch from Grannie Pattie. I don't know what's the matter whether she don't [sic] like for her grand baby to be so old or whether she has just neglected it...

Jean.

Kiowa, Kansas.

Saturday Morning.
[August 28, 1915]

My dear, dear Jean,

I am lonesome to-day and sad. I have heard nothing for the last two days but wrangles, and quarrels and threats. It is a terrible thing to say but I fear you have promised to marry into one of the worst families you could have found. We are in many respects like the MacDonalds of Kentucky, and I have one brother almost as mean as Richard,[47] perhaps meaner. I didn't know how bad it was before, and I had almost forgotten what I did know because I had been away so long. I must tell you about it when I come home, but it almost breaks my heart....

---

47. The extant fragment of "The MacDonalds of Kentucky" mentioned in the introduction to this chapter contains a character named Richard. In the play, he is David's sibling.

I am going with Ralph this afternoon to visit a number of the people of the country and talk some more about the church trouble. If Ralph's statement of the whole matter is right, the church here is scriptural, but from many things I have known him to do and say, I cannot believe my own brother without more proof than his own word. This is terrible and I will write no more about it, but will tell you when I come back. The mail carrier is coming—and I must quit....

C. S.

Sunday Afternoon

[August 29, 1915]

Dear Pataway,

... You can never guess what I told my sister last year about you. I had forgotten it. But when I told her that you had promised to be my wife she asked what had become of that other boy who went with you last year and that I thought you were going to marry. She said I had told her you were already just about "spoken for" last year. Then I had to explain. I forgot that I ever said such a thing....

I shall be so *very* glad, dear, when I can come back. I miss you more than I can tell and my people are different from me. You cannot understand yet, but perhaps you will sometime. Please do not forget me till I come, for I still *love* you with my whole heart.

Always,

Thine own, C. S.

Monday Morning

[August 30, 1915]

My dear Jean,

I have to go to Driftwood this morning with a load of wheat, and can write only just a little note to tell you how much I should like to write more. No one is idle at our house and I have joined the army of workers. Chances are that I shall be in the hay field before another day or working with the threshing machine....

Cline.

Tuesday Morning.

[August 31, 1915]

Dear Jean,

...Raymond's wife has joined the Russelite[48] [sic] class and is full of that doctrine. She has been trying to convert me since she has come. Yesterday we talked all afternoon and till ten-thirty at night, but neither could convert the other. She will not accept plain statements of the Bible, but always twists their meanings into something altogether unnatural and contradictory to other passages of scripture. There is no use for us to argue, because she only gets angry and becomes more confirmed in her belief just as I do....

Cline.

Tuesday, August 31. [1915]

My own dear Cline,

...I've been painting the front porch this evening and have the first coat on a little over half. I knew the old thing was large but I fully realize the fact now that I'm trying to paint it.

I'm going to town in a few minutes to get your letter. I'm coming home and to night I'm going to get my room straightened. I painted the floor the other day and all the furniture had to be taken out. I want to put that back and make some curtains, hang them and straighten the dresser. All after eight o'clock to-night....

Jean.

Wednesday, September 1, 1915.

My dear Jean,

...We went fishing yesterday and caught but one fish. I caught it and it was a crawfish. After driving over the whole country to find a good place to fish, we came home, bringing seven large, dark green watermelons with us—also some ice. Last night we made cream, and this morning we are making some more. I have been beating eggs, stirring milk, and so forth. In a few minutes I must turn the freezer. I am stealing a little time to write to you, for I don't want you to be lonesome if my letters can keep you from it.

---

48. I.e., the Jehovah's Witnesses, founded by Charles Taze Russell.

I should have enjoyed helping you varnish the stairway, even if we had to rub it all off, for you don't know just how much of paradise it is to be with you and how miserably miserable I am away from you. I wish I could take you with me everywhere...

Raymond and I have been singing some. He wanted me to sing to see what kind of voice I had. He had heard that I sang in a quartett [sic]. I wish I had as good voice as he has, for his voice is mellow and smooth, but not muffled like mine. If I had, I should not spoil it by so many "trills" and "trembles," as he does...

Cline.

Thursday, September 2. [1915][49]

Dear Cline,

I have just read your letter and I feel much better. Yesterday evening I was too tired to go to church and too tired to walk down to the post office. Bro. Blansette [sic] promised me he would get the mail for me but when he came home I didn't hear him. I went to bed dissatisfied but I feel much better now....

I'm glad of one thing it's just two more days until I can talk to you. I'm so anxious for you to get here I can't wait because *I love you* so.

Jean.

---

49. This letter was returned to Cordell so apparently did not reach Kiowa, Kansas before Cline left there.

2

Summer 1916

During the summer of 1916 Cline returned to the University of Oklahoma. Fellow Cordell teacher Homer Rutherford joined him as a roommate to take classes as well.

There were more breaks in the correspondence that year than the previous one largely because Cline and Pataway were able to see each other more often. In late June, Jack Armstrong held a protracted meeting in Lexington, near Norman. Pataway and Woodson joined him for much of that time, giving Cline and Pataway a chance to travel back and forth.[1] Jack then went elsewhere to conduct another meeting and the Armstrong women stayed in Lexington a while longer before returning to Cordell via a route that allowed them to visit some old friends.

Another reason for gaps in the correspondence is that some of their letters are now missing. Cline numbered Pataway's letters and numbers three, seven, and eight from this set have vanished. Even though he stopped numbering that year after the twelfth letter, others may have been lost as well.

---

1. Cline met Pataway and Woodson in Oklahoma City and took them to Norman where they stayed briefly. The three then proceeded to Lexington and Cline was able to make return visits to Lexington on a few weekends. Sears, *What Is Your Life?*, 73. The letters reveal that the Armstrongs stayed with Jack's sister and her family.

222 South Porter Street

Norman, Oklahoma.
June 10, 1916.

Dear Jean,

...I wish you knew how lonesome I am. I am lonesome enough to cry! That's saying a good deal for a boy. But I'm away over here a hundred and twenty miles from you in a *great big two-storied house by myself with no light except a single little oil lamp, and the rats and mice running through the ceiling and rustling the loose paper on all sides of me, and a lonesome old clock ticking away on the wall in a dreary monotone that makes the silence fearful, and an occasional squeak of a rusty screen door blown by the wind and the sound of footfalls on the sidewalk that always appear to be turning in to the house; and other sounds that may be mice or may be wind or may be—I don't like to imagine.* It's a fine place to think of robbers, thieves, and cut-throats—of cold-blooded murders—of anything that makes you nervous and lonesome for company. It's worse than Noah's ark with a *hundred* Johnny Smiths creeping all about! I have the jim-jams, creeps, crawls, fidgets, or whatever else bad there is.[2] If I were not a boy I'd go to Henton's to stay all night. There—! there went that clock! It struck! Striking in a two-storied house that's empty and dark and—and scary isn't like striking where there's a dozen people and plenty of electric light. Tell Homer to come over here, quick!...

I left Oklahoma City on the twelve o'clock car and got here at one. My trunks were certainly handled rough. The rope on mine was broken and re-tied loose, and one corner was torn up: [sic] But not a can was broken in either trunk. I don't think they could have handled them more roughly, and they couldn't have come through in better shape. I have everything unpacked and in the shelves. We have a fine place to batch as soon as I get some company. The house was rented by some people for school last winter and this summer they went to their farm. They left a fine large rug in the front room, a nice table, a davenport, and a rocking chair. There are curtains and blinds at the windows, two beds, matrasses [sic], covers, and all; two dressers with dresser scarfs [sic] (there were also nice covers for the standtables), a large clock, dining table, and a lot of dishes, pans, skillets, pots, etc. I used their dishpan to-night. I'll have to have the water turned on and the fuses put into the electric lights. We have a good bathroom too and can have a cold bath every night. Besides all this there are a lot of pictures on the walls. We are "fixed up." Our front room looks like a parlor. If it were just not so lonesome! I believe I'll die before Homer comes. You make him get well!...

---

2. Cline quotes from this letter in ibid., 69.

... I went to the treasurer to pay my fee and it was thirteen dollars. I didn't have thirteen dollars and I couldn't get it. There was no one to borrow from closer than town and I had to have it instantly. So I did all I could do. I wrote a check on the Cordell National Bank for that amount. It will take a few days for the check to get there, and Sister Armstrong will have to deposit some of her money in my name if Minor's check hasn't come yet. If it has deposit it. I wrote the check for ten dollars exactly. If she deposits her own money, then when Minor's check comes tell her to keep it. I still have two dollars and I won't have to get many books I guess ...

My work this summer won't be the pleasure it was last summer, but it must be done, and as well now. ...

Cline.

Sunday Night.

[June 11, 1916]

My dear Cline,

I am just home from church and so lonesome I don't know what to do. I had to go to church all by myself. I started out with J. D., but when we got nearly to sister Freeman's, he remembered that he had forgotten to bring his milk. I didn't want to go back with him, and I knew Beulah and Mae were not very far behind us, so I concluded to wait for them. They didn't know I was there, and they went around by the public school. Consequently, I went to church by my lone self. How I wish you could have been here and gone with me. I miss you so much.

Brother Wall conducted the service to-night different from any I ever heard. Instead of reading, he asked for any one to quote some passage of scripture. Six or seven men quoted passages, then sister Goodrum quoted one. That just hurt me all over. I don't like to see women do things like that, especially when we are in a large crowd as we were to-night.

When we got home from the train this evening and began to wash the dishes, I went to the refrigerator for something and saw a piece of ham that was left from dinner. That made me think of last Sunday when you came to me and asked if there was any more ham. I began to cry at once and I've been crying off and on ever since. I just can't help it.[3] After we got through with the dishes, I went out and tried to help mama hoe around the flowers, but still I cried. You can't find any place where it isn't lonesome, but I guess I'll live over it. ...

3. See Cline's reference to this in ibid., 72.

The light flashed. I'll have to stop and finish this in the morning.

Goodnight.

I'll try to finish this little note now. It's getting late, but I haven't had one single minute all day. Mama certainly has kept me busy....

Bro. Luther sent his grades over this morning. I'm going to put those grades on the cards and book just as soon as I can so I won't forget them. My memory's not more than two inches long any way....

Bro Boyd's check came in yesterday morning. It was in the post office when you left. Mama will deposit the check and send you the money right away—all except three dollars and some cents. The bank called her up this morning and asked if you were here. They said that the check from the Book Supply Company had come. Mama told them she would send the money down this evening.

I hope you have found a room now and can get straight pretty soon. I think Brother Homer will be able to go in a day or two. He is much better today Horace said....

Jean.

222 South Porter Avenue,

Norman, Oklahoma,
June 13, 1916.

Dear Jean,

Classwork began today. Had my first lesson in history and Chemistry. This afternoon I have another three hours long in Chemistry—laboratory work. We have to have a towel and an apron. I have no apron yet but I'll make one out of my towel while I'm not using it. I believe I shall like Chemistry better than I thought, for it is something new. I never have had anything like it before. I know I shall like experiments, for I always did like to find out new things.

The teacher of chemistry is a young man of about thirty, a fellow of the school, I think, and not a regular teacher. But he is good and knows, or appears to know, chemistry.

I don't like my history class so much. Professor Dale has it and I'm afraid he is no teacher. He has the finest, squeakiest, huskiest, thinest [sic] voice you ever heard. He sounds worse than you do when you are sick and let your voice go up five. It seems hard for him to speak at all. He is as thin as a rail anyway, looks as if he had consumption, and his voice is all that is needed to convince you you are in a hospital of consumptives instead of in a university with a learned professor before you. Anyone could beat him teaching so far as I have seen. Hope I'll like him better after while [sic].

Why, he actually does like John Harrel. He explains and argues and explains and makes his point more and more obscure and then points over at some one and with a sickening grin (just like Harrel's) says, "You get my point, don't you?" or "Did you catch my meaning?" or "Do you see my argument, Mr. Walker?" Of course, Mr. Walker always nods his head.—Anyone could have seen his point, if he had any! I know I saw one; that was the end of his nose. It is long, and skinny and hooks down to one side. . . .

What do you think I'm going to have for dinner? I'll bet you cannot guess. Lettuce! I have a nice bed of lettuce right by the side of the house. I can use it for a long time, and there's no one else to get it. If I only had some mayonnaise dressing for it, I should be complete. I thought Sister Armstrong made some for me, but I've looked through everything and haven't found it. I am going to use instead a little vinegar from my pickles—just a little. And since Sister Armstrong says salt will improve the taste of things, I shall use a pinch of it. I wish you could eat it with me—I do!

I had for breakfast cold boiled ham, bunns [sic], catsup, and syrup. For dinner I shall have lettuce, pickles, ham, and bunns. The reason I'm having so many bunns is that I got a nickel's worth last night and I haven't been able to eat all of them yet. They go a long way.

I haven't seen about getting milk yet. I don't think I'll get any till Homer comes, and just let him pay for it. If I need any soup I can make it with water. I'm going to have to live on nothing if I can. But I'll enjoy getting home that much more, where I can have you to cook for me—or where I can just *look* at you. . . .

Cline

Tuesday [eve]ning

[June 13, 1916]

My dear Cline,

. . . They brought out numbers and put them up to-day. and instead of living at 1010 North Grant we live at 1020. Mama likes it much better. She lived at 1020 South Spruce Street when she was a girl.

Cline, what is the matter? I saw the train go by and I just couldn't wait so mama and I went to the office. Again I didn't get any letter. I tell you, if I don't hear to-morrow, I think, I'll do something desperate.[4] It makes me so uneasy when I don't hear. I think of all kinds of things that might happen....

J. D. sold his pig to-day and got eighteen dollars and a few cents out of him. He feels mighty proud now. I see him take the check out of his pocket once in a while to look at it. I think, he is going to get him another pig pretty soon.

Mama and J. D. both are lying down here on the floor asleep. I wish you could come in and talk to me awhile. I'm so lonesome I don't know what to do. I must hear from you tomorrow. I wonder what you are doing tonight. I hope it isn't as hot there as it is here and that you are fixed so you can get to work now....

Brother Homer is a great deal better to-day....

Jean.

Norman, Oklahoma,

Wednesday, June 14, [1916]

Dearest Jeanette,

... Last night we had next to the hardest storm I ever saw. The cyclone at Cordell[5] was the hardest, but this comes next. It was raining a little before I went to bed, but I didn't think it would be hard, so I went to sleep. About twelve o'clock, I suppose, I was awakened by a terrific gust of wind that slammed the doors and raised the covers off my bed. I ran to the door and looked out. The rain was falling in sheets and the large trees were swaying and bending almost to the ground in the wind. I saw that a storm had really come, but there are no cellars to go to here, so I didn't know what to do. I saw, however, that the wind was from the northeast, and as cyclones seldom come from that direction, I felt easier and went to bed and went to sleep while it was still blowing and thundering. I thought I had rather be asleep than awake if I were to [sic] blown away.

This morning I had forgotten the storm till I stepped outside. There on the ground was one of the largest limbs of the large tree in the front of our house. I went to school and saw on the way five trees, some 12 inches or even 18 or 20, broken down by the wind. One tree about 12 inches through was

---

4. See Cline's reference to this in ibid., 73.

5. This is probably a reference to an incident Cline recounts as having occurred in approximately 1910. A cyclone that came through town narrowly missed the Cordell College campus. Sears, *For Freedom*, 12–13.

almost uprooted entirely.... I didn't know how bad the storm was till this morning.

The man who owns the house in which I am staying came in a while a go and rented it to me for five dollars a month. That means two and a half a month for each of us. If we can live on fifteen cents a day a piece (I have spent only ten cents for food since I came and have opened none of the things I brought)—if we can live on fifteen cents a day, it will cost each of us only seven dollars a month to live. That is fifteen dollars for two months, and I think we can live even cheaper. I believe we can almost live on five cents a day apiece—can most of the time anyway. I must go with the man and have the water and lights turned on, as soon as he comes back, so this letter may be a little short if he comes very soon. He went across the street after a key.

Tell Homer to write me when he will be here, so that I may meet him. He won't know where to go....

Cline.

Thursday, June 15. [1916]

Dearest Jean,

... I am sorry you didn't get a letter Tuesday, but I didn't write from Oklahoma City. I had no opportunity that night, for Willard took me directly home and put me to bed. In the morning I started to write, Tuesday morning, but when I went to get some letter paper I found that I had left my suitcase and pencil in it at the terminal station, checked and ready to go to Norman. So I just waited till I got here. But as soon as I arrived I found that Mr. Henton had no place for me to stay, and I had to hunt for a place. I finally came here, but it was about two-thirty then, and I had to enroll before four at the University, and it's a long way from here. So I had no time to go through town for stamps and I had none with me, but I went straight to the "U" and enrolled ("matriculated"). When I got back about six o'clock or after I got my stamps and wrote.

This stamp proposition is a hard one anyway. I have had to pay so many advance fees, etc. that I get back when I start home that I am about strapped. If you fail to get a letter pretty soon, you will know that I have no stamps. I had to pay a water fee of two dollars yesterday before the water could be turned into the house. Of course, they explained to me that I got the two dollars back when I left the house, but that makes me nothing for the present. The same thing is true of my library fee of two dollars and my chemistry fee of ten.

I am getting dinner while I'm writing to you. I have two eggs cooked and some potatoes on cooking now. I hear the stove just boiling them. They have been on for some time but are not quite done, not soft enough yet. I'm making potato soup. Then I'm going to fix some more lettuce, for I had better eat it while I can. The storm the other night almost beat it into the ground. If I thought they would get large enough to eat in time I would get some radishes and some more lettuce and plant them. . . .

— — — — — —

These lines mean that I stopped to take up my potatoes and eat dinner and wash the dishes. The potatoes were fine, but I didn't have any soup, for I didn't put in enough water and it all boiled away. Lettuce, eggs, and potatoes make a very good dinner. . . .

Cline.

1020 North Grant Street,

Cordell, Oklahoma,
June 15, 1916.[6]

Dear Cline,

Rain again. You remember I told you some of the young people were coming over to play tennis this evening. It's been beautiful all day long. It's been one of the prettiest days we've had all summer till just about five thirty. It began to get cloudy then and by six thirty—the time they had set to begin playing—it was pouring down rain. There is hardly any use to plan for anything at that time of the day. It will certainly be rained out.

I sent your letter this morning by old Brother Fogg. I hated to do it a little bit, and I thought he might forget to mail it, too, but that was my only chance so I risked it.

Brother Homer came over and talked just a few minutes. He's still swollen some, but he plans to leave here Saturday. Now are not you glad you won't have to be in that big old lonesome house all day Sunday my [sic] yourself? I am. . . .

I'm sorry, dear, that I can't write any more now, but I've had so much to do all day I haven't had time. I'll try to do better next time. . . .

Goodnight
Jean.

---

6. This letter is postmarked June 16, 1916. Included in the same envelope is the one from Woodson to Cline immediately below.

Cordell, Okla., June 16 1916[7]

My own dear son:

I have been too sick for a day and a half to try to sit up at all, but I am better this morning and will see if I can't churn for Pataway—she's had a pretty hard time of it but she's managed better than I thought she could. She did all of the cooking yesterday, house cleaning, dish washing, attending to the milk, and in addition nearly finished a chemistry apron for you. She is going to sew and cook alright. All she has ever lacked has been "the want to." . . .

If we can get ready we will leave for Lexington two weeks from yesterday and spend two weeks from today with you at Norman. If I am not sick any more I think we can be ready by that time.

Minor sent a check for $10.00 and I had to pay $2.96, I believe it was, for your overdraft. How do you suppose you did this? You'll have to get you a little check book and keep things straight. I am sending you in this a check for seven dollars. I'll take care of the $10.00 check you had to write at Norman. If you run out of money tell me at once. You must have the right kind of food this summer and plenty of it or you can't keep strong and do what you should do. I'm here at home and can get money if I have to have it.

I am glad you are taking chemistry and history. It will be a change and good for you.

I love you, boy—more than you can realize. Be good, work hard, and the summer will soon pass and you will be home again. I'll send you some more towels by Homer. You'll need them in your chemistry work. Use the oldest looking ones for that work. It will ruin them, I suspect.

Mother.

Friday, June 16, 1916.

Dear Jean,

. . . I am taking one course in English from Miss Berrigan, a two hour course in Old Testament literature—selections from the Prophets and poets. I don't know whether they will give me credit for it or not, but I shall have the good out of the work anyway. I think I shall wait a while before I ask for credit; they might be in better spirits to give it.

---

7. This letter is written on Cordell Christian College letterhead that lists, in addition to Armstrong as President, the following faculty members: S. A. Bell, Vice President; Batsell Baxter, Dean; B. F. Rhodes, History and Greek; H. H. Rutherford, Latin; L. C. Sears, German, English; Mary F. Shepherd, Primary; Louise Rutherford, Intermediate; Zoe Sparkman, Music; Woodson Armstrong, Expression; Lou Ella Utley, Art.

I positively don't like my course in history. I am getting nothing at all from the class lectures, for the teacher doesn't seem to have the least system, or energy about him. He gives a lecture on everything at once—a few words about the language of the Babylonians, then a few about their classes, next some on the topography of the country, then on the reign of Nebuchadnezzar, and back to the geology of the land and how the river basin was formed, which should have been the first thing mentioned. It is here a little, there a little till I get all out of patience with him. I wish you could hear him laugh. It is not a laugh, it's a cough, with a red face and grin accompaniment. I am pursuing some study on my own account. I'm reading a history of the Israelites, and I shall read other histories and take notes on them, but I expect almost nothing from the class except four hours' credit.

Yesterday, he handed around some books, which the university has, written by the Chaldeans about 2200 and 2300 B.C. They were little rocks shaped about like bed-pillows and covered by that strange cuneiform writing of theirs. Some of the letters were so small I could not tell exactly how many little marks composed them. These were not exactly books; they were records of sacrifices brought to the temple, of a pair of oxen sold, or of a field bought. One was a letter to a messenger telling him what to take with him on a journey he was to make....

Cline.

Saturday, June 17, 1916.

Dear Jean,

...Homer will be here in about an hour, I suppose, and I'll meet him at the inter-urban station. I'm glad he's coming at last, for it is mighty lonesome here all by myself. I'll have someone to talk to whom I know, for I do *not* like to talk to strangers.

I must take up my potatoes now—. There, I have them off and some apples on. I like the apples cooked. If I just had two stoves I could get along just fine; it takes too long to cook things like this. I am almost over my "hungry spell" before dinner is ready.

I'm going to open up some preserves now, for Homer is here to help me eat them before they spoil. It is not very hard work to cook, but it takes a good deal of time, and time is precious to a student of history who is supposed to read about six hours of history every day. I'm not doing it, and *will* not, even if I make an F. There's no sense in reading that much, for you forget it if you read too fast....

I had to get a new kind of Bible for Miss Berrigan's class. It has all the prophecies, Psalms, Job, etc. written in poetic form. Sometimes it has things arranged in dramas. It also includes three books of the Apocrypha, "Tobit," "Ecclesiasticus," and "Wisdom of Solomon." Then the Acts of Apostles is cut to pieces, and the epistles of Paul are inserted in it where they are supposed to go. It's a strange kind of Bible in arrangement, *but* the words and thought are the same as the King James and the Revised versions....

I have finished dinner. It got done and was cooling so I just stopped and ate. I knew you would not be delayed in reading this.

I'll have to get Homer enrolled this afternoon if he comes in time. It is almost time for his car now—three o'clock. You see I have a late dinner.

Sister Armstrong said you would start on Thursday, and get to Oklahoma City Thursday night. Then you will be here all day Friday. That is the day I have my laboratory work in chemistry and it takes me almost three hours. Do you want to see the laboratory work? You might get tired staying so long, though I guess you wouldn't much, for we can walk around talk and laugh all we please. They don't care just so we get our experiments finished and written up in our notebooks. I would like for you to see it, if you think it would be interesting. I want you to visit my other classes on that day too so that you may see some of their teachers and their work....

Thy lover,
Cline.

1020 North Grant Street,

Cordell, Oklahoma.
June 17, 1916.

My dear Cline,

In four or five more hours you won't be by yourself, for Brother Homer will be there. I'll be so glad when he is with you. It must be unmercifully lonesome in that big old house.

The iceman has just come, and I've had a piece of ice with a whole lot of ammonia in it.[8] Wouldn't you like to have a great big piece to eat? I know you would so I wish you had it.

The young people came over yesterday evening, and *we* played tennis. I mean we, too, because I played a set and got beat. I played with J. D. against Mae and Brother Fred....

---

8. At that time, distilled ammonia was used to make ice.

Yesterday evening Lou Ella and Mr. Westbrooks (he came in on the evening train) were at the tennis court and Lou Ella was telling about the wedding Wednesday night[9]—it's the first I've heard. They had the arch covered with green leaves but no flowers and then the looking glass was in the back as they had planned it. Claudine Williams was the only attendant they had. She was ring bearer. Lou Ella and Mae didn't think it was a bit prettier than Katies [sic] except their house was larger. They said Katie and Mr. Davidson made a much nicer looking couple than Ella and Mr. Forster. I suspect, they were expecting too much when they went to Ella's . . .

Jean.

Sunday, June 18, 1916.

My dear Jean,

This is Sunday, so I cannot get your letter to-day, but hereafter I think I'll get it, for Homer and I are going to get a box—maybe!—and have our mail put in it on Sundays. He wants Miss Mary's letters as much as I want yours.

I believe they have things more definitely settled than we thought. She writes to him every day, if I am not mistaken, and he talks to me as if they had a pretty definite arrangement. He said if he had the money he would go to Detroit and bring her down here. He surely knows she would come or he wouldn't make a statement like that.

I told him you were coming over here sometime and finish your A.B. degree and perhaps your A.M., and he said he didn't see any use for a woman to have so much education unless she were going to teach. He thought we ought not to wait so long. You will be an old maid by that time, won't you? But if we come some in the summer as well as in the winter there, we might cut the time down some. It's worth trying anyway, and when we get our degrees we can make a strong plea whether it does us any good or not. . . .

I wish you could have eaten dinner with us to-day. We had a fine-looking, and a fine-tasting dinner too. I cooked some canned beef and made gravy while Homer peeled potatoes and pared some apples. Then we both cooked them. We had meat, gravy, potatoes, apples, lettuce, mayonnaise, pickles, and catsup, and for dessert pineapple and cake. I am really proud of our cooking. I think we ought to have been born girls instead of old bachelors, don't you? . . .

I have about half a dozen other letters to write this afternoon and two large books in history and a chemistry lesson to read. Homer is going to take

---

9. I.e., the wedding of Warren Forster and Zou Ella Mamo.

chemistry with me. I am glad of it for we can help each other some perhaps on some things difficult of understanding.

Thank you, sweetheart, for the apron. It is beautiful, but I'm sorry I can't use it in chemistry. We have to have rubber aprons there for if any acid touches cloth it burns a hole through it at once. I took a towel up the other day—an old tea towel—and got a little nitric acid, weakened almost to nothing by water, on it and it turned it yellow in a second. Nothing that goes into a chemistry laboratory comes out looking the same, except people. I can use your apron to cook in, for I needed it badly there. I soiled it a little to-day, but I'll have it laundered before you come. I want you to see me in my best cooking clothes. Homer wants me to go mail this, so I must discontinue. I love you, my sweetheart.

Cline.

1020 North Grant Street

Cordell, Oklahoma.
June 18 1916.

My dear Cline,

...I came over to Beulah's for dinner and by the time we (Mae, Beulah, and I) got dinner, washed the dishes, fed the chickens, and made some ice cream it was about four o'clock. Then we went out into an alfalfa field just south of the house and took some pictures, and after that we played with the tennis balls a while. Now I'm sitting in here writing to the *dearest boy* on *earth*, don't you believe it?...

Brother Harrell's [sic] wife hasn't been well lately and Brother Harrell didn't get to come to church until twelve o'clock this morning. Brother Bell preached for him, so I haven't a new age to tell you about this time. Brother Harrell doesn't know whether he'll be able to get in to-nigh [sic] and it maybe [sic] we'll be spared again. I certainly sympathize with you if you have to listen to a man like he is *every* day....

Lou Ella and Mr. Westbrooks have just come over for supper. They are now in the other room playing and singing....

I am home from meeting and alas, we *didn't* escape. Brother Harrell preached one of his lengthy sermons while I sat back there and roasted and slept part of the time. I felt a little lonesome though because I couldn't wake up and see you with your head propped with a song book....

Oh! Cline, I got the prettiest new hat. (Excuse me, dear, I didn't know what I had written until it was down. It's not the prettiest in the world nor the prettiest I ever saw but I just meant it was pretty.)

Mama and I went to town about seven o'clock last night and stayed until pretty late—until about time for Mae to come home, we thought, so we stopped in Wright's. It was at least forty five minutes until she could leave, so we politely seated ourselves and waited. While we were sitting there, I saw a hat in the window that struck my fancy. I said a thing or two about it and finally mama told me to get Mae to get it so I could see whether it was becoming or not. When once I got it on it was a hard matter to get it off of me, so mama got it. Now I won't have to wear that old Indian chief's bonnet any more.

I could write on but the light flashed and I must go to bed. Writing is not such a drudgery any more, are not you glad? . . .

Jean.

Monday, June 19, 1916.

My dear Jean,

. . . Homer enrolled in the school this morning, and had to pay two dollars extra for being late. They will refund this charge, however, if he gets the certificate of a doctor there testifying that he was sick. He wants Sister Armstrong to send a statement to that effect, signed by Dr. Kerley or some other doctor.

We attended assembly this morning and heard a program by Miss Agnes Husband, a soprano, who has had training here and at Paris. It was pretty good, but I confess the soprano has lost its charm for me, as sung by most modern singers. I still like bass and tenor and some alto. There is too much screeming [sic], exploding, whispering, trilling, and yelling to suit me in the modern soprano. . . .

Homer visited my history class and came away with about my opinion of my teacher. He visited chemistry and likes it fine. He is going to catch up and take that class with me. It will be hard for him at first, because chemistry is made up of a lot of H_2O's & H_2SO_4's etc., that we have to remember and he has had none of them. There is also valence, mass, weight, conservation of energy, and a hundred other laws and things he will have to learn, some of which are almost incomprehensible without a good instructor to explain them. We will study together and of course I can help him some. . . .

I'm glad Miss Katie's wedding was as pretty as Miss Ella's, for I think Miss Ella was a little too "splavagaty" (ask Sister Armstrong if this spelling is right), and I know Mr. and Mrs. Davidson were the better looking couple. But all the pretty weddings have not yet passed. Wait seven years and ours will beat them all, especially in the looks of the couple. Won't it? ...

I am sending a letter to Sister Armstrong in this—and one to J. D. No I'll write J. D's another time. I must go to the university now. ...

Cline.

Monday, June 19, 1916[10]

Dear Sister Armstrong,

I didn't get to write yesterday, because it took too long to wash dishes and get dinner—and write to Jean.

The check of $2.96 of which you asked ought to have been in before I left. I sent it to the Book Supply Company a long time before I had you get any money. The company must have been slow.

I am sending you in this a check for five dollars, because I don't need it now, and you may need it before you get to Lexington. Homer will have enough coming in along to meet our expenses, I think, though I have had to pay two dollars for the water & two dollars on his entrance fee, and all the house rent for the first month. He will pay me back for this of course. I think he means to pay you for half of the things you sent with us, and I'll pay you for the other half. Keep the bill for them. My sister sent me the money she owed me to–day. That's why I'm so rich just now. I suppose I'll have to write to Minor about his $5 diploma fee; he ought to send it at once. That will help you some.

Keep Jean cooking! I am only beginning to realize what a blessing to man a good cook is. And sewing and darning will have to be done, as my clothes might show. Let her learn. It's just what a bachelor like me needs.

But I must go to the library now and do some studying. More history to read than the professor himself knows. ...

Your son,
Cline.

---

10. This letter is contained in the same envelope as the one directly above it.

222 *South Porter Avenue,*

Norman, Oklahoma,
June 20, 1916.

Dear Jeanette,

  . . . Miss Fenton says she took the examination in Ancient History, and even when I gave her [sic] D I felt that I had had her paper somewhere. Look in the book and take off the condition and give her whatever grade she made in her daily grades, for I must have lost her examination paper. Make out a new report card for her with this grade on it, but in other respects like the former. . . .

  I got a letter from Brother Armstrong about my English work. He understood that I had enough English for my A.B. If I were going to major in chemistry or science or history then I would have to take no more; but since I'm to major in English I *am going* to take some more. The requirement is so much English, so much language, ancient and modern, so much science, and so much history—the rest is to be elective. I will *elect English*, but I don't *have* to take any more—I could elect science or history instead. . . .

Cline.

Tuesday night.

[June 20, 1916]

My dear Cline,

  Will you be surprised when I tell you that one week from to-night I'll be in Norman *talking* to you instead of sitting down here writing to you?

  Mama has decided—if it is possible for us to get ready in time—to risk it and leave here Tuesday evening on the four o'clock train. Mama is going to write papa to meet us at Oklahoma City too. Wednesday morning we can go with you to the University and possibly visit the asylum . . .

  Eula's and Delilah's paper's [sic] came to-day but I don't suppose there will be any use in sending them to you. We can bring them in just a few days. . . .

Jean.

Cordell, Okla., Wednesday morning[11]

[June 21, 1916]

My dear Cline,

If we can, we will leave here on the four o'clock Tuesday evening. I don't want to make the day trip that it would take to go by Hobart. It is so hot, I know I'd reach there with a bursting headache. I shall write Jack that we'll be in Oklahoma City Tuesday night on the 9.30 and he can meet us there or at Norman as is most convenient for him. I think it will be best for us to go to Norman Tuesday night. There is no use in paying a hotel bill in the City.

Jack closes his meeting at Ardmore Sunday night and begins at Lexington Wednesday night, so I think he can spend the day Wednesday with us at Norman. I hope so, I think it will be good for him to visit the University as often as he can.

I received the check but you did not need to send it.

[word(s) missing] much love,
Sister [Armstrong]

Wednesday, June 22. [sic]

[June 21, 1916]

Dear Jean,

... Yesterday our laboratory work took us till half past six and then we didn't complete it. I completed my experiments but didn't get them written up. I must go up this afternoon and finish them. The experiment was extra hard, because we had to do a lot of weighing, and it had to be done so accurately that when the experiment was finished and the acids and liquids had changed to salts, our weight had not diminished nor increased by the weight of a feather—and a very small one too. I think I have mine all right when I get it written out. But the whole thing made me cross enough to fight a bear....

I am going to a lecture to-night on eugenics, which I expect to be good. From now till the close of the week we have every night full. I hope we—I started to say I hope we can hear something good when you come, but we won't be here at night any if you don't come till Friday. If you can, I wish you would come Thursday and stay all day Friday and Saturday. You could get us something better to eat perhaps, although we are fine cooks, I can tell you. Anyway I want to see you, dear, more than I can tell.

---

11. This letter, written on Cordell College letterhead, is enclosed in the same envelope as the one directly above it.

Homer ... is pleased with his Latin teacher, and I think this study of Latin will help him wonderfully. Homer has never taught enough history and literature in his Latin. He knows the Latin grammar by heart but he doesn't see that one sentence has more beauty of expression than any other, and he doesn't realize that the study of a few legends and myths with his Latin will make it a live thing to his students instead of the common "dead language." It is something of a revalation [sic] to him. I only wish I could have taken a similar course in German.

The Robinson girl from Cordell is here. She is taking Chemistry IV and is doing it on the strength of her Chemistry work in the high school there. She took their high school course and they exempted her from Chemistry I, the course we are taking, and as they are not offering Chemistry II this summer, let her take IV. We will have to build up our laboratory or the high school will beat us after all. . . .

Cline.

Wednesday, June 21. [1916]

My dear Cline,

... You need not be afraid mama won't make me cook for I've been chief cook and bottle washer on this place nearly ever since you left. To-day I washed and dried the dishes, washed the cooking vessels, and swept the kitchen floor all in fourty [sic] minutes. Don't you think I'm getting to be pretty expert along my line?

The Odessa school is in an awful fix.[12] Commencement morning Brother Gardner whipped his wife! Got her down in [sic] the floor and whipped her. The next day he whipped her twice and bruised her all over. This time she went down town and showed some of the business men the bruises and told them what had happened. The whole town was in an uproar and came very nearly horse whipping him. Sister Jones, Sister Bell's mother, Brother Gardner's sister, and a Brother Covey and his wife stayed at Brother Gard-

---

12. Pataway's reference is to Western Bible and Literary College that Armstrong, R. C. Bell, and R. N. Gardner cofounded in Odessa, Missouri, in 1905. This was an area where Daniel Sommer's influence was particularly strong. The college occupied a two-acre campus, the dormitory of which was financed by A. D. Gardner. The Armstrongs left in 1907 and R. N. Gardner succeeded Armstrong as president. He was in that position at the time of Pataway's writing. By that time, the College was also in severe financial straits. Young, *History of Colleges*, 116–21. Even though the school closed in 1916 some of its buildings have survived into the twenty-first century. Information obtained from Odessa resident, 2013.

ner's home that night. Just about dark he disappeared and no one knew where he had gone. There were several automobiles coming back and forth all night watching the house but they had no trouble.

Sunday morning at church Brother Gardner made a three hour talk—when his wife wasn't there—explaining matters, but he didn't show any penitence in any shape, form or fashion. He said he whipped her because he thought he ought to. He had thought over the matter and prayed over it and he did just what he thought was right. Sister Gardner sent word to some of the brethren that she wanted to see them and when they came Brother Gardner got up and left. She told them she'd rather talk to them in his presence and asked them to come again.

The whole trouble has come up over a young girl they have had in their home for years, a Miss Grace Puett. Sister Gardner has done every thing she knew to do to get the girl out of the home, but she won't go and Brother Gardner won't have her go. She is a poor girl, so some of [sic] brethren told her that they would see that she got a place to stay and some where to work if she would only leave town. She told them that she guessed she'd stay right there that nothing could hurt a Christian.

The brethren came back in a few days but again Brother Gardner left. Sister Gardner just told them then that she had done every thing that was unbecoming in a wife. She had struck him and she had lied to him and she was sorry she had done that way but that he had driven her almost crazy. She said she would be far from saying that this Miss Puett and Brother Gardner had been guilty of anything criminal, but that he had sought her on every hand. If he wanted anything done, he went to Miss Puett instead of her and if any trouble came up he sought this girl. When Sister Gardner would be out of the room they would laugh and chatter like two young people.

This girl got her A.B. degree there this spring and Brother Gardner eulogized her for twenty five minutes. Several of the people timed him by the clock that was on the wall. What he has done is enough to make any woman on earth desperate. I think it's the awfulest thing I ever heard of. He told papa his wife was crazy when he was here. I think he is the one that's crazy. I don't think he is mean and I am compelled to think one or the other. But in spite of it all, it doesn't make me fear the double harness one bit. It would though if I wasn't sure I loved the man I'm going to marry after seven long, long years have passed, and if I wasn't sure he loved me.

It's strange isn't it how circumstances change a persons [sic] ideas. Not very long ago Brother Homer thought any girl ought to go on with her school work until she gets her A.B. degree anyway. I admit that some girls can get through this world on less education than others because some marry men that don't know everything themselves. But when a girl is going to marry a literary star, it is a law of the Medes and Persians that she must have her A.B. degree....

Jean.

Thursday, 22, 1916.

My dearest Jean,

... The war with Mexico has called for the Oklahoma militia and many of the boys from the university have gone. The army has a company of engineers stationed in the city and composed chiefly of university boys; it is going to-morrow, I think. The war spirit here is pretty high. The citizens are calling a mass meeting to-night to give the solders a send off.

I must quit now and go finish that old experiment. I just about had it yesterday, but by mistake I put in nitric acid instead of hydrochloric. Now I have to evaporate all the nitric and it is taking several hours.

I *love* you, sweetheart. Ich bin nur Dein, meine liebliche Jeannette.

Cline.

1020 North Grant Street,

Cordell, Oklahoma.
June 22, 1916.

My own dear Cline,

... What do you think? Lou Ella is going to marry Brother Westbrooks Wednesday morning before that eight eighteen train and leave on it for Texas. They intend to spend the summer there and come back here next fall. She is going to marry in a coat suit. Deliver me from such a wedding—one on such short notice at any rate. They went to Clinton yesterday to have their announcements printed. Brother Westbrooks told Mae that he wasn't going home and leave her out here if he could help himself. I think if I were in his place I'd leave her here a while to try her. After they are married it will be to [sic] late to see whether she will stay by him through thick and thin. I go to another shower Monday night. I thought the shower proposition was over. I don't know whom we'll have to shower next. There is not much telling. I never was more surprised in my life than I was this morning when Mae handed us an invitation....

What do you guess happened to me to-day? This afternoon some one knocked on the front door. I went and opened it and there was some strange man standing there. He asked me if this was Mr. Armstrong's home and I told him it was, and then he asked me if I were Mrs. Armstrong. I told him no I was not, but that I'd call her for him. I went to get her and just left him standing there. I was so rattled that I didn't have sense enough to ask him to come in and have a seat or anything that was courteous. I have been taken for her over the telephone but never before did I experience such a thing as this so I didn't know just how to take it. . . .

Jean.

Friday, June 23, 1916.

Dear Pataway,

. . . Homer has been telling me some of my faults and I have not enjoyed it specially.[13] Of course, I know I have them, but I am already trying to overcome them as fast as I can. One was my impoliteness in not saying "please," "thank you," "yes, sir," "yes, ma'am," etc. But "yes," said right, sounds better to me usually than "yes, suh" or even "yes, sir." The other principal fault was that I was *overbearing*. I told you. But I have let him have his way almost absolutely since he has been here, so he hasn't seen much of it lately. He has been wanting to buy an oil stove for about a week, argues for it, talks about it, dreams of it, I think. Yesterday, however, when he mentioned it, I could hardly hold in and I said, "Buy it, nothing!—" and might have said more but caught myself in time to keep cool. I told him, though, that I didn't have any money to put into a stove (for I have lent him about all I have), and he wanted to get about a five or ten dollar one. But last night we went to the second-hand store and got a two dollar gasoline stove. It's the only thing that would satisfy him, and we really did need something. It's about as good as his five dollar new one would have been—at least, as good for our purposes, and I'm glad we have it.

The trouble at Odessa *is* bad. I believe Brother Gardner is partially insane, for surely no one but an insane man or a brute would beat a woman. The trouble will hurt the church in Odessa beyond measure. It's a pity for a man to be so dogmatical and aggressive as Gardner. Such men always cause trouble, and their absence is a pleasure. . . .

Cline.

---

13. See Cline's references to this in Sears, *What Is Your Life?*, 70.

Friday, June 23. [1916]

My dear Cline,

Oh! I'm so tired to-night—so tired I could drop. It was stormy last night and we went to the cellar and stayed until a little after one. I took my book along and read while the others slept. I didn't get my usual amount of sleep so I was tired to begin with this morning. Just about ten o'clock Syble [sic] came over and wanted me to help her and Laura give Lou Ella a shower in the chapel. I was glad to help them and so we have been decorating the chapel and the music room all the evening. I've carried chairs, and tables, some of those great long benches, the oleander and swept floors until I am nearly dead. I hope everything goes off nicely. We are going to serve ice cream and cake on two little tables in the music room and are going to use my little pink and blue plates. Mama wanted me to christen my spoons by letting the bride and groom eat out of them but I objected. I want to wait until you can be here to eat with one too. Now do you blame me?

J. D. took his cream to the creamery this morning and got eighty one cents for it. If we had churned it and sold the butter we would have got only about sixty cents. He is going to sell his separated milk too from now on and get a cent a pound....

Jean.

Saturday, June 24, 1916.

My own little Jean,

... Monday, I think, I have to make a special report in the history class on Greek philosophy and philosophers. We have to go up in front of the class and stand by Professor Dale's desk as we make our reports. Wouldn't you like to see me turn pale? But I don't think I shall be much afraid....

I am a little surprised at Luella. I don't exactly understand her, nor Westbrooks either. I almost believe she is marrying him because she promised to and cannot break her word. I should be terribly afraid if I were her. It would be a terrible thing to marry a man you did not love. It's bad enough to marry one you do love; a girl makes a big sacrifice to do it. I know I should hate to marry any old boy I ever saw—even in a *mirror*. Well, he can have her, I don't envy him, for I have the sweetest little girl on earth, and I don't have to be afraid of her, but can trust her as long as the world shall stand....

I must go up to the university now and finish that experiment. It is getting late....

Auf Wiedersehen,
Dein eigener.

1020 North Grant Street,

Cordell, Oklahoma.
June 25, 1916.

My own dear Cline,

Oh! Cline all our work for the shower was lost. It began to rain about six o'clock and kept it up until about nine thirty with the exception of about forty five minutes; but the lull came just too late for nearly any one to come. The worst part of it all is that the bride and groom themselves didn't come. Why, I could cry if it would do any good. There were twenty one of us there anyway, Brother and Sister Bell and Catharine, Sister Davis, Thelma and two of her brothers, Sister Rhodes and Willis, Sister Wood, Miss Wood, Miss Nellie, Katie Freeman, Bro. Fred, Brother Short, J. D., and Christie besides us three girls. I forgot to name old Sister Bell. The presents brought were few, of course, but they were every one nice. A good deal nicer than most of the things Katie got. Mr. Westbrooks came over just after we got there and told us they would get ready just as soon as possible and come over. We waited and waited and just about nine it began raining again, so they never did come. Lou Ella hasn't said a word to us about not coming but Mr. Westbrooks told mama that they got ready to come and started just when the shower came up and then they couldn't come. She said they were so disappointed they didn't know what to do. I don't think that was any excuse at all. That last rain didn't last but a few minutes, and we stayed up there an hour and a half or two hours after it had stopped. They could have seen the light if they had just looked out of the window. . . . I must stop thinking about such unpleasant things. It doesn't help me in the least to get over my hurt feelings. . . .

We didn't think there would be a soul here for dinner to-day except mama and me, so yesterday we didn't order any thing or prepare any thing at all for dinner. Brother Blansett and Brother Fred were both here and not a thing cooked or anything to cook. I venture you can't guess what we had? First we had to eat the little bit of ice cream that was left from last night because it was just about to melt. Then we had pan cakes, sugar molasses and cantaloupes. Now could you have guessed it? It wasn't very appatizing [sic] but it kept them from being hungry. . . .

Brother Homer is better to you than he is to me for he is telling you some of your faults. Last summer he told me I had some but I couldn't get him to tell me what they were. I can't remedy mine because that man who is so capable of seeing and telling one of his faults has refused for once to tell me mine....

Papa wrote mama that it would be all right for us to stop at Norman, but that he was so very tired and so behind with his paper work that he felt like he couldn't come to meet us.

Don't think you are overbearing, dear, because you are as far from that as day light is from darkness. I think I am every bit as competent to judge this case as Brother Homer is....

Jean.

P. S. Don't ever write to "Pataway" any more please. I love you.

J.

July 3, 1916.[14]

Dearest Jean,

I got back this morning and went directly to school from the train: I read my chemistry lesson on the train, or rather finished reading it. I was so sleepy at my first history class and at chemistry that I could hardly keep my eyes open. But I didn't miss any questions on account of my thick-headedness.

To-day was the time for my report on Greek philosophers and philosophy. I thought I had put the notes for the report in my suit case so that I should have them with me, but when I looked I found that I had put in the wrong notebook. I went home at once (I had two hours before my second history class and after my chemistry) and threw myself down on the davenport and went to sleep. I slept about half an hour, I think, but I got up feeling fresh, looked over my notes and went back to school. I was just in time for my class.

I didn't know I was going to give anything extra; in fact I was only hoping I should not make a complete failure, but I think I won Dale completely. I kept my ears open to see what they said and this time for once I received compliments from almost every one; even Dale complimented me to my face—and to my back too. I didn't have quite time to finish my report; so the class demanded that I finish it the next time. In the morning then I shall have to face the stern assembly again.

Walker told Dale that "Sears is the Professor of German, English, and Expression in Cordell Christian College." He said he knew it. I wonder how he found it out.

14. This letter is addressed to Pataway in care of Mr. N. O. Ray, Lexington, Oklahoma.

I have been asleep for about two hours this afternoon. I was just so tired I had to do it; and I could do it very easily for I have only my history class in the morning. Porter released us from chemistry till Wednesday. To-morrow then I shall have nothing to do—all day. I wish you could be here with me; we should take in the Fourth of July in old style fashion. You could put on your yellow and red dress, I could wear my flaming scarlet neck tie, and we should walk up and down the streets, buy ice cream, peanuts, and cold drinks, shoot firecrackers, and sit in the public park to be looked at. Wouldn't that be fine? I have seen it done more than once by some angular, bashful, rubber-necked couple. We could almost do it—we're about angular enough, and are not over loaded with brass, while all will admit that my curiosity is enough for forty ordinary people. Therefore my neck might stretch. . . .

Give my love to Brother and Sister Armstrong. I'll try to see about our library equipment this week so I can discuss it with them when I come back Saturday. . . .

Cline.

Monday, July 3, 1916.

My dear Cline,

It's almost time for every one to come home from church. Aunt Ora went this morning and I stayed at home with the children. I was so tired any how that I felt like I *could not* walk way down younder [sic] in the blazing hot sun. I knew I was worn out last night, but this morning when I got up I was almost past going. . . .

I have a great big dictionary here, and if I mis-spell any words, I'm sure it won't be the dictionary's fault. It's such a pity I can't excange [sic] dictionaries with my learned professor, since he has informed me that he has out grown the small one that he has.

Dear, you are not the *only* stubborn man on earth. This evening Aunt Ora asked uncle Onzan when he was going to get that corn for the chickens he had promised, and some how it struck him wrong. He told her he didn't know when he'd get it, and it was too hot to get it this evening anyhow. After supper he repented and told her he'd go get it. Aunt Ora laughted [sic] and told him she wouldn't ask him any more if the chickens should happen to dry up right out there in the yard. He went though in a little while and got the corn. I think aunt Ora knows how to manage a stubborn person pretty well. I'm keeping my eyes open so I'll be able to manage one after a while. No, I really don't think I'll need the lesson after seven long years have passed, if my sweetheart keeps on trying like he has lately . . .

Tuesday morning.

I will just have to send this letter with out quite finishing it. We have meeting this morning at nine instead of ten because it's the fourth and the Bookers want to go on a picnic. But they don't want to miss the meeting this morning. It's eight o'clock now and I'm not quite through cleaning up . . .

Jean.

Fourth of July, 1916.

My own Jean,

I don't think I can get your letter to-day for it is a holiday. I wish such holidays did not come. They don't let us out of our classes and they make us miss our letters too. They are not worth their trouble and are a positive bother, and when I get to be President I'm going to abolish them altogether or make all places throughout the country (schools included) dismiss for a *whole* day, instead of for a few hours.

This morning I finished my report in history. I hope it will be a long time till I have another one. It is not pleasant to face fifty-seven students, some of whom are college teachers and one a superintendent of the Tulsa public schools and try to tell them something they don't know.

My chemistry didn't meet, so I visited a German class. Professor Steitz was the teacher, a German who can speak that language twice as well as English. I think, however, we can equal his class work in most ways in our school. I know he had second year German students and they didn't know the use of "es ist" and "es giebt." He had to explain it to them. And only one or two could give the principal parts of "kann," and "weisz." I don't think they know as much as my first year class does. I am going to visit his classes all I can and learn everything I can from him, but I have a lot of new ideas of my own for teaching next year.[15] They may not work, for I have never heard of their being tried, but I don't see why they should not work. Anyway we are going to learn to speak next year and speak well. It isn't hard to do if we go at it right.

I talked to Professor Steitz after the class a while. He asked where I was teaching and I told him. Then he bluntly remarked that he thought we had

---

15. Cline convened a German conversational table in the dining room during the academic year 1916–17. "The German students were encouraged to speak nothing but German at this table. Conversation was slow at first, but gradually increased through the winter." Sears, *What Is Your Life?*, 74.

too many schools in the country already. We could easily despense [sic] with about two normal schools, a half dozen agricultural schools, and with *most* or *all* of our *religious schools*. I thought he was very impertinent to say such a thing to me when I had just told him I was teaching in one. I almost resented it, but caught myself in time to smile and say "Perhaps." I don't want to turn him against me for I have to do some more German work with him. Anyway what do I care if he doesn't like our schools, just so they keep growing and prospering. He is a German and perhaps an infidel and he cannot understand the way in which we regard religion ...

We had the Fourth of July speeches at chapel this morning. Miss Anderson read the Declaration of Independence; and I never noticed till this morning how weak she was on anything but comedy. ... [S]he doesn't have the personality to hold an audience in anything that requires calm strength and dignity. On comedy she is all right.

Mr. L. Q. Campbell gave an interesting address. He has great power as a speaker, I think, except in the use of his hands. One of them he used in a short forward gesture of reference; the other he kept persistently in his trousers pocket....

The best thing was the singing of some national songs by the assembly ...

Cline.

Lexington, Oklahoma

July 4, 1916.

My own dear Cline,

We are just home from Sister Bland's and we had the finest dinner I nearly ever ate. We had fried chicken, stewed chicken, tomato salad, creamed potatoes, gravy, and cucumbers. For dessert we had pineapple salad and marshmellow [sic] cake. It looked like there was nothing there that could have been any better. Sister Bland gave mama the receipt for icing of the cake she had, and is going to write the receipt for the cake itself for us. When I get home I'm going to try it. I wish you could have been here with us to-day. That is the only thing that was lacking to make it a perfect day.

Mama said for you not to forget to write Delilah about the work she has had with us so you can fill out that blank and send it to President Brooks before her school is out.

I wish you could be here to-night and help me shoot some Roman candles. I guess I never will grow up if liking to shoot fire works is baby's play. I went down town this morning to get them and I tried to get a sky rocket too but the druggist told me they were not allowed to sell them. I can't understand why. They are not half so dangerous as fire crackers and no more so than Roman candles . . .

Last night at church several of us were talking about names and Sister Booker (the queer woman) said she thought Robbie Jo beat all the names she had ever heard and then she said she'd take that back and pointed at me. I think a person whose name is "Mickey" [sic] has no right to talk. I think it's another case of the pot calling the kettle black. . . .

Jean.

Wednesday, July 5, 1916.

Dearest Jean,

. . . I saw about the Rhodes scholarship this morning.[16] I can get it I think by reviewing and taking some more Latin. I hate to do it like everything for I am not exactly in love with Latin. I'll talk to Brother Armstrong about it when I get down there again. . . .

Cline.

Wednesday evening.

[July 5, 1916]

Dear Cline,

If I were a man, I don't think I would preach more than one summer. At the end of that time I'd be dead. I've been here only about a week—six days I think—and I've gone to every meeting but one. I don't know whether I'll be able to stand it a week and a half longer or not. I take a nap nearly every evening, but it "don't" do me much good. . . .

Last night when I got to church, one of the old ladies handed me a box of flowers that she had gathered at home. They are pretty as they can be, and they smell so sweet you can smell them both in the front room and the dining room. I wish she had waited until later in the week so you could see them. I hardly think they'll keep until you can get here. . . .

I hope your plans will work, and I will be able to talk *some* German by the time school closes next year. I know I will be too if I just let myself loose and do what you tell me to. . . .

16. See Cline's discussion of this in ibid., 72.

Jean.

Norman, Okla. July 6, 1916

Dearest Jean,

... I have been reading about the Rhodes scholarship. W. S. Campbell who was a Rhodes Scholar and graduated at Oxford gave me some books and pamphlets about it. I think if I work a little I can get it. He said he tried only four of the ten problems in arithmetic. It is about the easiest of all university examinations except in Latin where it is the hardest. My only trouble would be in being elected after the examination, for I know with some study I can pass it.

There is only one thing I don't like about it. That is that I cannot take you with me the first two years. They make the Rhodes scholars stay in the colleges, where they have their rooms with the other students, each man having a private sitting room and bedroom. I don't know whether they would allow a man and his wife to stay in these rooms or not; but I don't think it would be quite the best thing for us to stay in the rooming house of the boys of the school. The third year, however, they will let the students get houses out in town anywhere. They can live much cheaper in this way. During the vacation after the second year I could make a quick trip home and take you back with me. We could then spend the third year there to-gether, and do it on much less expense than I could by myself. After the third year was out we could travel some through England and Europe and come back home again.

There will be several advantages in getting the Scholarship. I shall have my expenses paid, have opportunity to travel, can visit Germany and France and learn their language at first hand, and shall bring to our school a strength that I could not bring by attending Harvard or Columbia. But then there is the great sacrifice of having to be away from you for about two years (I hardly think it will be quite that long). I don't know exactly what to do. I feel that our school needs the best that we can give it; that the cause of Christ ought to have all the scholarship and all the ability we can put into it even at great sacrifices to ourselves. I don't know what is best, but if it is the sacrifice, we can make it for two years, can't we? ... I almost feel that we ought to sacrifice ourselves for *two* years ... that the church of our Saviour may be strengthened and built up in this country. I know there have been much severer sacrifices made for Him—men have given their lives for his sake—surely we can give two years in preparing for his work. And yet it is bitter to think of now. I can hardly think of leaving you for two years. We shall have to let our Father direct us and lead us into what we ought to do. Let us ask Him to decide it for us....

Cline.

Lexington, Oklahoma

July 6, 1916.

My dear Cline,

...Robbie Jo has decided she isn't going to church unless she can ride. Brother Bland has spoiled her by letting her ride every night. He carries the mail every morning, and so, of course, he can not take us to the morning service. This morning Aunt Ora decided to go—she usually stays at home and keeps the children. When Robbie Jo found out she was going, the child began to cry and beg her mother to stay at home. She cried for at least twenty minutes even after I told her I'd stay with her. When Uncle Onza got a little switch and started to use it she became reconciled and stayed with me just as contented as could be. The only thing is, I would have had her contented about fifteen or twenty minutes sooner than he did. I *think* I would.

Aunt Ora put the baby to sleep before they left but in a few minutes she was awake again. I put her back to sleep, read my Bible lesson,[17] strung some beans, and did some "tacky work." By that time, they were all home from services and it was time for dinner. After dinner I helped mama and aunt Ora wash the dishes. When we got those done I hemmed the other end of the little towel I was fixing at home and put the tatting on it; then I washed and ironed it. That is all I've done to-day except help with the breakfast dishes and clean up the house a little. I haven't fooled any either or taken my nap but it does look like I never get anything done....

It's after six o'clock and I must set the table for supper. I *love* you sweetheart.

Jean.

---

17. While Pataway may have been reading in direct connection to the evangelistic meeting in progress, she may also have been following a practice employed by J. A. Harding of reading approximately three and one-thirds Bible chapters per day. This routine allowed for one complete reading of the Hebrew Bible and two of the New Testament annually. Hicks and Valentine, *Kingdom Come*, 80–82. Harding, in turn, may have adapted his practice from that of George Müller's. See a reference to Müller's Bible study habits in Garton, *George Müller and His Orphans*, 132.

Friday morning.[18]

[July 7, 1916]

Dear Cline,

Pataway is sick this morning. She has a sore throat and aches all over. Her throat is not ulcerated but is very red. She slept little last night but has been asleep for about two hours now. I am doctoring her throat and I think she'll be alright. It frightens me for her throat to get sore.

Mother.

Norman, Okla., July 10, 1916

My own Jean,

...I was a little sleepy in my chemistry, but managed to get through all right. German was interesting enough to keep me awake, but in my second history class I did *go to sleep*. Professor Dale didn't see me though, because I was behind some other boys who were tall enough to hide me. I had a very pleasant nap and am not so sleepy now. Homer is in the other room sleeping, and I think he'll sleep almost all afternoon....

We opened another can of peaches for dinner but they were sour. We tried to eat them in spite of this fact till Homer found a piece of glass, which he was just ready to swallow; then we both quit. I think the chickens have enjoyed the remnant. I wish I had such a tough digestive system—I hate to be extravagant, and peaches are rather costly chicken feed....

Cline.

Monday night.

[July 10, 1916]

My dear Cline,

...Papa and mama went to Sister Manheart's for dinner to-day. I didn't go. I haven't gone anywhere except to Sister Bland's since we've been here. I don't like to go anywhere, and somehow or other I have had a good reason for not going every time except the one. To-day I simply couldn't have gone no matter how bad I might have wanted to. I have not done a thing all day except lie on the bed in the front room and "roast." I feel better to-night but I was

---

18. This letter is written on the back of the one immediately above it.

afraid to tackle going to church till to-morrow. I doubt whether I'll be able to go to-morrow morning, because I will have to walk and it will be so hot then. I'm sure though I will be able to go to-morrow night. Mama and Margie are staying with me to-night but Robbie Jo wouldn't stay. I think she would have died a natural death if she had been made to stay. She likes to ride in a car better than any child I ever saw. The other night her mother tried to get her to stay at home with us but she said she just had to go hear papa preach. But in the day time she *didn't have* to go hear him preach. She can make the nicest little excuses some times you ever heard....

They have all come home and are in here talking, so I can't think....

Papa told me I must go to bed so I'll have to finish this in the morning. I love you, dear.

Goodnight.

Tuesday morning.

It is just a little while until uncle Onza goes to the office, so I must be in a hurry.

Mama and I got a letter from Granny Pattie yesterday. She has a lot of flowers started both out in the yard and in pots. She said she didn't see how I got along with out you for she missed you herself, that you were always in a good humor no matter how hard pressed with work you were. She said she thought you and I should congratulate each other every day that we had the good fortune to meet. Granny Pattie thinks we have made a wise choice, and I think so too, don't you?

Granny Pattie sent a letter from uncle Ben. I think he is doing good work in Alabama. He will not put a report in any of the papers and papa has asked him to I don't know how many times. He said in this letter to Granny Pattie that he has six meetings to hold, beginning now pretty soon.

Charlie Klingman is married already and his wife hasn't been dead quite six months yet. I think that is terrible. He married Brother R. A. Zahn's old maid sister. She is, at least, four years older than he is and will make two of him. She is not fat but is just big all over. She is a nice looking woman and is neat in her clothes but very much too large for a little man like Brother Klingman. And just think! His first wife hasn't been dead quite six months. I don't think he loved her in the first place and I don't think she loved him. They both loved some one else but couldn't get either one so they decided in a short time to marry each other. Even if he didn't love her he ought to have more respect for her than to marry so soon. I tell you I don't understand a man that will do such a thing. Of course, I know he had four little children to take care of. But Brother S. A. offered to take all of them next winter, and I am sure Sister Bell would have taken just as good care of them as Miss Zahn will do....

Jeanette.

Wednesday July 13. [sic]

[July 12, 1916]

My dear Jean,

... I talked some more with the German teacher this morning. I asked him about Wilhelm Tell as a classic for the 2nd year of German. He thought exactly what I did about it—that it is too hard for the ordinary 2nd year student; does not afford the chance for conversation which an easier work does; and will not be appreciated by students of that development. I had already decided not to use it, but I am glad he agreed with me. I also asked him about "Im Vaterland" for second year work, and again he said exactly what I thought with a little addition. He said Im Vaterland was too costly (which I had not considered); that it was too monotonous (which I knew full well); that it was poor German (which I did not know); that it did not afford a good chance for conversation (which I was sure of); and that it required too much time for the little good received (the which I had already discovered).

So in consideration of all these facts, I am excluding for my German courses Wilhelm Tell, Im Vaterland, Gluck Auf,[19] and Pope's Composition, which is too advanced for most third year students. I am putting in place of them in the first year's work a new German grammar by Spanhoofd[20] and little classics by Benedict.[21] In the second year's work I am going to use an advanced German grammar as a reference book, a conversation book and simple classics, beginning with Benedict's and Immensee and ending the year with hard work; such as Das Edle Blut, Das Mädchen von Capri, Hochzeit auf Capri, etc.[22] All these books afford opportunities for conversation and the words are not poetical and seldom used, as they they [sic] are in Wilhelm Tell. Our second year's work, with the exception of Wilhelm Tell and Immensee, was absolute drudgery. No student could learn to speak German by using Pope's Composition first. It is not a book for conversation but for writing. We attempted to use it in conversation but it was just too difficult....

Cline.

---

19. This is a basic German reader.
20. I.e., Arnold Werner-Spanhoofd, who wrote a number of German textbooks.
21. This reference is unclear.
22. *Das Edle Blut* is a German history by Ernst von Wildenbruch; Julius Grosse published *Das Mädchen von Capri* in the mid-1800s; and Paul Heyse published *Hochzeit auf Capri* in the early 1900s.

Wednesday morning.

[July 12, 1916]

My own dear Cline,

...Clyde Utley and his wife are having some trouble, I understand. Not very long ago he took the bankrupt law. He don't [sic] seem to care to do any thing and they are way down to rock bottom. You know yourself that the Utleys won't stay at one job long enough to make anything out of it. He has already become a socialist and he doesn't come to church like he ought to.[23] His wife's people have been trying to get her to leave him. She hasn't done it yet, but I don't know what the results may be. It will be terrible if she finally leaves him. They are both young and they'll be ruined for the rest of their lives. People ought to know what they are marrying. I don't know how long she knew him but not long, I think. I guess that little girl that went crazy because he didn't marry her if she had known him to be what he is would have rejoiced instead of going crazy, poor thing!

I've made enough tatting of a different kind to go on one end of another towel. I think I'm getting to be an expert, for when I first began I couldn't have made that much in a week. This I made in three days I think....

Jean.

Wednesday evening

[July 12, 1916]

Dear Cline,

O dear me I'm so hot, I'm so hot! I don't know when I ever was as hot. It's so hot in the house you can't do anything. I have got my paper and pen and come out here on the back porch. I'm writing on an old box that has a little middle and two side pieces on it. I have my pape [sic] in the little middle and nearly every time I make a stroke I hit one of the side pieces.

We have all decided to go to Sister Burkett's to-morrow. I do hope she'll have some of her good cake too. I'm so hungry for something besides beans, corn, potatoes, and chicken I don't know what to do. I'm different from some people I guess, but some times I have to have something except plain old solid food....

---

23. Socialism was remarkably strong in Oklahoma at the time. There were twelve thousand dues-paying members (more than in New York) in the state the year before Pataway wrote this letter. Zinn, *People's History*, 340.

A while ago mama read of a boy she used to know getting married and she made the remark that the boy must be getting pretty old. He is some where around twenty eight. From now on, Sir, you need not say that there will be an old maid in our wedding for there will be an old bachelor as well. I think the man in the party will be a little past twenty eight.

Thursday morning

I couldn't finish this last night.

I had a terrible dream last night for a while, but it finally turned out some better. I dreamed mama and papa were almost making me marry some boy whose name I didn't even know. He had had a wife already and she wasn't dead either, but still they wanted me to marry him. I thought they told me that in seven years that he would die or something would happen to him. After awhile I consented to marry him and the wedding day was set. By the time it came though I could hardly stand the boy. He was even repulsive to me. The guests were there and had brought their present [sic] when I decided I could not marry. I thought you were there but you didn't say anything. I felt like I'd rather die than to live seven years with him, and too, I thought it wouldn't be treating you right to make you my *second* husband. I went to papa and told him how I felt about it. Finally he and mama told me I need not marry the boy if I could fix it with him, so I went to work at once and in a little while I was released. I tell you I felt good when I awoke and found it was just a dream. I tell you I was miserable for a little while because it was so real. It was as plain as could be....

Jean.

Thursday afternoon,

July 13, 1916.

Dearest Jean,

... Granny Pattie doesn't know me quite as well as I know myself or as you know me, or she would never have said I was always cheerful. No one can be more melancholy sometimes, unless it is you. I admit that you can equal me and perhaps surpass me a little. I must write to Granny Pattie again. She hasn't answered my last letter yet, but I must not let her utterly forget me. I can readily say "Amen" to the statement that I ought to thank God that I met you, but I don't see why *you* should be so thankful. I really believe you have made a bad choice instead of a good one, but if you are satisfied, es ist mir gut....

I have sent for my two German grammars; that is, the two which I think I shall use.... I am attending the German classes *almost* every day. I think I have missed two or three times in the last two weeks. I can understand all the German he speaks easily and can speak anything he says in class....

Cline.

115 McLendon Ave., Atlanta, GA.[24]

July 7th 1916.

Dear Cline & Homer:

Your letters were a very pleasant surprise to us all. Sue enjoyed them very much too. It has been pouring down rain here all day and last night it did not stop. When I came home as soon as I could I put in a very small garden Dr. Paine had ready for me to plant in flowers, so I put in peas, radishes, turnips & cantelopes [sic]. besides I made a border of flowers Cosmos, [illegible] geraneums [sic], cannas, & six [illegible] roses white, red, pink, & cream. When you come to see us I hope to be able to have enough to decorate with. I know you both enjoyed Woodson's & Pataway's visit. Surely I would have been glad to have been with them and would have enjoyed some of the nice cooking you both are able to do. Now a compliment for each of you. I think the girls who are so fortunate as to be Mrs. Sears & Mrs Rutherford will be blessed indeed. I mean every word I have written. Cline I am glad you were so fortunate in receiving such a nice place for your summers [sic] work. And I am glad you & Homer are together, to comfort & help each other. Mr. Harding seems real well since we came home and he has gotten used to things again, for surely he was upset on the way.[25] We carried our lunch box all the way and after eating along the way all we wanted, there was [sic] some very nice things in it untouched, so I thought Sue would be so glad to eat some of our lunch, but Mr. Harding left the box on the street car in Atlanta. Just think of it, and after bringing it so far lost it in sight of home.

July 15th 1916.

My dear Friends—

---

24. This letter from Pattie Cobb Harding, along with one from Sue Harding Paine that Cline mentions in his next letter to Pataway, was sent in an envelope dated July 18, 1916.

25. This is likely another reference to Harding's ill health. The description of their travels may concern the Harding's trip to Cordell during the 1915–16 academic year. See Sears, *Eyes of Jehovah*, 261.

I want you to know my heart has been perfect toward you by sending you the above lines under date of the 7th. Since that time Sue has been real sick and just as she was getting out of bed I was taken sick. Of course I was not as seriously sick as I felt or I would not have gotten well so soon, but I suffered a great deal. Dr. Paine soon relieved me. It certainly is good to have a fine doctor at hand. Well the time for your return to Cordell is not far off. As you only expected to spend six weeks in Norman. I enjoy reading the Herald, and will enjoy hearing from you again any time you find you can give to write me another letter. Our protracted meeting has been in progress one week tomorrow. Last night we all went and took Gertrude & Charles Jr. They enjoyed the ride over and we brought them both home asleep ready after redressing for bed. I believe Charles is the best Baby I ever saw. Gertrude is very interesting, and is learning very fast.... I know you enjoyed having Woodson & Pataway to visit you. I would like just such a rare treat myself. I was about to forget to tell you we had one Confession last night. A young lady. Our young preacher just 21 years old is a fine, earnest good proclaimer of the Bible. I like him very much. R. N. Luton of the Nashville Bible School. A Kentuckian by birth.... I was forgetting to tell you that we have been overflowing with company up to the time we got sick. Sue & Charlie think of going to Valdosta for a two weeks visit in Aug. Mr. Harding & I will keep house while they are gone. Now if the air ships were common you and Homer could fly over and see us while they are gone remaining of course until they return to see them too. We have had a big preparedness parade in Atlanta recently, but we did not go to see it. Dr. Paine was too busy to take us and we did not care to go on the street cars with two babies. Are you interested in the war any more. I read more of it than I did in Cordell. Germany is a greater nation than I ever dreamed she was.... Ben's protracted work begins the last of this month and he expects to hold six meetings. Beth expects to go to Bowling Green to the home coming in Sep. Elizabeth is there now. I had a letter from L. J. & Eulalee Gilbert in which they told me about seeing Elizabeth at the Orphan's home (Old P.B.C.) and how she clung to them after she found out and remembered who they were. Said they missed us all very much. Especially did L. J. miss Paul Harding. It will be nice when we can have the final reunion in the Great City of God. Let us work and pray for this meeting. Devotedly your friend & sister in the Lord
Mrs. J. A. Harding

Monday Afternoon,

[July 17, 1916]

Dear Jean,

...I was put into a very embarrassing position this morning—Homer and I both. They are raising $125 among the students to buy a *flag* for the Oklahoma regiment in the Mexican War.[26] I don't know whether I am right or not but I felt that I could not sacrifice the principles of Christ in regard to encouraging a war and "patriotism." Every man who gave to this fund received a small flag which he had to wear about with him as a sign of his *patriotic devotion*....

I know this "patriotism," as they call it, is contrary to the great principles of Christ's government, and for me to lend encouragement to such a spirit would be to forsake the very principles of Christ. I could not afford to do it. So when one of the girls who were selling the little flags came to me I had to tell her I could not take one. Of course, she thought I had no money, and I let her think it, for that wasn't as bad as to make myself a veritable fool to her and everyone else around by telling her just why I *could not* take it, and besides this having the doctrine of Christ in regard to governments laughed at and despised. In my class another girl asked me to buy one of the flags and I had to refuse again. This time it was even harder, for this girl was in one of my classes last year and knew me well. She even offered to sell it to me "on time." Everyone is so intensely patriotic to-day; everyone has a flag and sometimes three or four, tied to his button hole. A man or woman who goes around without his flag to-day is a mark for criticism and wonder. Therefore I am remaining quietly at home this afternoon with my books.

There is a great difference between the people of the world and of the popular churches, and the people of the churches of Christ. Anything that is respectable and respected by society and the world is engaged in by the popular churches. War is not condemned, but is encouraged by the ministers. I heard a prayer recently for the "success of our arms in Mexico,"—which necessarily means the destruction of hundreds of lives and the ruin of hundreds of homes, yet because the world praises it as patriotism the preachers pray for it, and buy flags to lead the army in battle....

Cline.

---

26. This refers to the border incidents between Mexico and the United States that took place from approximately 1913 to 1916. In June of 1916, President Woodrow Wilson had dispatched National Guard troops to the border between New Mexico and Mexico.

Monday, July 17. [1916]

Dear Cline,

    This certainly has been one day of leisure. I haven't done anything all day except help wash the breakfast and dinner dishes, make enough tatting for the other end of my towel, and read my Bible lesson. Mama and aunt Ora haven't done any more than that either. We all feel very much like we have been going to a three weeks meeting.

    Brother Booker's niece was talking to mama last night about *you*. She said she thought you were an excellent young man and asked if she and papa had not "raised" you. She said she had heard that they did. I guess she thought she would like to captivate you and would have more chance to get you if they had reared you and you were only coming down here to see your little sister. . . .

    I hope Brother Homer got enough sleep while you were gone. I tell you he's queer but since Miss Mary is so good and has no faults at all maybe they'll get along all right. I hope so any way if she ever quits keeping him guessing long enough to marry him. He must think she is as good as the Lord himself since he thinks she has no faults. I suppose it is a little mean in me but it makes me tired to think he is every once in a while comparing me unfavorably with her. I guess after I've lived eleven or twelve years longer I will have overcome a *few* of my terrible faults anyhow. . . .

                                                                                         Jean.

Tuesday, July 19 [sic; 18], 1916.

My dearest Jean,

    . . . I got a letter from Granny Pattie and Aunt Sue this morning. They told me everything to be told, it seemed—from the babies to the garden. Granny Patty has planted a lot of flowers and vegetables. I hope she has better luck then we have had. Our garden was growing nicely and our lettuce would have been ready to eat in two or three days, but some chickens found the place about Saturday and when I came back Monday there was no lettuce or radishes to be seen. I was tempted to catch the chickens and use them instead of lettuce—they would have made a pretty good substitute.

    Granny Pattie seems to have fallen in love with Charles Jr. too, for she wrote much more about him than about Gertrude. The new baby is always the pet. They always forget the first one as soon as the next is born. Such is the irony of fate. But that is not the worst yet. The wife usually forgets her husband as soon as their first child is born, and gives all her attention to the baby. Then poor, neglected, forsaken "hubby" wants to spend his time at the club, or with the "other fellows"—or at the *bottom of the sea*....

Few women realize how a man must feel. I am sure I don't remember how I felt when I was a child and my little brother was born. I was too young to know whether to be jealous or glad, I suppose. Anyway, I place myself now emphatically and eternally on the side of the child or husband who is being woefully neglected for the first newcomer....

Cline.

Wednesday morning

[July 19, 1916]

Dear Cline,

...I don't think the Baptist meeting is going to prove to be "Lexington's big meeting." Monday night Brother Bland went and there were only about seventy five there under the tent and in the cars too. Yesterday morning uncle Onza was down town so he stopped to hear him and there were only twenty there. The preacher said it was a great improvement over Monday morning. I suppose he didn't have anyone that morning....

Brother Nichol wrote papa and told him that he had asked Brother Showalter to give one issue of the Firm Foundation for an Educational number. Brother Nichol wants each one of the Christian schools to send a cut of there [sic] building and it's [sic] president and two or three of the members of the faculty. He wants papa and three of the teachers—the ones he sends cuts of—to write an article each. Brother Nichol made it plain that there is nothing to be said in any of the articles which will "reflect" in any way on the other schools. They are much afraid something will be said some time that will reflect on Thorp Spring. But they can say any thing and expect us to sit by and take it....[27]

Brother Baxter is coming to Cordell about the first of August. I am so anxious to see him. I believe now I'll like him better than I thought I would at one time....

Jean.

---

27. Austin McGary had begun *The Firm Foundation* in 1884. He shared some of Daniel Sommer's antipathies for what he saw as innovations within Christian practice. Hooper, *Distinct People*, 20.

Wednesday Afternoon,

[July 19, 1916]

Dearest Jean,

Your letter came this morning and I am rejoicing. It is a great pleasure to have a letter waiting when I come home from school. It's a great relief to come from the presence of a stern Professor of So & So and sit down for a talk with you. I wish you were here indeed, it would be much better—infinitely better. Some day, dear, you can be here, to go to school with me, perhaps, and come back with me. I hope you can do it after next summer. You will if I don't go to Oxford, won't you? You said you would do anything, you remember,—now keep your word, and with all your might persuade them to let you come after next summer.

I got back my examination paper in history this morning. When Professor Dale gave the papers back, he prefaced it with a long talk about grading. He said he hardly ever gave an A, just once in a great while, because he thought it was hardly ever merited. He considered B a fine grade and even C– was nothing to be ashamed of.... Dale advised us not to feel discouraged if we got C's, because according to his standard of grading a C was a pretty good grade. His speech alarmed me. I was afraid I had failed entirely. When he began to give out the papers I watched, Most of them were in B's and C's. I saw only one or two in A's, and when mine came toward me I was almost afraid to look. But it was an A, not even A–, but an A. I was surprised, but very glad.

I saw Ramey this morning and had him give me a list of books for our library. Dale is to help me with history tomorrow....

It is fearfully hot this afternoon. I am smothering. I think I shall go out in the shade to study. I am going to get my chemistry and spend the rest of the afternoon taking notes in English. I am trying to get some things that will help me in teaching and in other ways. I have been studying about the translation of the Bible by Wycliff, [sic] Tyndale, and by the authorized translators. It is exceedingly interesting to read of the keen sacrifices these men made, of their profound reverence for the Scriptures, and their zeal and enthusiasm for the work of God. They were wonderful men. To read of them inspires one to a greater faith in our Father. It would be great only to equal some of them in self-sacrifice and religious fervor. I hope I may sometimes attain to the noble spirituality which they possessed....

Cline.

Thursday, July 20. [1916]

My dear Cline,

...Brother Booker, the one we visited Sunday, went to Oklahoma City yesterday morning and got him a Saxon car. Bernice was so jubilant over the idea he telephoned Aunt Ora before she got up yesterday morning and told here [sic] they were going to the City to get a car. Sister Booker said just after Brother Bland got his car that she *wouldn't have* a car. It's a little amusing now to see how happy they are over getting one.

I finished When Knighthood was in Flower[28] yesterday, and I certainly did enjoy it. I haven't had a chance to read a bit for about two weeks until yesterday. When I got a chance I stuck on to that book till I finished it. I wish I had something else good to read now, but Aunt Ora hasn't anything and no one else around here that I know.

I'm sorry you were put in such an embarrassing position, but I am so glad you had strength enough to keep from helping to buy that large flag. I don't know whether I would have had strength enough to keep from helping them or not, especially if some of them had offered to sell me a little flag "on time." I'm mighty glad you didn't help them....

Jean.

Thursday, July 20, 1916

Dearest Jean,

Women are awful things! It's impossible ever to tell just what they will do. Professor Vosse had a woman in his class who was studying law in the law school, intending to become a suffragette, I suppose. Well, she began her suffragette career before any one thought about it. She independently persisted in coming to the class ten or fifteen minutes late. At last Professor Vosse got tired of her carelessness and since repeated admonition did do [sic] good, locked her out of the room one day. Then came the opportunity for her to show she was "equal to any man," and she went straight home, got her hatchet, broke open the door, and came in. Vosse was startled, she was angry, and the students were tittering. The school expelled her, and because she was not yet quite even with the "men" and had been cheated out of her right (which was clearly the liberty she exercised in coming to class late), she sued the institution for about $15,000. Once again she proved unequal to the "lords

---

28. A novel by American author Charles Major, first published in 1898.

of creation," and let a man lawyer defeat her, although she plead [sic] her own case. Such is an example of the incomprehensible things a woman will do.

Homer received his credit yesterday. He got 62 hours in all. This was because he was an A.B. graduate. They will not give our A.B. graduates less than 62 hours. To do this they had to give him credit on his Bible work, and let him make up physiology, civics, and so forth. So his 62 hours mean that much when he has studied these other things. As it is he has 54 hours clear.

I have written to Brother Armstrong for a statement of my work in Bible as well as in German and Greek. I am going to try to get credit too. They may not give me credit on my Bible work, however, for I have enough work besides this to make my sixty-two hours of entrance standing. The way they have accepted Homer's work means that they give our graduates at least junior standing, and I believe they will accredit anything we do.

I am going back to the library this afternoon. Professor Dale is to help me select some histories for our library, and I must meet him there in exactly thirty minutes. That means that I must go. . . .

I am anxious for school to close. I want to be at home awhile before our school begins, especially if I am to board somewhere else. I want to be with you. Will you please do something for me, dear? I know you ought, for your sake and mine, and for the sake of everyone. Will you try your very best to do it? I know you can, if you try, for any one can do anything, if he tries hard enough. Then if you will do it, I want you to drive out of your breast all the jealousy you feel toward those who others think surpass you in any way. I know it's hard, but you must do it to be the woman you want to be. How could you teach a child not to be jealous, if you were jealous too. Or how will you become a woman others praise, when you show sometimes jealousy and anger when others are praised. I am giving *myself* a lecture as I write, for I am as guilty as you or *more guilty*. It is a continual fight with me. But that is all the more reason why both of us should fight it with greater strength. We must do it. I *love* you, and you'll try with me, won't you?

Cline.

Thursday night.

[July 20, 1916]

Dear Cline,

. . . To night is the night that I am to make a simpleton of myself. I'm going to say My little Newsboy[29] and then two or three short ones from James

---

29. Probably a reference to Louisa May Alcott's short story "Our Little Newsboy."

Whitcomb Riley. I have not said them a time to Mama, but I want her to hear them once any how. Then I'll trust to fate. I can't do anything before a little crowd thought [sic], and I'd rather do anything than try.

Papa thinks he'll be home for a week just after his Kirkland meeting, so that may change our plans some. We may have to go home a little sooner than we expected. You find out just as soon as you can when your last examination comes....

I am so glad you got the grade you did on your history examination. I knew you would make one of the best grades in the class anyhow. But it makes me feel so proud of you to know you made an A after Professor Dale made the speech he did.

I will certainly keep my promise if you'll just do the thing my promise is based on....

Jean.

Saturday morning.

[July 22, 1916]

My own dear Cline,

... Well, I got through last night about half way. No one came except Brother Bland and his family, so I thought I'd get out of saying those readings. I had a cold and my throat was sore too. The more I sat out on the back porch the hoarser I got. I thought surely that would be excuse enough when there were so few here. They insisted a little bit so I had to try to do what I could. I did pretty well on the short things but [word(s) missing] the long one I made a complete failure....

The escapade of that suffragette is the most absurd thing I ever heard of a woman's doing. It looks as if she didn't have as much sense as she ought to have or she would have known she would be defeated and [wo]uld never make anything [word(s) missing] of the university. I think you have found out one reason women are so interesting. They always have something new for you and sure enough you never know what to expect next. However, most of them never attempt anything so surprising as this woman undertook....

Jean.

Norman Okla., July 22 1916

My dearest Jean,

... My last examination is on Friday, August 4. I hoped to get away sooner but I cannot, I guess. We will be through our examinations by twelve o'clock and about one we will start home. You can arrange just as you think best about your trip, but let me know what you decide, and by all means come past as soon as you can. I wish I could see you to-day. My weekly trip spoiled me, I think, for I am almost unable to stay away from you more than a week.

... I must copy Brother Armstrong's recommendation this afternoon and hand it in next week, so I may get my credit. ...

Cline.

Sunday evening

[July 23, 1916]

My dear Cline,

... I was taken again to-night for mama's sister. I went over to the well for some water and one of the women said to me, "You are Mrs. Armstrong's sister aren't you?" I smiled and said, "No, I'm her daughter." I'm getting used to such remarks as that until now I can answer with a smile. I'm going to look so old by the time you marry me people will take you for my little son instead of my husband. ...

This certainly is a house of old maids and "widow women." Six of us here and not a man or a boy on the place. I do wish there was, at least, one man on the place to keep anything away that might come. They have all gone to bed except me and if I don't go pretty soon I'll be to [sic] afraid to get any where. ...

Jean

July 23, 1916

Dearest Jean,

This morning I made a talk at church, which I enjoyed immensely after it was over, but it was not very good because I was too hoarse to speak. Yesterday afternoon I washed some socks and underwear and didn't have time for them to dry thoroughly before I put them on. As a result my larynx was dammed up and my [word(s) missing] appendage suffered an overflow—in [word(s) missing] of Cicero, I catched a cold. I [word(s) missing] bad however, since dinner.

We went to Brother B[word(s) missing] for dinner, and had a regular old fashioned *Kentucky* meal, as Homer called it. I guess it was so, for it was not like Oklahoma dinners in *one* respect, which I shall tell you later. We had chicken and good gravy, and almost everything else you could think of except vegetables and potatoes. They had blackberry preserves, grape jelly, honey, and two other kinds of preserves which I did not taste. It was all good, except this one thing, which, as I said, distinguished it from Oklahoma dinners. It was this. I had taken one piece of chicken and enjoyed it extremely, for, as you know, we are not flooded with chicken here. When I had finished one piece they pressed me to take another and I did so with a show of reluctance but with a very ready mind and appetite. This piece was odd looking to me, but I thought it must be the gizzard, and I am especially fond of it. So I took it, and plunged my fork into it and pulled. The brown [word(s) missing] on the outside broke off, and laid bare [word(s) missing] [chi]cken's *eye*!! Horrors!! A frog's eye is [word(s) missing] compared to a chicken's eyes cooked [word(s) missing] dinner on chicken was over; thenceforth [word(s) missing] pie and cake. But the *dinner* was *good*, though it was a Kentucky meal....

Cline.

Norman, Okla., July 24 1916

Dearest Jean,

... A fellow the other day offered me a position he has as principal of a public school with a hundred dollars a month if I would take it. I considered it a step downward, however, and declined the offer. Anyone who would exchange a position in our college for the principalship of a public school is unworthy of a college. His forehead is too low to be a teacher in our school.

To-morrow night, Tuesday, a pageant is to be given on the university campus. It is directed by Miss Anderson. It was to have been given on the Fourth of July, but because of the accident and the killing of the boy, it was postponed.[30] It ought to be pretty good, I think. I wish you could see it, but if you don't come till Wednesday you won't be here in time....

I shall hand in my credit to-morrow. Dean Buchanan is not here to-day. His wife is sick and he had to take her to Oklahoma City. I think she

---

30. On July 4, 1916, a train hit an automobile occupied by two men. The incident occurred at the Daws Street crossing in Norman. One of the two automobile passengers, a young man of 25, was killed. Since the accident seems to have attracted considerable attention, it is likely that this was the incident to which Cline refers. "Fatal Automobile Accident," *Daily Transcript*, July 6, 1916.

has heart trouble and is not expected to live long. She has had several severe attacks, it seems.

Infantile paralysis[31] is again spreading over the country. There is a case or two in Oklahoma City, and the mayor has forbidden all children to attend the moving pictures. It is pretty bad farther east, but is only beginning here. I hope they can get it stopped. Nothing much is known of its cause nor its cure. It just has to kill or let live of itself....

Cline.

Monday, July 24, 1916.

My dear Cline,

... Papa wrote mama to-day that he was so anxious for me to get my college work and a good deal in the university. He said I just must do it and I think I must too.

I certainly would have enjoyed eating that "Kentucky dinner" with you. It has been three long years since I had the pleasure of eating a Kentucky dinner, and then it was not shared by you. There are no cooks like the Kentucky cooks, and no chickens quite so plump, high headed, and high stepping as a Kentucky roaster of the frying age. I have really thought they have brighter eyes then other chickens, don't you know. While I have never had the pleasure of eating an eye fried, the good lady who is such a perfect imitator of a Kentucky cook must have thought it quite a delicacy. Oh, that I had been there to see you *un*cover and *dis*cover it!!

By the way, you remind me of an old man I have heard my grandfather Armstrong tell about. The old man came to Grandpa's one bitter winter's night. As he sat hovering over the fire thawing the frost from his beard he said, "It's cold! Mr. Armstrong it's cold!! This is shore a bad night on dumb brutes and sheeps." Your "Kentucky dinner" had every thing but "vegetables and potatoes." Oh Cline, you are great! Come with me to Kentucky and I'll show you fried chicken, corn, beans, potatoes, tomatoes, jellies, cakes, pies and ice cream that would make a bull dog gnaw his chain as uncle Paul used to say....

We have decided to come to Norman Thursday morning unless that is one of your chemistry days and I do not think it is. Since you can't get home until Saturday we will have to get home first.... I must go read my Bible lesson now. It's after nine and the rest of the house have gone to bed but I have neglected it for two days. So I must read it to-night....

Jean.

31. I.e., polio.

Norman, Okla., July 28, 1916[32]

My dear Jean,

…I am altogether done with chemistry laboratory this summer. To-day I wrote up my last experiment and washed all my apparatus. Tuesday we check in our things to see if anything is missing. I have one bottle and a long-handled spoon gone. I know I haven't broken them, so the only conclusion is that I happened to leave them on the tables and some one else got them. I took some bottles over to Rutherford's table to work one day, and I suspect one of them was displaced then. They won't cost much, however, and I can easily pay for them if I can't find them.

I am not going out to the lake with the class. They are going this afternoon instead of Saturday, so I just told them I couldn't go. I was too tired for one reason. I don't think I got to bed till twelve o'clock or after last night, and I worked this morning at my chemistry till one-thirty this afternoon. Then I have about two or three hundred pages of history to read this week and Sunday. And best of all I *didn't want to go*. So I am not there now. I don't care much for picnics if you are not there anyway, and I wouldn't want you to go on a "swimming picnic," if the girls wore bathing suits. So even if you had been here we would not have gone, would we?

Homer and I had a little discussion about bathing at dinner to-day. He said he didn't mind seeing girls go bathing with their little short-skirted bathing suits on. But I do. I don't think such a costume is any more modest on the bank of a lake than it is in the parlor or at a banquet. He said he wouldn't like to see a girl dress like that for a reception, but on the lake it was all right. Every one, of course, has to have his own idea of modesty and modest dress, but there isn't much danger of being *too* modest.…

                                                  Cline.

239 South Draper Street.

Shawnee, Oklahoma.
July 28, 1916.

My own dear Cline,

---

32. This letter is addressed to Pataway in care of Joe W. Warlick, Shawnee, Oklahoma.

... We certainly had an experience here that I never did go through before. When we got off of the train it was eleven o'clock and no one was there to meet us. We had forgoten [sic] the name of their street so we didn't know what to do or where to go. We saw two cabmen a little way off and we asked them if they knew where Joe Warlick lived. They didn't know but they thought they could find out. They already had a load so one of the men took those people to their destination while the other waited around there keeping his eye on us a little bit. As it happened I remembered the house number and thought I could recognize the street if I were to hear it. I suggested to mama that we go out and ask him to name some of them for us and sure enough he hadn't named more than three or four before I recognized the one Sister Warlick had given us. It was fifteen or twenty minutes before the first man came back but when he did they had no trouble in finding the house. I was certainly glad to see somebody I knew. Sister Warlick never did get the card mama wrote her....

I am sitting here writing by a gas light and I'm sure it's fine and some cheaper than electricity but I'll take the electricity every time if I can get it. I am just a few feet from the light but it's so dim it is hard for me to see....

Jean.

Sunday morning.

[July 30, 1916]

Dear Cline,

... Yesterday mama, Sister Warlick, and I went down town to see some things. We walked to the library and up the street through the best part of town, then back by the public school. The most interesting thing to me though was a little brown bungalow just up the street here from us. It's the home of a young couple. Both the boy and girl have been working in a garment factory here. They had both been saving there [sic] money for some time. They got their house built and almost furnished before they were married. Some one on the place has fine taste, too, because the cannas around the place chime in exactly with the dark and yellow browns of the house.

Sunday night.

We are just home from church and all of us so tired we could drop.

I haven't seen much of Ira. He goes to work before I get up and doesn't come home until dark. Usually after supper we've been sitting out on the porch and talking until half past nine or ten. I mean all of us. But to-night we came home and every one has gone to bed except me. Ira will go to work to-morrow before I get up and we'll start home before he gets through work. I won't see him anymore except maybe go by and tell him goodbye. Do you feel a little bit easier now, dear? I think you have been almost afraid for me to be here where he is. You have no reason for being that way because the more I'm with him the more I wonder why I ever did like him at all. You knew we were going to get home before you did even if we did stay here till Monday and I can't see any other reason for your insisting that we leave here Saturday or Sunday evening except that you felt a little uneasy when I'm where Ira is long.[33] Cline, I'm so sorry you feel that way for I love *you* and always will love you more than any other boy on earth....

Jean.

Okla., August 1, 1916.[34]

Dearest Jeanette,

... This afternoon I have to check in my chemistry apparatus, and see how much money I get back. If we don't have everything clean and shining they fine us $1.50 each. I have inspected my outfit very carefully since they made that announcement. I shined them more than I do dishes when I dry them.

Jean, you are mistaken about my being jealous of Ira. I am not jealous of anyone, for I know you could not love any one else now, and I trust you too much to be jealous. I just thought you didn't want to stay at Warlick's anyway, and I was telling you what I should do if I were in your place. I think you said you didn't want to go, and were only going to please Sister Warlick, didn't you? I should have been selfish enough to please her as little as I could. You are always better than I am about such things.

I have an aversion to visiting anyway, and I must outgrow it. I think we ought to do more of it this winter than we ever have done before. I am sure it will help matters between the church and the school. The church people hardly know us except from hearsay. They are not among us enough to learn to love us, and the same thing is true with us. We ought to get acquainted....

Cline.

---

33. This may reference an in-person conversation because there is no such discussion in the extant correspondence.

34. This letter is addressed to Pataway at her home in Cordell.

Okla., Wednesday

[August 2,] 1916

My dear Jean,

I have no time to write to-day, so I'm just sending this note. I have to review history and chemistry, do all my packing, get my money from the bank and water plant, and go over to our milk woman to pay a small debt I have there—all this afternoon.

But I love you just as much if I cannot write, and I'll soon "see thee face to face"[35] and talk as much as you wish. I am going to Opal's to-morrow afternoon just as soon as my examinations are over—and shall wait there for Homer. We'll get home Saturday before you are up, I suspect. This is my last letter till I see you. Be good till I come, and *love* me as *much as ever you can*, for I love you, dear, with my whole heart. Du bist mir alles in der Welt.

Cline.

---

35. Probably an allusion to 1 Corinthians 13:12.

3

Summers 1917 and 1918

The entire Armstrong household spent the summer of 1917 in Norman so that Jack and Cline could study at the university, strengthening their credentials as they worked toward the College's accreditation. Pataway took a couple of courses there as well. The family rented a house that included a room for Cline, hence there were no letters exchanged that summer.[1] The years 1917 and 1918 did, however, did bring profound changes to the couples' lives, both of which are documented in this brief chapter.

The first change was that they married several years before the date they had set for themselves. The reason for this was that the United States' entry into World War I (April 1917) precipitated military service notices going out to millions of American men. Cline was one of those men and multiple appeals for a deferral failed. Eventually, the only option seemed to be for the couple to marry since the draft board was not taking married men. Their wedding took place on September 17, 1917, and Cline received his discharge notice less than two weeks later.[2] Even though Jack Armstrong ultimately went along with the plan and performed the ceremony, his letter written several weeks before the wedding clearly communicates reluctance.

The second change in Pataway's and Cline's lives involved the closure of Cordell Christian College under Armstrong's presidency. Cline's letter of 1918 recounts crucial events leading up to the closure. The upheaval

---

1. Sears, *What Is Your Life?*, 75.

2. Woodson seems to have been behind the idea of the early marriage while Jack was initially opposed. Ibid., 81. Draft notice and certificate of discharge in possession of the editor.

prevented him from returning to Norman that summer and he had to wait until 1919 to finish his bachelor's degree.[3]

Howe, Texas

c/o Willis Harrel[4]
August 10, 1917.

My dear pataway and Cline:

About two years ago now I received a letter from you telling me of your promises to each other, and your plans for the future. This letter as you know was a source of no little grief, not because I objected to those plans' being carried out sometime, but because of pataway's age. You both expected this to be my serious objection; in fact, your own good wisdom told you your age was objectionable. So in the letter referred to you assured me that your plans would not be consumated [sic] for *five* or *six* years. While I have for a long time thought long engagements are unwise, yet in your case it was a comfort to me and made your plans bearable to me, or, at least, made it possible for me to be reconciled to them. I had no objections to your promises to each other then and I have less now. But it is so unwise for you to make so short the *five* or six years. Personally, I should prefer the marriage right now were it not for pataway's age, and incomplete education. For a long time I have had plans for her and it is a keen sacrifice to give them up. I know you have plans about this that you think will be all right, and should everything go as you plan and work out as you hope for it to work I readily grant you it would be well. But there are a dozen ways for your plans to miscarry. While your early marriage may seriously interfere with your own education, Bro. Sears, it is not so likely to hinder yours as it is pataway's. The chances are all against her. A Ph.D. and a high school graduate are a great way apart, the gap is too great for the greatest service and happiness, and you both know this is strongly possible with an early marriage. But this is not the worst that might be. Sister Bishop under great burdens has been trying to fit herself to care for her children. Our Lord wisely veils from us the future, but he wants us to be wise and prudent. When your mother and I were married, I never dreamed of your mother's teaching and bearing the part in our work that she has. I am quite sure she did not dream of her part in our business. What you may need for the Lord's work in your hands in ten years from now neither of you

---

3. Ibid., 88.

4. This letter is addressed to Prof. Lloyd Cline Sears, Cordell, Oklahoma, and postmarked Howe, Texas.

could have knowledge of to-day. You are both young and with a small sacrifice now you can so prepare that whatever might be your needs you could supply them. Remember that self-denial, a little waiting now, will yield you a great income in the years of your pilgrimage when you will most need that income. Even pataway's health is in the balance and a few more years now of care may mean many years of peaceful living to-gether. I am making this plea for you and your usefulness and happiness, not my own. I want you to be happy and I have great plans for you.

I want to ask your serious and prayerful consideration of putting off the marriage until the fall of 1919. This means four years from the time of your promise to me and you assured me that it would be *"five"* or *"six"* years. I do not hold you to your promise. I release you altogether and promise you my help and support in every way possible whatever may be your decision. But you will be unwise and hinder your otherwise great future of service and happiness by an early marriage. Remember what I say, and be wise. To be selfish at this time in which so much of your future is bundled up is certainly not expected of those with your opportunities.

With much love I am your father,
J. N. Armstrong

Cordell, Oklahoma[5]

August 16, 1918.

Dear Miss Mary,

We have just received your letter and the money order for $15. We appreciate your gift and the love and interest it shows more than we can tell you. But the school has closed. We have had such severe persecution from brethren and the county Council of Defence [sic] that we have had to discontinue and there will be no school this year. Nothing has ever pained me so much—except the early death of my father. I could hardly stand it if I did not know that in some way it is best.

You know when Brother Bell's article came out the Council called Brother Ray, Arthur Tenney and me into a meeting and questioned us about the matter. They tried to draw the school into it then, but failed. Then Brother

---

5. This letter was written to Mary Shepherd and so represents the sole piece of correspondence in the volume not addressed to a member of the Armstrong or Sears families. Its significance to the historical record warrants inclusion here, however. The transcription was made from a photocopy that, regrettably, is missing a few lines. A few sentences of this letter appear in Casey, "Closing of Cordell," 28.

Armstrong came home and the [sic] called him before the council. They accused him and the school of teaching Randolph and the other boys not to do any work. The school has always taken the position that we could do some non-combatant work, but they would not believe Brother Armstrong's statements, and asked for a statement from the Board endorsing him or stating their position on war. Brother Hockaday and several other members met the council and told them about the same things Brother Armstrong had already said about our position, and answered fully their charges. None of us have ever influenced Brother Randolph to take his position, but have tried [to] get him to take non-combatant work. They also charged that we had four students in the Federal penitentiary—we have only two, and both of them there because they would not listen to our teaching and do non-combatant work.

Then the Council demanded that Brother Armstrong resign and said that I could not teach and for any other member of the faculty or board who endorsed Armstrong to resign, and a complete reorganization to take place so as to endorse and encourage "fully and [word(s) missing] the government with respect to the war, and that "no half-way compliance would be tolerated." Our Board suggested three different forms of arbitration each of them perfectly fair to both sides, leaving the case to the higher federal officers at Oklahoma City and Washington. They refused to consider it and demanded the closing of the school.

Hockaday and Dial then went to Oklahoma City to the State Council and asked for an investigation. It was promised and last Tuesday Judge Owen, judge of the supreme court, came to investigate for the State Council. Hockaday and Dial came to Cordell for the investigation and got here several hours before Owen. When Bingaman, the Chairman of our Council, heard they were here he saw them and ordered them to leave town at once with an open threat of mob violence. He slapped Hockaday half-spitefully, half-angrily, and told him he never wanted to see him in Cordell again. Hockaday told them to begin at once if they wanted to mob him, he was alone and there were fifty of them present. (Bingaman had called in men from all over the county and told them a lot of lies—they knew nothing about the trouble except what he and our Brethren told them. [word(s) missing] Harrell, Cook, etc—our brethren). Bingaman replied in a manner as if shaking his fist in Hockaday's face, "Instead of fifty men, there will be *five hundred* men here to attend to you if you don't clear out at once. Do you see the door? Go!"

I have never known in my life such extreme and superlative insolence from any one. But as they were starting home, Owen came into town and called for Brother Armstrong who told him the Council had ordered the board to leave town and had prohibited any investigation. Owen called in Bingaman and gave him in plain terms to understand that it was none of his business whether the investigation took place or not and if we wanted a hearing we should have it in spite of Bingaman and the county Council, and he wanted no rough house about it. Bingaman got quiet for a while but had to be called down once or twice during the hearing because he became so loud. Several times he went over and consulted with Crumley and then came back to question our witnesses.

Crumley has shown himself a bitter enemy—to be a snake in the grass. He has done some of the meanest work against us. Fleming has figured the same way. Crumley used to hold our position on the war, but to be popular and escape public sentiment and persecution he has changed completely and now persecutes those who do not believe in resisting.

Judge Owen has not reported the decision of the state Council, but he assured us that he understood the case and believed we were good Christian people. Billups told him Armstrong was a "Christian of the highest type." But they are still threatening mob violence against us, and we have been forced to close on that account. The main business men of the town do not endorse the action of the Council, but they have never been able to learn the facts and to handle the matter.

We will leave Cordell in about a month. Harper offered me a position as soon as our school closed a[s] teacher of English. I may go there. Brother Armstrong will make his home where I go, but will evangelize most of the time.

I suppose I have a little surprise for you. On August 12 at 10:10 a.m. Master Jack Wood Sears made his debut. Pataway is doing just as fine as anyone could possibly do. This is the fifth day and her temperature has never been more than 100.6.° It is normal to-day....

Miss Mary, I am not sending back the money order right now. We got a five dollar order from another class. It was sent by a boy named French. I wish you would thank him personally for us. Our appeal was made to pay for new equipment the coming year, and since we are not going to run we cannot use it for that. But the closing of the school leaves over $1000 of debts for back equipment and expenses. We are writing some of the people who have promised [illegible] to the school to see if they want to put them on this back debt. If not, of course they are just released from their promise. Brother Tipton, I think, is going to help us pay these back debts, but what are left Brother Armstrong and I will handle. We would appreciate putting these two $5 gifts on this debt, if you like, but if the class would rather have it in new equipment we will send it back or give it to the Harper School, whichever they like best. Write me [word(s) missing]

With love, L. C. Sears (Cline)

4

Academic Year 1920–21

Cline did accept the offer to teach English at the Christian college in Harper, Kansas.[1] B. F. Rhodes had already gone there to teach history and his recommendation brought Cline to the position. Armstrong, who had planned to support himself by holding a number of protracted meetings, was forced to cancel many of those engagements due to the influenza epidemic that year. So, he and Woodson moved to Harper and stayed with the Sears family. By the spring of 1919, the Harper College board approached Armstrong about becoming the School's president and asked Cline to assume academic dean duties.[2]

That same year, Cline completed his bachelor's degree at the University of Oklahoma and soon began considering master's degree possibilities. By 1920, he was able to take a leave of absence and, at age twenty-five, enrolled in the University of Kansas, Lawrence.[3] Of this decision Cline wrote,

> Remembering my homesickness at Norman, it is strange that
> I had decided to spend another year away from my family. We
> had resolved never to be separated again, but the need of the

---

1. Harper operated from 1915 until 1924 when it merged with Arkansas Christian College to form Harding College. It had been established by members of the Churches of Christ in that region who had been sending their children to a Bible College in Gunter, Texas, because they were so dissatisfied with the quality of public school education in Kansas. Young, *History of Colleges*, 129.

2. Sears, *What Is Your Life?*, 86–87.

3. Ibid., 88–89. This was also the year when the school had its highest enrollment: 232 students. Young, *History of Colleges*, 132.

college for a stronger faculty prevailed over our personal feelings, and in September I left for the university.[4]

Pataway, now twenty-one, remained in Harper to care for their children: two-year-old Jack Wood and James Kern, an infant. While they talked of her visiting him in Lawrence, this seems never to have happened. Moreover, while Pataway corresponded with Cline, only his letters have survived. This regrettable loss may have occurred long ago since Cline appears not to have had the letters when writing his autobiography.[5]

Cline's own correspondence also contains considerable gaps because he was able to travel back to Harper several times during the year.[6] A few of the letters that remain are missing salutations, signatures, even pages.

Sept 13, 1920.[7]

Sweetheart,
   ... I took a sleeper from Wichita because it cost only $1.73 more, and I was tired. They let me sleep till seven at Topeka and I had just time enough to dress and get the train to Lawrence, arriving here at 8:20. I went directly to the YMCA building at the University, and asked for a room. They told me of a room for $11 but on phoning found it already taken. The next one was $12.50 and not taken; so I walked about eight blocks to it. Such walking you never saw. The entire campus is on a mountain. It wears you out to go up or down. When I reached the place, I found the woman wanted a roommate for a boy already in the room. Then I set out to find a room for myself, carrying my "vanity case" with me. I travelled every street near the University and finally persuaded an old couple to take me in. They did not want any one but

---

4. Sears, *What Is Your Life?*, 90.

5. There are no quotations from her letters in his chapter discussing the year in Kansas and this differs from the practice he employed when writing about their time in Cordell. Additionally, he talks speculatively about her reactions to his letters. See, e.g., ibid., 91.

6. Ibid.

7. The first two letters of the series are contained in the same envelope, dated September 14, 1920, and addressed to "Mrs. L. C. Sears, Harper, Kansas." They, and a number of others, are written on Harper College letterhead. This letterhead contains only the names of Armstrong and Sears in their respective positions as president and dean. The letterhead also confirms that Armstrong had obtained a master's degree by that point.

finally agreed to take me. I have a nice little room, just four blocks from the campus; in fact the library is in the fourth block. The walk to the university is right up a steep hill westward—but all walks to the university are up the same steep hill so this does not matter. The room has a good Simmons bed and is furnished with a study table, rocking chair, book racks, etc. The bath is just at the door. It is heated by *gas*, but is on the south east corner and shielded from the cold by other rooms. It has one outside entrance in case I do not wish to go through the living rooms. The lights are also of *gas* but make a brilliant light—about as good as electricity. I shall do much of my studying at the library anyway. This entire room costs me—. Maybe I had better not tell you. I could have got a room the third door north of it about the same size for $22.50 a month. I could have got another about two blocks further away from the university, gas-heated, electric lights, and on the north side of the house, with no sidewalk for one block, for $18 a month. But I preferred the one I have, which is much nicer than either of the others, for $10 a month. There is no one in the building but me and the old couple who live there.

I have engaged board on the same street about the fourth or fifth house north for $7 a week. Other boarding houses are charging $8. I do not like this one much for it is too crowded. One cannot use one's elbows at the table; we are packed like sardines. I may be able to find a better place for the same price. At least I shall try.

My board and room at the present rate will cost only $38 a month. This is much cheaper than I expected to get it. But the fees at the University are higher than I expected.

I went the first thing after finding room and board to see Dr. Blackmar and presented my credentials from Okla. Uni. He gave me a permit to enroll in the graduate school and sent me to the gymnasium where they are registering. He said it might be impossible for me to do enough educational work to get the Teacher's diploma this year. I do not care much. I can get it later—and there is nothing compulsory about it anyway. I went, after dinner, to the gymnasium and registered and paid $36 worth of fees—$10 matriculation fee, $6 hospital fee, and $20 marked "Inc." What that means, I do not know, but I suppose it is about the same thing as our "tuition." At least this whole thing was $36, which leaves me $79 in the bank and $7.50 in my pocket. The latter will pay my first week's board and the former ought to buy all my books. I shall have to wait a little while on a suit I suppose.

Everybody is talking athletics. It is about all I can hear. . . .

. . . They expect over 4000 enrolled. I was the 2138th to register.

Tell *Jack Wood* and *Kern* I love them. Jack Wood had no idea how long I should be away when he kissed me goodbye. Kiss him a hundred times for me. *I love you all.*

Cline.

Sept. 13, 1920.

Dear Pataway,

I have enrolled at last and have nothing more to do until the first classes meet. That will be Friday. I could have stayed at home several days longer had I only known it, but I might not have got my room if I had. I have changed boarding houses and like the new place better. They serve much more and have a greater variety of things. It only costs me twenty-five cents a week *less*, too. Board and room now cost me $37 a month. I have no more to eat I believe than you have there and my room is not nearly so nice. The boys and girls ought to be glad for what they have at Harper....

I am trying to decide on a subject for my thesis to-day. They have given me two Seminars in English of three hours each, one each semester. I give my entire time in research work for my thesis. This research work is given the six hours of credit. My thesis will then receive the two or four hours of credit extra, I suppose....

This year the university plays football here with, Nebraska Uni, Okla, Haskell, the A. P. M. college, and some others. There is at least one big football game scheduled for each month and some months two or three. I don't believe the football players can do much actual school work....

I am eager to hear the results of the Mangum meeting. Let me know at once. If I need to make out an order for books I can find a number here to order.

Cline.

1332 Ky. St.

Sept. 15, 1920.

Dearest Pataway,

This is Wednesday morning and I have received no letter from you yet. I have given the University post office my address and they would have delivered anything to me at once. Consequently there is but one conclusion—you have not written. Am I not logical?

I have been studying subjects for my thesis this morning. What do you think of these:

1. The Minor Writers of Blackwood's Magazine.
2. The Greek Element in English Drama.
3. Autobiography in Samson Agonistes
4. History of American Drama.
5. William Vaughn Moody.
6. The English Historical Novel.
7. The American Novel.
8. Sidney Lanier's Poetic Art ...

They require at least fifteen hours of strictly graduate work for the M.A. and I am enrolled for nineteen. By strictly graduate work I mean courses from which undergraduates are entirely excluded. I have only eleven hours of my work in classes that will include undergraduates, and four of these are in education.—all but seven hours of my English is graduate work. But I am taking this year all the strictly graduate work they offer here in English except four cours [sic] or ten hours. It will be impossible for me to take Ph.D. work here....

I am going to try to find the church here to-day. It may take me a long time. All the churches are supposed to be listed in the City paper but it is omitted. I bought a university publication put out by the Y M C A which was supposed to include all the churches in town but the Church of Christ is left out. I suppose it is so small they are ashamed of it or more likely have never heard of it. I'll write over to Hillsdale as soon as I get my work started and see what they are going to do.

Tell your father I had no opportunity to stop at Topeka this time. I thought it better to drop those two normal training classes anyway and lighten the burden of the teachers. When I come back I want to stop at Topeka and bring with me the forms and instructions for applying for both the normal training work and affiliation as a junior college.[8] We can fill them out while I am there and I can bring them back to Topeka with me. I hope the laboratories will all be arranged by that time. There is still much to do on the library for I could not finish the job.[9] It is usable but not as it should be. Even the library here has its books catalogued minutely. To do this requires a librarian's full time and requires one who understands how to catalog the books and make new subject headings, etc. Students will constantly call for

---

8. Harper College's normal training program was approved that year. Young, *History of Colleges*, 132.

9. Cline had been cataloguing the Harper College library. Sears, *What Is Your Life?*, 89.

material on subjects which are not mentioned in the catalogue; at once a card should be made out for that subject.

. . . I cannot tell yet how heavy my work will be but it looks like *lead* instead of feathers. All the teachers but two, however, are old men, grey or bald, or dried up, and so their work may not be so rigid as it would have been fifteen years go.

I must go to dinner. We have for breakfast each morning either cream of wheat, grape nuts, or post toasties—one or all (they are put in large bowls on the table and we help ourselves),—a half or whole banana, and a cup of chocolate or coffee and butter and toast. There has been no variation so far. There is no meat, eggs, bacon—nothing but the above mentioned. . . .

Cline.

Sept 16, 1920.

Dearest Pataway,

. . . I met some of my classes to-day. I have one of my classes in English this semester under Sisson, one under O'Leary, and two under Whitcomb. I like all of these men (except O'Leary, and I do not know him yet), but I don't like the fellow who handles my class in education. He is too cocksure and egotistical. He thinks his department is all of it. I am thinking of changing his class for another under a different professor. I have been advised to make the change, because his class pertains nearly altogether to elementary school work. What do I care about elementary methods?

I have no text for my class under Dr Sisson and the one under O'Leary. That means I must do extensive library work. In my class under Whitcomb, one of them, I have to use C. H. Dickinson's Chief Contemporary Dramatists. I used it at Norman the last year, and I think it is in my bookcase in the reception room. Please send it to me at once. It would cost here $3 or $4. . . . I don't think I'll need many books, for most of my work will be in the library. My seminar begins to-morrow. This will be strictly research work directed toward the preparation of my thesis. Dr. Whitcomb told me he did not want to scare me, but only about one-third of the graduate students ever took their degrees the first year. This is because it takes so much work on their theses that they cannot finish them in nine months. He said they did not demand a doctor's thesis for the M.A. but wanted them to be of a very high standard. They publish an occasional one which is especially fine. He wants me to begin work as soon as possible on my seminar and select a subject. The subject will have to pass the scrutiny of every teacher and be hammered on and picked to pieces before it is accepted. They will have to question me closely about my ability to handle the subject selected and my knowledge of and preparation for it—all of this before it is approved. I am getting along well with them so far, and I do not intend to cross any of them unpleasantly....

For next Tuesday we are to read Synge's Riders to the Sea and be able to criticize it from the point of view of dramaturgy, histrionics, and "higher criticism"; point out the theme; read it from the view point of comparative aesthetics and comparative rhetoric; and be able to explain its bearing on the Irish situation, religion and ethics, and world politics. Then we are to make a bibliography of fifty or more titles bearing on our course. I have about thirty-nine books already, but I have to glance through each of them to find out the general purpose, bearing, and value of the work and make a note of it in the bibliography. I don't know whether I can get to Luther Marshall's list of books or not. I will, if I can.

Two teachers here, the only teachers I have heard express themselves, discourage copious notes. The education man said he thought all the notes necessary for each assigned reading of fifty pages should be put on a card three by five inches in size. Whitcomb recommends only a few class notes. He says one should put the instructor in his head instead of his notebook.

Haven't seen a biscuit since I left Harper. All of it is light-bread except for breakfast; then we have near-toast. I mean that white, soft toast which is served merely warm. Some of it is not that bad....

Cline.

Sept 17, 1920

Dearest Pataway,

I have just come from chapel—the first one we have had. It was held in the gymnasium because the auditorium would not hold the people. The whole floor was filled; must have been three thousand there with others standing in the doors. The new chancellor, Ernest H. Lindley, made an address. Ex-chancellor Strong opened the meeting and introduced him. I am inclosing [sic] a program of the whole affair. Only the college yells are omitted. They yelled and cheered until it was nearly bedlam—I despise it all.

The new chancellor is a very slender fellow with a very slender face and a big shock of iron gray hair like a cap on his head. As he stands facing you he is the personification of the burlesqued timid preacher or minister in popular plays. He seems to be a thoughtful and capable man, however, in spite of his appearance at first.

There are fully twice as many teachers here as at Norman. They marched into the chapel two and two and it took a long time for them all to come in; the whole stage must have had three hundred seats and all of them seemed filled. That may be a little large but such was the appearance, and I saw one professor down in the audience, one of the older ones....

Cline.

Sept. 18, 1920.

Dearest Pataway,

...I am going to church here to-morrow. I don't know how they will receive me, and I don't care much. I called up Sister Draper and found where they meet. Brother Draper is away in a meeting. They live a mile from where I stay and I have not gone to see them yet.

I met the Shepherd boy who used to be at Cordell. He took his M.A. at Oklahoma and has a fellowship here this year in Sociology. He is doing a little work toward his Ph.D. but plans to go to Chicago and finish it there....

We have a typical German at our boarding club—that is, typical from the present day American opinion. He is so fat he resembles a dumpy pig with a short stubby nose, and is egotistical, gruff, selfish, and a perfect glutton. Some have to wait once in a while but Mr. Schutz never waits. He knew it was about time for the bell to ring one day and he jumped up suddenly elbowed his way through a big crowd at the door and got first in the line. He dump [sic] the whole dish of potatoes or peas into his plate at once and lets the next man go hungry. In fact the whole club does this more or less. They help themselves as if they thought they should never get any more. I may catch the same disease, so you need not be surprised if I come back and turn into my plate all the meat on the table and let the rest of you beg....

Cline.

Sept. 19, 1920.

My own Sweetheart,

...I came near missing church this morning. I had called up Sister Draper and found that the church was meeting in an Adventist house on N Y street [sic] in the 1400 block. I waited until about time to go; I wanted to get there just before time to start the singing. When I got to the 1400 block on NY street I could find no church house anywhere. I walked on to the 1500 block and ran finally into a big green house built squarely across the street stopping all further progress in that direction. Then I turned and started back down NY street, finally finding the church in about the 900 block. They had begun the Bible class when I got there.

There are only a very few meeting. Four or five meet on the other side of the river. The service was absolutely of no worth at all except to keep them hanging on. It was as dry as husks. Bro. Mitchell taught the class, but he could think of no questions whatever to ask and no one else was any brighter, it seemed; finally in desperation we ran through the chapter and stopped. All the comments made as we read had something to do with the old law. If there is one thing in the world our people know it is the fact that there is one "old law" and a "new"; that the old law has been abolished and the new is still in force. Every question that did accidentally arise was put instantly into the category of one or the other of these laws and, whether it had any bearing on the laws or not, some far-fetched connection was sure to be formed. I hope we shall never forget that the old law is dead!

They welcomed me heartily, and I hope they will let me teach the class each Sunday. I believe I may be able to give them some better things. I did not tell them to-day that I was teaching in a Bible college. I told them where I lived and that I was a brother of M R Sears, whom they had read of in the Review.[10] They know too that I am here to go to school and that I preach. I mean to be frank and open with any of them about where I stand but I don't think it necessary or good here to press my beliefs on them or even mention them of my own accord. I don't want to turn them all against me from the start. I may be able to do them some good. They are all very ignorant, it seems. Brother Draper is not here at present; out in a meeting....

Cline.

1332 Ky St.

Sept 20, 1920.

My own Sweetheart:

... I have been working pretty hard lately. I have read more than half of the Nibelungenlied and the first three books of the Odyssey, also "The First George" by Thackeray and made my bibliography in the Drama. Tonight I am going up to the library and look up some on Sanskrit literature, especially the two epics Ramáyana and Mahabhárata and also look over the theses that

10. I.e., Daniel Sommer's *Octographic Review*. Cline's brother, Ralph, admired Sommer and regularly read his paper. Sears, *What Is Your Life?*, 35.

have been printed and placed in the library. I have not yet decided on a subject for my thesis. I like Moody, and if he has not been treated, I'll do it, I think. They are encouraging me to take him if he has not already been dealt with. We had a long session with Prof. Whitcomb to-day. He is a peculiar fellow—a little egotistical, I believe, but also very scholarly and exacting. His Doctor's thesis at Columbia, he said, brought him a letter of appreciation from Roosevelt.[11] It was on some phase of American literature, I think. He urges us to make our theses fit for publication; said if I could publish my thesis it would go far toward securing me a fellowship in an Eastern university where I could continue my work on the Ph.D.

You asked about taking the PhD here. Whitcomb says they have never conferred one here. They do not have enough graduate work in my line catalogued. I am this year taking all of the English work they offer above the AB work, except only nine hours. That is little more than a fourth of one year's work. I could do all of this in one summer, provided they offered it all in a single summer, and then I should be *done* here. They have only about six or eight working toward their MA's this year. Before the war he said they had as many as twenty-five graduate students in the English department alone; now they have four, I think. He said the war nearly ruined the higher work. I really wish I could have taken my work this year in a stronger school. But I'll get as much good from it here perhaps, and this is far stronger than the Oklahoma University. There is no comparison between the two schools in the English department. I haven't seen any teacher who could go to sleep as completely as Ramey. They are all really scholarly men. Whitcomb has published several books, one on the novel, one his doctor's thesis in American literature, one his chronological outlines of American literature, and some books of verse written by himself. Blackman [sic] in the department of Sociology has written and published eight or ten books, I believe. I looked through his cards in the library catalog and found a large number of cards giving books he had written, I do not remember the exact number. But I think the scholarship of the school far superior to that of the Oklahoma University. Still they do not do PhD work yet.

I don't want ever again to spend another year away from home. When I go for my doctor's work, we both go together and old Jack Wood and Kern too. But I want to prepare my thesis so that it may be printed and secure me a fellowship at Columbia or Harvard if possible. For that will make it possible for us all to go.

I don't imagine you would like one phase of the school here. The negroes and whites are in the same classes. You see them talking together

---

11. I.e., President Theodore Roosevelt.

sometimes very familiarly. The other day I saw a white girl walking down the street with a tall fellow as black as you nearly ever saw. Both seemed to be enjoying themselves in conversation. I don't know whether he was a negro or a Filippino [sic]. They have a large number of Filippinos, Hawaiians, Greeks, Japs, Negroes, etc and sometimes you can't distinguish between them they look so much alike....

I went to the Christian Church last night. The whole thing was nauseating. It was an effort to entertain, and as entertainment it was flat and insipid. They had singing with Prof. Downing of the University leading. This and the chorus sung by the choir were the only really good things in the program. The preacher then "sandwiched" in a "sermon," as he called it, of about fifteen or twenty minutes length in which he strove to say some nice and learned things without offending anyone.... Only a few people were present and yet it is about the biggest church in town. They have a $60,000 building....

Cline.

1332 Ky. St.

Sept. 21, 1920

My own Sweetheart,

I have been at work! I don't know whether I would *have* to study quite so hard, but I do enjoy it. I have at last found my thesis. It is to be "William Vaughn Moody, Poet and Dramatist." How does that sound? I don't know just yet how the English department will make me limit it, but I want to deal with it in about the following larger divisions: (1) Life. (2) Poetical works (3) Dramatic works (4) Letters and editorial work (5) Position in American literature. This is a big plan and may not be finished in the nine months or again it may be limited by the department.

I have been hunting up material on him and have about twelve pages in my note book filled with references to magazine articles, reviews, and papers treating him and his work. I showed Professor Hopkins my notebook when I had only about six pages full and he said he did not know there was so much material on him. Hopkins is the professor of American literature.

Listen; I may have to make a trip to Chicago in the spring for about a week or two if we are able to stand the cost. Moody taught at Chicago University and his wife, they think, still lives at Chicago. Hopkins thought it might be well to go up and see her. At least I am to write her now. Perhaps I can get all that will be necessary without a trip; I hope so anyway, for we have no money to make it....

I don't see how the boys and girls get their work at all. They are on the streets all day and dancing and playing and at the show every night. At the library last night there was a mere handful; but as I came back, I passed a house where twice as many were dancing to their jazz music. I hear the jazz going now as hard as it can, and I suppose they are dancing somewhere with it....

Cline.

Sept 22, 1920.

Dearest Pataway,

It is raining a slow dreary rain outside. I came through it from the University this afternoon, but the trees kept me from getting very wet. I believe there is more shade here than we have at Harper; every street is lined on each side with big trees. It is a beautiful town and has three or four parks that are pretty.

I wanted to go to the picture show to-night and see Douglas Fairbanks. You know I have never seen him act in my life. But it is raining too hard and besides I have too much to do instead. I have to read Sir John Mandeville's travels[12] through before to-morrow's lesson. It is a whole book of three hundred pages or more, but I can read it hurriedly. This is an indication of how heavy some of my work will be when we get started right. I am also to read the Niblungenlied [sic] through—I have finished only 190 pages of it and there are about 400; then the Song of Roland of about 250 pages; Rāmāyana, the Sanskrit epic, of more than 100 pages and much more. This is all in the epic class. I read to-day and yesterday nearly a whole book on Sanskrit literature, a history of it. I don't know whether I have to remember such names as Samaveda, Rigdveda, Sutrās, Bhagāvad-gita, or not but there are a plenty like that and worse in that history. Tasso's Jerusalem Delivered, Dante's Divine Comedy, Paradise Lost (entire), Paradise Regained and many others come in this course....

Cline.

I hear the jazz again. It goes every night. If my feet don't catch the jingle and bring me "tripping" down the church aisle sometimes I must be thankful. Such a thing would be ruination to what little reputation I have.

---

12. This fourteenth-century work is attributed to Sir John Mandeville but its authorship has long been a matter of scholarly debate.

Sept 23, 1920.

My sweetheart,

I am so lonesome this evening I could cry; in fact I have been crying some. I have just finished reading Moody's "The Death of Eve." ... I had never thought how Eve must have felt when her first-born was driven from her presence with the mark upon his brow; but Moody shows her to be a real mother with all the strength of a mother's love. I hope you will read it sometime. I only wish he could have finished the piece.

I feel so little when I think of dealing with the work of a real literary genius. I have felt many times after an effort to interpret a play in the class as Moody said he himself felt. He was a teacher in Chicago you know, but ceased teaching in 1902. He was urged time after time to take only a lecture course and many times courses were organized for him but were withdrawn before the session opened because he would not consent to take them. One day [word(s) missing] him [word(s) missing] would never consent to take a [word(s) missing] he replied "I cannot do it; I feel that at every lecture I slay a poet." It is so hard to interpret a real work of art. It cannot be done without analysis, and analysis always destroys its beauty, for the moment at least. Poetry and drama are made to enjoy but not to be taught nor to be dissected by some dry-brained old practitioners of literary surgery. (I must go to supper.)

I have written your father that I have applied for a fellowship. If I get it we are easy sure enough for it will bring me $350,—or $39 (nearly) a month. This will pay all my expenses except paper, clothes, and railroad fare. It will cost me only six hours of work each week for that is all they are allowed to ask ... I like this better than teaching a class, because I would be so anxious to make good in my teaching that I know I should give too much time to it and perhaps slight some of my own classwork.

I have one teacher who is a curiosity—Professor Whitcomb, who handles most of my work and conducts my seminar. The students hate him; and he is provoking. He talks low as if speaking to himself or thinking aloud, and mumbles his words, when he gives his lectures, until it is often difficult to understand what he is driving at. He knows a great deal, but he is not very connected in his lectures—seems to be making them up largely as he goes. He gives us a good deal to think of and has a philosophical mind, but we have to arrange his material largely ourselves, if it [word(s) missing] [a]rranged.

There is a negro in [word(s) missing] class I have taken up. You know the class in education in which I went first was for elementary work, and I have changed to another in High School Administration. It is dry as dust, and all the students seem to despise it. Professor Johnston conducts it. He told me of the vacancy in fellowships, and advised me to apply for one. He asked me why I did not change my work to the educational department. I didn't tell him I should become a raving maniac in two years at his work, but I believe it is true....

Sept 24, 1920.

Dearest Pataway,

...Professor O'Leary and Professor Whitcomb said they would speak a good word for me to Dean Blackmar about the fellowship. I referred them to Ramey and Haskell[13] too, and they will wait until they hear from them, I think. O'Leary said I had a mighty good chance to get it....

They had chapel again to-day but I didn't go. There is too much heathenish, barbaric yelling for me; it grates on my ears. They had nothing anyway except some short talks from the students—the head of the Y M C A, Y W C A, foot ball team, and some of the other student organizations.

Boy at my boarding place belongs to a fraternity. It costs him $15 a month. It takes about $3000 a year to be in a fraternity if one boards and rooms in the building and engages in all their active work. At least that is the estimate made by me of the students, perhaps a little exaggerated. I can get through the year on about $500.

I have been enjoying Mandeville, He and Swift are about the biggest and handsomest liars I have ever met. I admire their way of telling them....

Me.

Sept 25, 1920.

Dearest Pataway,

...I wish you were here. I am so lonesome sometimes. I'll never go off like this again. If I didn't have to work all the time I should die. I have hardly time to eat and sleep. I'm trying to keep up my Bible readings, but I have missed a few times. I don't see how I'll have time to get up a sermon if I go over to Hillsdale. I haven't written them yet, for I have been full of other things. I should have written to Topeka before this, but have done nothing yet. I'll try to do it to-day. I want to fill out our application for Junior college standing as soon as I get home.

---

13. Cline apparently means Sardis Roy Hadsell. See his reference in Sears, *What Is Your Life?*, 89.

Had to buy a book for my class in education cost $3.25. We have a copy of it in the library but I thought you might need it there this year. I think I'll do very little reading in that class outside of the text-book. I don't think it will require any. The English work is the recent work in [word(s) missing] there is nothing quite like the study of a language, for in it you get the thought of the greatest men. One reads not merely for the beauty of the language but for the thought as well. I have noticed this in all of my work through the Okla-university and so far in this one—the English teachers seem to be the broadest minded men in the school. They have an appreciation for art, music, opera, sociology, history, sciences, philosophy, etc and they refer to them as they teach. But the teachers of education think there is nothing else but their "field," and they wear out the word "function," and many others. I have yet the first time to hear them do anything but criticize the methods of English teachers, etc. It is the opinion of all that one has no idea of "method" until he takes a course from some young upstart in the Theory of teaching or in some branch of Pedagogy. But you can sit in the class till doomsday and fail to see any superiority in the "method" of the man who is teaching you "methods." Professor O'Leary gave us in the bibliography for his course several histories of England covering the 18th century, and asked us to read them. One is a big thing of 8 or 10 vol., but he recommended it highly and though [sic] we ought to read it through some day. Here is appreciation for things outside one's own work. You never see it in teachers of education. The correct study of English takes in more than the mere language. It includes it, of course, but it includes as well, history, sociology, philosophy, religion, fiction, drama, poetry, opera, science, education, and a thousand things not included in anything else. This year we'll read Milton's Aeropagitica—it is a paper in *government*, the freedom of the press. Burke wrote largely on political subjects and we make a special study of him. *I hope no one will ever ask me to change to education again.* And yet it is a *valuable* line of work—but there is something else as far superior as the soul is to the body. . . .

Cline.

1332 Ky St

Sept 26, 1920.

Dearest Pataway,

. . . This morning the [sic] asked me to lead in prayer, and I think will treat me all right after a while. Oh, they are nice enough but I haven't told them yet exactly who I am. They only know I am Ralph's brother.

Tell Brother Croom, I think the Hornbaker boy from Stafford is here. Sister Draper at least asked me to find out if I could where he stays and bring him to church next Sunday. He is in the freshman class she says, and comes from Stafford. You see his people, and perhaps he, were afraid of the "Christian College" but he comes here and misses church the very first Sunday. Of course he may not have been able to find it, but so many boys and girls do not want to find the churches here. They nearly all stay at home on Sunday and make fun of the idea of going. Old Daniel Somer [sic] and a few others may have a heavy debt to pay sometime.

We have nothing at all to-night, but I think I'll go down to the Methodist church to-night and see them. I went to the Christian Church last Sunday night you know . . .

We had a pretty good dinner to-day: smothered steak with bowls of gravy; peas; tomatoes; creamed potatoes; sweet pickle; and brick ice cream and cake. Sunday breakfast is a little different, for they give us, besides the regular supply of breakfast foods, French toast and syrup. I make my meal entirely of the two last for it is the only relief to the monotony of breakfasts. They serve sweet potatoes here once in a while for dinner or supper, but there are enough other boys to eat them; so I make it a point to be generous to them.

Professor O'Leary's son left last week for Harvard. He graduated from Yale with his M.A., I think, but is to take additional work at Harvard this year. O'Leary himself is from Oxford, England . . .

Cline.

Sept 27, 1920.

Sweetheart,

. . . Some of the boys said there is a girl here who stays on the streets all the time to entice the boys, and they wondered that they let her take classes in the university. But the school would not care much if they knew . . .

I got a letter from Ramey yesterday saying he had sent a recommendation [sic] Dean Blackmar. He regretted that I had not told him I was going to school, for they could have given me all the teaching I wanted this year, and very likely for the future. He didn't like my subject for a thesis of course, for he loves Anglo-Saxon and linguistic studies and thinks one should do all his work in that line. Here the critical, and the literary and historical side is emphasized. I showed Whitcomb his letter, partly to let him see what Ramey thought of me, and partly to get his opinion of my subject. He talked for an hour or more with me about the subject and [illegible] subjects, but he feels that the subject is a good one, provided I am anything of a "stylist," as he put it; that is, if I have a literary style. It should be well written to be worth much. I am just a bit shaky about my "style," for I have not written enough to have one, I fear....

Cline.

Sept 28, 1920

Dearest Pataway:

...I am glad to hear of the number of baptisms you are having. It sounds incongruous, with the noise of jazz and dancing beating on my ears all the week here. There is absolutely nothing to encourage or inspire students to a cleaner life or to a respect for the church. The Christian school is the only place in the world where Christian boys and girls should go. I found the address of the Hornbaker boy to-day and will go to see him about coming to church. He may not know the location.

Percy Tuggle is a *good riddance*. He belongs *here*. Tuggles are here as thick as Mandeville's devils—they walk all the streets and are sitting on every porch you pass. By the way, I have finished Mandeville and shall tell you about the "most beautiful" passage of all when I come home. He is a consummate, irredeemable liar! And the ease and perfect equanimity with which he does it is astonishing to all who are not themselves of the duo-linguistic genus. Perhaps it is for this reason I can appreciate him so well myself. It may be gratifying to you to learn that we are now reading Mallory's Morte D'Arthur, which, as you know, is a very religious and a very clean, healthy book.

The city of Lawrence has a fair on this week. The bill of entertainment includes auto races, horse races, baseball, football, and picture shows each night. The last is a wonderful attraction, seeing that the good citizens of this town seldom have opportunity to see these shows oftener than each afternoon and night in the week except Sundays, and that no less than three houses run them simultaneously...

I am inclosing Ramey's letter. Professor O'Leary said "He seems to think you ran away from them down there." I believe if the time ever comes that I need to do it, I can get a place there. Whitcomb told me they seldom get graduate students here who have much sense about English; many of them cannot write a correct sentence. After this year's work I could perhaps get a place here, but I don't think I should want it. Somehow I don't like the place as a whole as well as I did Norman; there seems to be a coldness about it all that Norman did not have. Still all of this may be imagination and may be different when I know it better. . . .

Cline.

Sept 29, 1920.

Dearest Pataway,

. . . The dean of Education wants to see me I have been told, and I believe it concerns the fellowship. He may want to see if I could take work in the educational department for Johnson [sic] told me they needed some one very much and asked if I could do it. I tried to see him yesterday but could not find him. I'll try again to-day.

I have resolved to give up Moody. After reading more from him I don't find him the great writer I at first considered him. He is a great writer, but somewhat smaller than I believed at first. Then it would be so hard to get at the facts of his life without going to Chicago and seeing his people and his friends such as Schevill, Levett,[14] Hapgood, etc. Another difficulty in free and open criticism is his nearness to us and the high prejudice people have regarding him, some believing he is one of the greatest of American poets, others thinking he is far overestimated.

I am looking for a subject back further. Joanna Baillie a contemporary of Scott wrote some very interesting plays, one or two of which should be edited and made available for modern use. I believe it is impossible at present to get hold of her work at all. Her life has never been treated and offers a most interesting subject. I am going to see about her and about several others back in the same period, for I believe they offer a much better subject than Moody. One should write only an appreciation of Moody, while one could write a critique of an older author. I should give an extended treatment of the author's life and works and her position in her own age and in the development of literary history and edit one or two of her plays. Such a treatment should be published at once. If I can I want to get a standard publishing house such as Ginn and Co., or Macmillan, or Dutton to publish it, for I should share in the profits of the sales. If the university publishes it, I would receive fifty copies, I think, for my own share, and the profit from all sales would go to the university. There is only one difficulty in getting it published by a standard book company, and that is the extreme shortage of paper and the cost of the work. They are making as few books now as possible. . . .

14. Cline apparently means Robert Morss Lovett.

The first football game is with the A & M college and comes next Saturday, but I shall not go. Season tickets sell for $4.50. Nearly a thousand tickets have been sold for the lyceum or concert course. This means between four and five thousand dollars....

Cline.

Sept. 30, 1920

Dearest Pataway,

... I saw the dean of education to-day. He only wanted to know if I would accept the principalship of the Junior High School in town. They have lost the principal somehow, and can find no one at all for the place. I told him "No, thanks." It seems they are in hard straits.

I am exploring the ground around John Home, Sir Thomas Noon Talfourd, and Joanna Baillie to see which of them I want to work up. They are all interesting, but I am inclined to the men a little, unless they have been treated already.

It's time for supper. I'll finish when I come back.—Well, we had beans, potatoes, an egg, & bread, butter, etc. This is the usual thing for supper, except that usually we have no egg. Our meals are monotonous, but I don't mind that. We have plenty always, and I don't tire of "solids" like potatoes, beans, meat, gravy, corn, peas, etc....

Cline.

Oct. 2, 1920.

My own Sweetheart,

I love you more than usual to-night, or I am more than usually homesick. Your letter did not come yesterday, and none came this morning; but this afternoon I got two. Jack Wood's letter was mighty sweet, and so was Kern's except I am afraid his was not entirely original. I know I have the dearest and sweetest wife and the sweetest and brightest babies in the world. (Don't let anyone read this but you, for it might produce sensations of nausea in anyone but us.)...

Well, I have been through a new experience for me. The University beat Emporia to-day forty-seven to nothing, and they are wild about it. To-night they are having a shirt-tail parade down Main Street. I wish you could see it. Fully two thousand boys, some with night shirts over their clothes, some with pajamas on, some with plain union suits, others with shirts pulled out over their trousers, but nearly the entire crowd in some kind of white underwear or night dress—all of them singing and shouting to split the air itself—are marching double-file, or rather parading with a snake-like course from one side to the other, down the main street. On both sides of the street the sidewalks are thronged with masses of spectators. At intervals along the curb where the line of parade touches the sidewalk, some store keeper is handing out treats to the boys. I saw one man with a great stack of Hersheys, box upon box, handing out a Hershey to every boy who passed, and they "rahed" him in return. At the head of the parade is the University Band playing all the rollicking songs you can imagine. I didn't know any but "There'll be a Hot Time in the Old Town To-night." I think I can hear the shouting and singing away out here, more than eight blocks, I suppose. Yes, I know I can.

Hundreds of hours and hundreds of dollars are foolishly thrown away by the students in just such things as this. And yet there is a fascination in it even to me as soured on such things as I am—a fascination in the enthusiasm, the exuberant overflow of animal spirit in it all. Compared with most of the boys in the world, I have sat all of my life like an old owl moping. But it is my nature it seems.

The boys here sweep everything before them. No one would attempt to interfere with the parade to-night. Street cars don't break through the line, but wait. Still they have an order of their own and a system of honor. To-day they were talking about hazing at the table. The custom is to let the freshmen run the gauntlet between two long rows of upperclassmen with paddles to strike him as he runs past. One fellow said one could get through easier by running faster, and another suggest [sic] that some one might trip him. A freshman spoke up instantly "No, they always give a man fair play." Even in the roughest practices they have their ideas of honor which they cling to tenaciously. The life of boys is hard to understand; it is one of the biggest problems in the world. I believe girls are easier to understand....

Cline.

Oct. 3, 1920.

Dearest Pataway,

... The boys say their parade last night was a tame affair. They did not break into the stores last night as usual and take what they wanted. All the merchants along the street donated five dollars into a common fund till they had twelve hundred dollars, and with this they bought the treats, candy, cidar

[sic], Vienna sausages, apples, etc. The boys are complaining that they didn't get more than thirty-five cents worth apiece. Last year they ran through the stores and took what they wanted. Last night, however, two of them went into a restaurant and ordered their meals. After they had finished they went up to pay and the man refused to take anything. No doubt other boys had similar treatment. Many of the stores locked up before the parade that usually stay open late on Saturday night.

Chancellor Lindley was out too, and made them a speech both at the University and down town. The boys all like him because he comes out and takes an interest in what they are doing. They say Strong never turned out for anything. Of course they know Lindley may be doing it merely to gain favor with the students and people while he is new, but still this is a commendable thing, they think. It is all right to gain favor, but I would not like to encourage shirt-tail parades to do it. . . .

Cline.

Oct 5, 1920.

Dearest Pataway,

. . . I heard Franklin D. Roosevelt, candidate for Vice-President, speak to-day. He is a very earnest, persuasive speaker, polished and of more than average force. He put the league[15] issue in a way that would be hard to meet. I heard several of the Republicans went away expressing themselves in full accord with his views. He did not sling mud, but all his references to Harding and Coolidge were nice and gentlemanly. Only in one instance and in a story about Harding did he reflect on the Republican candidate in any way. He said he did not intend to sling mud at Mr Harding for "he is an *amiable* gentleman—a *thoroughly* amiable gentleman." In his repetition and his slight stress of the word "amiable" I thought I could detect the kind of irony used by Antony in his oration. That is the trouble with Harding, he is too *amiable*. I don't think any one hardly would have noticed it and it may not have been intended for irony.

His story on Harding is too long to tell here; I'll give it when I come home. At any rate it shows how Harding courts popular opinion and waves to every wind of republican sentiment. He makes Taft think he'll be all right on the League and Hiram Johnson believes he is against it.

15. I.e., The League of Nations. The League was generally supported by Churches of Christ leadership on the basis that it could help secure world peace. Hooper, *Distinct People*, 114–15.

I don't get to see the papers much, but the ones I get here are all Republican. I bought a K. C. *Post* Sunday. Cox spoke in K. C. last Sat. night to an audience of 16,000 people. He seems to have taken them by storm. The demonstration after his speech lasted a long time, and the applause when he came in to the stage lasted eight minutes. Harding is to speak in K. C. soon, I have heard. I suppose he has at last come off his porch. Roosevelt [spe]aks i[n]K. C. following Cox. Lawrence is a Republican town. The boys at the University ridiculed Roosevelt's speech, except one or two. They are all against the League, because "such a thing has never yet been done and therefore cannot be." That was the argument at the table.

I have finally and unalterably settled on my thesis. I am going to make an extended study of Miss Baillie's life and works, and write an entire *book* on her. I suppose it will be a book, for the [illegible] be big enough for a large book if it is done right. Now comes my *study*. I've already found some material on her but there will be much more to go through. I'll have to read every line she wrote at least twice and make a careful study of it all. Then there will be reading of contemporary lite[rat]ure to get her relation to her times, the authors who influenced her, etc. . . .

Cline.

Oct 16, 1920.

Dearest Pataway,

. . . The house is not rented yet but I expect it to be to-day.[16] You would be surprised at the numbers that have come to look at it. It will be an easy matter to rent, for people are walking the streets looking for places. I am keeping back the kitchen for us, and this throws some of them off. Let them walk the streets a little longer—they'll finally come back and take what they can get. Two girls have just been in. One of them is married, and she and her husband are looking for a place [word(s) missing] to phone me or let me know about it to-night after she sees her husband. The other girl is a freshman from Wisconsin. She and her mother want a place for the winter, and the rooms just suit her, she says, but she can't engage them until her mother comes. That will be Monday, Tuesday, or Wednesday. . . .

Cline.

---

16. The couple from whom Cline originally rented moved out and he took over the lease of the entire house. Sears, *What Is Your Life?*, 90.

Oct 19, 1920.[17]

Dear Pataway,

... The new family moves in next week. There are only three and one is a baby about six months old. The man works in a store in town and is gone all day.

Yesterday some one wrote some words on the steps of the law building. It is thought some upper classman did it, but the upper classmen, of the law school especially, laid it on the freshmen. They got several pieces of brick, and compelled every freshman who passed to scrub off the steps with the brick. They had paddles and forced them to do it. One fellow was run through the gauntlet. One of the professors passing by gave them a lecture and warned them that some of them would be dismissed from school if they kept up their course, but it had no effect.

I have escaped writing a thesis in my drama course by agreeing to read several Russian plays instead. He gave me this permission since I had my master's thesis to write.

They haven't asked me to do any work yet in my fellowship—I hope they won't for I have my hands full...

Cline.

Oct 19, 1920.

Dearest Pataway,

Monday is gone and it is my hardest day. Friday may be hardest this week, for we have a test in education. I am not going to worry even if I flunk, for I am so torn up just now I can't study.—There is no one in the house but me, and the only furniture is a stove, a chair, and a couch. I am sitting on the chair and writing on your father's brief case across my knees. It is the best table I have. I feel like a step-child or rather an orphan. But there is no help for it; I must "dry my tears" and comfort myself in my affliction with the gloomy thought of how much worse it could be or may yet be.

I had a new experience last night. You are missing much by not being with me. I went to the Catholic Church. They had a big show. I suppose more than a hundred boys and girls were "confirmed," and they made it a great occasion. They had eight or ten priests and a bishop to carry out the forms.

I got there early and could observe the congregation before the service began. As each person entered the aisle, which led directly to the figure of

---

17. Cline appears to have written two separate letters on October 19, 1920.

Christ on the Cross, he touched one knee to the floor. Sometimes this was omitted until one had come down to his pew, but before he entered, his knee hit the floor. Sometimes you could hear the whack. But many of the rheumatic men made only a pretense and merely gave a bob with their body and went on. Many of them knelt whenever they crossed this central aisle; the ushers were constantly bobbing. Not all of them took the holy water as they came in, but most of them crossed themselves. When a party came in together, it seemed that one could dip his finger in the water for all. Some of the girls crossed themselves very gracefully by pretending to be putting back a lock of hair or arranging something about the dress.

When they came to their seats they knelt on a kneeling-board a minute before they sat down. I could not understand the reason for this, for all the time they were gazing about over the house or talking to some one near them.

When the service began the pipe organ played beautiful slow music, and led by a priest bearing the cross before him, the Bishop dressed in red attended by the other priests marched in followed by the boys and girls to be confirmed. After all had taken their places, the Bishop accompanied by certain priests knelt in front of the Christ statue. Then standing they began to undress the bishop, taking off all his red clothes; then the [sic] proceeded to put on him piece by piece other elaborate and beautiful robes and capped it all by a peculiar crown-like hat. After all this appareling [sic] in which every priest assisted the Bishop read certain passages from the Latin prayer book assisted by the priests, and then shook holy water at the statue. They then moved over to Mary's statue and carried out the same ceremonies, and a third statue which I did not know received similar worship.

The next thing was a sermon by one of the priests who said some good things and some striking things. He said one-fifth of the U. S. is Catholic now and in a hundred years more nearly the whole country will be Catholic. He gave three reasons for this. The first one was that all the schools are ceasing to teach the Bible and religion. He said "Whenever you put the Bible and the teaching of God out of your public schools, you are hastening the time when the country will be Catholic. For if no no [sic] religious teaching is given to the young, they get its opposite and become irreligious, caring neither for God nor for the church. But all the time the Catholic Church is increasing its schools and making multiplied [sic] converts to the true church, while the protestant world is failing to teach the bible in any of their schools." I did not know why the Catholics opposed the teaching of the Bible in the schools, but this explains it. He dwelt on this at length. Their schools are turning out Catholics by the hundreds, while the protestants fail to build schools and exclude the Bible from the public schools. The Catholic schools have increased from 271 with 11,728 students to 975 with 56,182 students in the last nineteen years, a total of more than 322%. Schools of all protestant denominations have increased but slightly if any. The second reason was that the American women would make the country Catholic in self-defense. They are getting tired of the "strange civic institution of divorce"; they want homes that are held in honor by their husbands; and the only way to have them is through the Catholic church. He referred to the increasing number of divorces none of which would be tolerated by the Catholic church. Then the third reason was that the men would make the country Catholic because they loved justice and the Catholic church is the *only place where justice exists*.

Well, after the sermon the children passed to the railing before the pulpit and knelt. The Bishop & priests then pulled off some more clothes and put on others, and then came to each child and rubbed water on his forhead [sic] and chin, repeating at the same time some Latin ending with "sancti." After all were confirmed the Bishop was again disrobed while a song was sung. Then he was robed again with more care and splendor than ever before, and by all the preparations I knew the climax was approaching. The large cross was taken out of its place, a box was opened and a shining thing with spikes out from it on all sides was set up where the cross had been. I was afterwards told this thing which looked like an attempt to make a little sun contained the *host*, the body and blood of the Lord—nearly like God himself, I suppose. Anyway they all knelt to it while more Latin was chanted. This ceremony finished the Bishop disrobed and put on his red robes again, and with the priest attending marched out the door. As he passed the priests motioned for all to kneel. I was standing right by the side of the aisle, because I could find no seat. All the people knelt but me, I think—and I was too stubborn to do it. There seems to be a slight difference between this Bishop and Paul when the people started to kneel to him. The priest looked like a picture of one—he was an enormous fat old round-faced fellow, and walked like an elephant.

Sweetheart, I have used nearly an hour and a half to write this letter and have written so fast I have failed to spell some words out fully. If you were here this hour and a half could be spent more satisfactorily in conversation or study...

Cline.

Oct 21, 1920.

Dear Pataway,

... The upperclassmen are talking of making the freshmen rise and give them their seats in public assemblies when they come in. They used to make them do it, but gradually quit it. I think it may just be talk now.

Last year a student went home because they forced him by beating to wear his cap. He had some kind of religious prejudice against it, and made them a speech, quoting the Bible as authority for his belief. But they used their paddles on him, and he went home.

Sam Amidon from Wichita speaks here Monday night. He is about the biggest Democrat in the state, and I should like to hear him. He discusses the League of Nations especially. It won't be long now before we know the result of all the campaigning this summer. I care little one way or the other.

My examination in education comes to-morrow. I have no idea what we shall have for we have covered very few things so far. I believe teachers can waste more time in a classroom than anybody unless it is the preacher in the pulpit. I heard Bro. Love (a young fellow near here) preach last Sunday on "Standing fast in the faith." I certainly learned that we should "stand fast," but how, or for what, or what the thing meant, he never explained....

Cline.

Oct 22, 1920.

Dearest Pataway,

... I don't have the least idea how I came out in the exam to-day, but I think at the bottom. He asked questions we had never heard of before—especially new to me, for I have never had any work in education before. One was to outline the curriculum of the Latin Grammar school in the days of Quintilian. We never touched on it in the class, and I have never had the history of education. Some other questions were nearly like it. I made the most brazen guesses you ever saw. I hope they will get through in some way. Surely one who teaches education should somehow make use of his own principles!...

The new people move in next week. I hope they are nice and agreeable. The girl looks like she might be; she is rather pretty; but I don't like the man's looks much. She doesn't look like she does either, but she may....

Oct 23, 1920.

My only Sweetheart,

... K. U. played the Iowa A & M to-day and beat them 7 to 0. They have not lost a game so far. The [sic] expect stiff games with Okla., Nebraska, and Missouri. I have not seen a game; I couldn't understand what they were doing if I went and couldn't enjoy it....

There are some letters of Miss Baillies' kept by one of her distant relatives at Long Calderwood, Scotland that I'd like to see. I think I'll write her to have any of them that would be valuable to my work copied and sent to me. I think the university would pay for the work of copying them, and if they wouldn't I'd pay myself to get them. The letters have never been published....

Cline.

Oct 24, 1920.

Dearest Pataway,

... We had a kind of prayer meeting to-night and they asked me to make a talk. I think I talked too long for Bro. Bradley; the others all seemed to enjoy it. I think Bradley may be a lover of the chief place, but I may judge him wrong. I am walking on eggs here and shall not put myself forward in any way. They are talking of getting a Bro. Scott to hold them a meeting this fall. When Bro. Mitchell recommended him as a "sound" preacher and a Review man, an old brother said "Sound! That's what we want. Sound!" Sound means no college man; loyal means none of the *first* digressives.

Joanna Baillie grows continually. I find out something every day or two.

It is positively winter weather to-night. I have had my fire on just a little all day when I have been here. I can turn it nearly out and keep any desired amount of heat in the room. The finest thing I've ever seen unless it's a furnace.

I have finished Paradise Lost. I hated to lay it down; it was like parting from a close friend. The two closing lines, like those of the Eve of Saint Agnes, pull at your heart strings but leave a deeper ache and void behind them; the sadness of them is inexpressible. I don't quite approve Long's criticism of Adam. His passionate love for Eve may be so strong as to unman him, but it makes him more human and loveable. He is no fop. I have to admire his firmness and resolution to eat and suffer death rather than part from the only creature on the earth he loved. His characterization of God is too Puritanical; he is too adamantine and unbending, too altogether icy and hard, without compassion and warm sympathy; there is no suggestion in him of Jesus' grief for Lazarus. Once in the character of Jesus he gave a suggestion of such warmth, but so hurried and fleeting that we can only wish he had done better. His religion colored his views of God. Eve is a delightful, exquisite creature, I hardly see how he could have imagined her and yet been able to treat his wives and daughters as he did. But he makes Eve inferior in intellect to Adam—superior only in beauty. The first thing she does when she wakes from the sleep of creation is to gaze into a stream, where she is so fascinated by the beautiful creature in the water that she would have stayed there forever. Some one has said "how natural!"....

Cline.

Oct 25, 1920.

Dearest Pataway,

... The new people have moved in, and are below. I meant to scrub the floors before they came but had no time. I swept everything out and the house was clean....

The business men of the city are having a meeting to begin a drive for a fund of one million dollars to be put into a stadium, a big "grand stand," for the university. They certainly think more of football than I do. The university plays some other school every Saturday and sometimes both Friday and Saturday of every week. They have not gone away yet, but beginning with Saturday they make trips to Manhattan, Emporia, Norman, Missouri Uni, Drake Uni, Des Moines, Iowa, Ames, Iowa, etc. Every trip will require at least three days to complete, and they come every week. Tell me, if you can, how any of them can study and get their work.

I have some comfort in my Education exam. It took every one else by surprise too. No one expected what we got.

Sam Amidon speaks at the court house to-night but I don't feel like going. I think I'll go to bed pretty soon, & sleep off my cold.

You must let me know what Dr. Hertzler says about your father. I don't know what the school could do without him this year; if it were not in the midst of a session arrangements might be made. But whatever we do this winter, he must give the summer to rest and recreation.

... Everything here is done in a very formal manner; the teachers write letters to each other when they have offices in the same building and have the U. S. mail deliver them. This sounds ridiculous but it is nevertheless true. They could step down the hall to the other office more quickly than they could write the letter, or they could deliver the letter themselves far more quickly than the government will do it....

Cline.

Oct 26, 1920.

Sweetheart,

... I am going to write to Miss Baillie in Scotland and see if she will give me the information I wish about her grand aunt. I am writing also to the Library of Congress for titles of any works about her which we do not have.

It has been gloomy and chilly to-day. and rained a little this morning. I suppose the weather there is about as cool, though you may lack the rain. Situated as it is in the Missouri River valley this place gets more rain than you do at Harper. Every body is wearing an overcoat or raincoat just now.

... I haven't seen the people below since they came. We all keep scrupulously within bounds. I'll have to go down and visit them sometime *when the man's away* and see what kind of people they are!!

Well, I love my family. Maybe when we all get to heaven we can be together again for a little while, unless you are sent to take care of the moon and I am sent to direct another planet.

I had a curious dream. I thought I had married a girl at Cordell a long time ago and had forgotten all about it, for immediately after the ceremony she had been called away and had never come back. But now she had written or sent to me to come to her. I didn't want to go, but I thought you and I had never been married at all but had only been living together and she had the only legal claim on me. I thought you wanted me to stay and were willing to live with me without marriage. I finally decided since the marriage with the other girl was only legal, I'd have it annulled and marry you. So it came out all right in the end. A story I had just seen was just a little like that and I suppose I tried out all the rest asleep.

Cline.

Oct 27, 1920.

Dearest Pataway:

... They have begun to give me work in my fellowship now. I am to conduct an examination Friday for Dr.—I forget his name. All I have to do is to hand out the exam questions and collect the papers at the conclusion....

I am inclosing a statement about the religious life of the University which the Chancellor asked us to read and send home.[18] They are doing a good deal—about all they can do, I am sure—and on the whole the

---

18. The statement is no longer with the letter.

environment is a little better than I expected unless my failure to get into it keeps me ignorant.

Oct 30, 1920.

Dearest Pataway,

    ... You should have been with me yesterday. The Masons have been initiating their new members, I suppose, and promoting others to higher offices. Yesterday the street was covered with them—about a thousand in all they say. All were dressed out in picturesque costumes—high red turbans, knee breeches, green silk, or white, or varied in color, jackets of various colors with embroidered designs, swords, and *cowbells*. One old fleshy fellow was in motley and wore a hideous false face—his patches were the flags of all nations sewed together. I was in at Kress's getting some wire to hang the mirror when I heard a deafening noise outside: a big bunch had got cowbells of all sizes and shapes, tied cords to them, and were pulling them along behind them as they marched down the street. The bells bounced on the sidewalk and made such a noise you could hear nothing else. I believe old men can be as foolish as boys; the parade yesterday dressed out in such variagated [sic] costumes and making such hideous racket was fully as bad for old men as the *shirt tail parade* for boys. I didn't stay to see the conclusion of the show; I was ashamed of it. It was funny to see how *unconcerned* some of the old fellows tried to appear as they marched along jerking their cowbells over the cobblestones—it was an every day matter with them!

    The football team went to Manhattan yesterday. They won fourteen to nothing this afternoon.

    No effort is made here to teach honesty, it seems. The boys organized their "Club of *Bums*," and about two-hundred of them "bummed" their way on freight cars down to Manhattan. The round trip costs over five dollars, I believe, and this means the railroads were cheated out of a round thousand dollars. They always do this when the team goes away. So many boys left that some of the clubs[19] closed to-day; only about half of our bunch was here. Next Saturday they play Oklahoma at Norman. I'd really like to see that game, for Oklahoma has about the best team they will meet this year. It played Missouri Uni. to-day and the score was seven to nothing in favor of Oklahoma at close of third quarter, but no word has been received since the finish. The boys do a great deal of betting on the games....

19. I.e., boarding houses.

I certainly enjoy my research work on my thesis. Something new turns up every day, and every book I read refers to another, and the chain is endless. I have no idea when I shall find out all—perhaps too late to write my thesis this year; yet I don't think so. You can help me very much when you come by reading my notes as I read my manuscript, for every quotation and statement must be exact—in spelling, punctuation, grammar; etc—every mistake Scott makes (and they are many) must be written out just as he made it. I take comfort from seeing how very careless Scott was in his letters—never uses a mark of punctuation and often makes positive mistakes in English. He says "The boy was astonished at hearing Harry Mackenzie and I talk—"; and uses "definitively" for "definitely," etc....

Cline.

Sunday

[October 31, 1920]

Dearest Jean,

... This has been a gloomy day—rain most of the morning and till after four. I think it has been raining to-night a little for I haven't been out. Got wet coming from church but not much. I didn't go to-night because of the rain. Got several complements on my talk last Sunday night. I think it was new to every one, for all they hear in this country is "The Proper Division of the Word" and "Differences between the Old and New Laws." They have been fed continually on milk, which is a good food, but needs augmenting a little.

Instead of two hundred bums there were three hundred and eighty-six that beat the railroad. Total car fare for all of them would have been two thousand dollars. The brakeman tried to keep them off when they started back and fired a couple of shots, but they knew he would not dare to shoot any one and boarded the train anyway. There were about two box cars full.

They are afraid of Oklahoma whom they play next Saturday. Missouri beat Kansas last year, and Oklahoma beat Missouri yesterday 28 to 7, I believe. I look for Okla to win next Saturday, but I haven't said so to any one....

Jerusalem Delivered is a very entertaining story, I hate to break off without finishing. I have read Euphues the Anatomy of Wit.[20] Such an abominable style! The worst reading I have had so far with the exception of education. I have read education for four hours together to-night. Found many interesting things, but all in the most unimaginative, dull, verbose or

---

20. "Euphues the Anatomy of Wit" is a sixteenth-century work by English writer John Lyly.

learned language. What is the study of education? Is it not a study of *how* to educate or train in arts, sciences, or vocations? Merely a system, a method! How then does it presume to become itself a science or an art? Should one study education purely for its own blessed sake, what has he acquired when he has finished?—a method!—But upon what art or science shall he use his method?—He knows none! Should one study music, Belles Lettres, pharmacy, medicine, what has he when he has finished? An art or a science which is either a great pleasure in itself, a source of inspiration to humanity, or a useful and remunerative profession!—a tangible thing! And therewithal he has no less surely the *method* of procuring and the method of imparting....

Give my love to Jack Wood, Kern, and their granny and granddaddy. Don't let the babies forget they once had a poor miserable thing for a father; and that he'll come home as soon as his wife will let him. My love and my life to my sweetheart.

Cline.

Nov 1, 1920.

Dearest Pataway,

... It is genuinely cold to-night—the climax of a steady day's growth. This morning I went to school without my overcoat and thought I should freeze by noon. This afternoon it was even cold inside an overcoat. Really, however, I expect no colder weather here than you will have there. So long as the gas pressure stays strong we have nothing to fear, for my little stove must be kept turned down to make the room comfortable.

I must correct another statement. They say the number of bums was slightly over five hundred by actual count. That would mean $2,500 to the railroad. Then instead of paying their way into the game they organized and forced their way through the gates without charge. This cheated the teams playing out of $1000, for the tickets were two dollars, I believe. Well, it may be worse yet. A Professor to-day gave them his mind about such dishonesty; but one of the boys remarked that he was only a hard tight-fisted fellow—and was too hard on his classes; someone ought to tell him this was the twentieth century—let him ease up!

I don't believe we ought to tolerate class cutting for any excuse. It is hard to label excuses good and bad—so many are on the borderland. Professor Hopkins here, and I think the other professors also do, give an examination every once in a while to all absentees. Those who have missed one day must answer one *hard* question—and they really give some hard ones—those who have missed two days must answer two, and so on. Besides all this *a certain number* of cuts, for sickness or any other cause, removes credit for the course. I think each day's absence is counted a full *zero* for any cause whatever—and only by the examinations are the zero's cancelled. Should one fail to take the examinations, which are extended as a special grace to allow the student to win back, or make up for any unavoidable absence; his credit is cancelled at once. It certainly brings them to the line here. They do not miss classes much.

Professor Johnson (education) believes we should have separate high schools for boys and girls. For, he says, in these days the teachers cannot secure the cooperation of the parents to deal with it, and this social side of school life has run away with itself. Students are doing less work in all the high schools than ever before, and there seems no way to stop it except by training the boys and girls away from each other. It is all athletics, clubs, societies, parties, socials, class meetings, and absolutely no serious work. He is about right. The fewer distractions of this kind the better. The French boarding schools allow almost none—no athletics at all. . . .

Cline.

Nov 2, 1920.

Dearest Pataway,

. . . Phew! I have been formulating a letter to Miss Hunter Baillie, Long Calderwood, Scotland. It is a task to write to one whom you have never seen, and who may not now be living, on a matter of such delicacy and importance. I hope I have not been too abrupt nor yet too stiff and formal. I think I'll write to a Mr. George Plarr somewhere in England or Scotland also, for he has recently published some correspondence of Miss Baillie and Scott in the Edinburgh Review. I don't know who he is or where to address him, but the Edinburgh Review would forward a letter, I suppose.

The big contest ends to-day. By to-morrow either Harding or Cox will be in the ditch, and I imagine the latter. I am really a Democrat, I believe, for I find myself antagonistic to every one here. I really feel like arguing for the Democratic party. . . .

The love case of Brother Croom and Miss Harris may be all right. I believe Miss Harris is a good girl and marriage makes one get sober soon enough—sometimes even sours people. I hope we can pay Croom back before he starts to school next year. . . .

It is getting so late I must go to bed. I have a nice loud bed; if you listen closely you can hear me get in. I try to lie still all the night for I make so much turning over that it wakes me up. It will be better when I get a mattress on the springs. At present I sleep on the springs without a mattress . . .

Cline.

Nov 3, 1920

My own Sweetheart,

. . . I give an examination to one of Professor Whitcomb's classes tomorrow. He said he might want me to teach it once in a while for him. It is a course in literature in which the [sic] read the Odyssey, Paradise Lost, Alcestis a Greek drama, the Rivals, Henry IV, etc. His health is poor and he shields himself as much as possible.

When is your father going to finish the application for Junior College standing and send it to me? The application for the Normal Training work should have been sent in long ago; it is supposed to be filed as soon after the opening of the term as possible. I hope you will remind them of it and have them finish it at once. I hope there has been no trouble about getting the necessary laboratory apparatus. . . .

. . . Please don't work too hard sweetheart. It will make an old woman of you before your time to get up so early. It is a fact. Every book on health and beauty advises caution on that point and especially about getting up too fast. You ought to take a little time to think about and get thoroughly awake. I don't like for you to work hard.

Cline.

Thursday night.

[November 4, 1920]

Dearest Pataway,

. . . The students are having some kind of parade [illegible] in preparation with the Oklahoma [illegible] which comes off Saturday. The band has been playing out on the street near here, and the whole bunch yelling. This game settles the championship for the "Valley Conference."

The election was complete for the Republicans. People must be more tired of Wilson than I thought. I'm afraid the League is out for a while. Even Oklahoma and Missouri went Republican as well as Tennessee. I feel sorry for Wilson; it must be a hard blow. He could have averted it all and have kept his popularity if he had only used a little more wisdom and policy in dealing with men. His statement at the election of congressmen last time cut off his head.[21] I believe he is one of the greatest presidents we have ever had, but it will take years for the country to realize it....

Cline.

Nov. 6, 1920.

Dearest Pataway,

...The rain is still pouring down, knocking the leaves off all the trees. The ground is all yellow with them. I meant to rake the yard this afternoon but the rain prevented me. I wonder if you have rain every time we do, for it seems we have an unusually large amount. It will turn cooler now, I suppose....

I haven't heard how the game with Oklahoma came out. At the close of the first half the score was 9 to 7 in favor of Kansas. I'll learn the outcome at supper. This was the game they dreaded most. Next Saturday they play Nebraska, whose team is supposed to be stronger than Oklahoma, but it is not in the Valley Conference and they don't care so much about beating them. Nebraska plays with the eastern Universities—Pennsylvania, Wisconsin, etc. They are selling tickets now. I thought once I'd go, but I can't throw away $2 for such nonsense—you can't get in for less....

Cline.

Nov. 10, 1920.

My own Wife,

...We have a vacation to-morrow in honor of the *armistice*. It unfortunately comes on my easiest day, when I have only one recitation. If they had only made it Wednesday or Fri! Friday I am to conduct two lessons for one of the teachers. Classes are in Rhetoric and they have written work; so I shall have nothing to do but gather the papers, call the roll, etc....

Whitcomb is a curiosity. He told one of the girls in our class that she was "crazy," when she couldn't answer a certain question. I am not used to such *manners*. He seems to be a philosophical, careful teacher, with a good

---

21. This most likely refers to President Woodrow Wilson's "Fourteen Points" speech given to Congress on January 8, 1918. The speech outlined steps that Wilson thought ought to be taken to end World War I and secure lasting world peace. The fourteenth and final point was a call for the organization of what would later be known as The League of Nations. The United States never joined the League.

memory stored with wide reading, and I like him very much. I was surprised at his speaking to the girl as he did, and I really believe his tongue slipped, for he seemed to try to catch the word when it was more than half way out, and his immediate change of tone and treatment was apologetic....

Nov 12, 1920.

Dearest Pataway,
 ... The alumni and friends of the University have been planning for a year a big million dollar drive to erect a big stadium and a Recreation Building (for dances etc). Monday they have a big convocation and the drive will begin among the students, then be extended to the business men of Lawrence, and then be carried through the entire state. They will raise the money in time. I wonder how much the students will give. They throw away enough. Some of the boys at our club have been playing pool & cards, etc. and I have heard that one fellow lost fifty dollars in one night....

Cline.

Nov 14, 1920.

My own Sweetheart,
 ... I am a little blue since supper. I was watching a game of checkers and saw a "cheat." Before I thought I called attention to it, but the green horn who was cheated didn't know what I had said and went on undisturbed. The other fellow, however, didn't like it much, it appeared, I don't care, but it made me feel a little like kicking myself....

We have had our first snow! It fell Sunday afternoon, all night, and all this morning—enough to make the ground slightly gray as if some one had sprinkled it with salt. But it was beautiful as it fell. It always brings the smell of the cedar, the red and green of the holly, the gay, shining tinsel, and lights, the candy and nuts, and the mysterious, beautiful gifts, and with all this such a genial warmth and sense of security and peace and such infectious laughter and good spirits! I felt like a mere boy as I looked at it. I hope I can always be a boy when Christmas comes, for it is the happiest day of the year. But it has been so long since I have given a gift! I hope sometime we can celebrate Christmas as we would like to do.

The university started its drive for the million dollars to-day. They want the students to raise $160,000; and have requested each student to give $40 as the minimum amount. This is to be paid in four years in semi-annual payments of $5 each. Nearly all the students I have heard talk say they will give their $40. I don't intend to do it, because I have better use for it....

Nov 20, 1920.

My dearest Wife,

... The money drive has gone through here. At noon $158,000 had been subscribed by students, with much that had not been counted yet. It is thought that it will pass $200,000 by Monday. And all of this is from the students. When you have 3,500 to give things move pretty fast. But a Bible school can never have this many students, for if it ever should get half that it would no longer be a Bible school. You think the boys are hard to control there, but here it would be an impossible job. The students rule absolutely, and the professors merely lecture. When this has become the rule everywhere, what can we expect in our school but the same kind of spirit?...

Cline.

Dec. 2, 1920.

Dearest Pataway,

... I am reading Richard Hooker's *Laws of Ecclesiastical Polity* for Sisson this week. It is very hard reading but has some interesting things in it. Deals of course with the laws of nature, God's laws, laws of the church, etc.—a philosophical thing. I have got nearly half through the first volume of it....

I love you dear and would give anything if I could make you happy. I want you to be my *sweetheart* once in a while yet—you are not too old. It is all right to be a mother and a housekeeper and all that—but be a mother to Jack Wood and Kern and a housekeeper to the house—when I am there, please just be my sweetheart, like you were before so many babies came and even before were [sic] were married. You don't understand me? Well, I'm a fool anyway—only fools dream once in a while. Forget about it. I love you more than you think.

Cline.

Jan 20 1921

Dearest Jean,

... I am preparing for my final exam in the epic to-morrow, and have also to write a paper in education to hand in Monday. Then I have three exams Monday, and must by all means finish Whitcomb's papers by that time. So I have so much I feel like throwing everything down and running. I get nervous when I'm pressed like that. I am not going to worry about the grades I get—they may all be B's for all I care. I am getting a great deal out of my courses, and what do I care about the grades? ...

Cline.

Feb 4, 1921

My dearest Sweetheart,

... They want to get G. K. Chesterton here for a lecture if possible. He is the biggest modern critic and is in America at present. He is also a writer of some good short stories and other literary work. He lives near Beaconsfield, I think, where Burke lived and of which Disraeli was made Duke.

I wish you could have had some of my corn to-night. It was extra good—crisp, and buttered and salted to taste, or perhaps I should say "oleoed" to taste. ...

When does Judge Lindsey come on the program? I have just read of his being fined for contempt of court. He carried the case to the Supreme Court at Wash. D. C. but the Sup. Court confirmed the judgment. I think his fine was about $500—for refusing to give as evidence in a trial what a prisoner had confided to him. ...

C.

Feb 9, 1921.

Dearest Pataway,

... I have sent to Harvard for some more books on my thesis—two of them in German again, which will give me some more pleasant work. Four different German Dr's have written Doctor's Dissertations on Miss Baillie, while so far as I know, I am the first "white man" to make a study of her. One of her songs was set to music by Beethoven and I am getting it also. I want to bring it home and have Miss Baxter or Miss Pittman play it for me—that I may get the music of it....

I am sorry about our domestic science for next year. But I really shouldn't be, for I don't believe we'll have any to be sorry about. It's this that makes me sick.

I hope the teachers are going to get out our application for Junior College standing sometime before the millennium, for 'twill be no use then. Nobody will care to go to school, and if they did I fear affiliation with a state school would be no high recommendation....

Cline.

Feb 11, 1921.

My little Sweetheart,

... I signed the pay roll to-day for I don't want to run two months any more. They have given me no work at all to do lately, but Hopkins asked if I would be willing to grade the papers of the High school contestants later. All high schools of the state contest in composition work and have judges from different schools to grade the papers so he is to turn the Univers[ity] judgship [sic] over to me. The students, of course, will never know but what Hopkins himself graded them. It's a pity to treat them so shamefully....

Cline

Feb 15, 1921.

Dearest Pataway,

We are having a typical March wind to-day. One can nearly lean against it and rest. It is usually so calm here when you wrote about the wind there that I wonder if you are able to hold the dormitory to the ground....

Dr. Dunlap located a second-hand copy of Joanna Baillie, full morocco binding, for me. It costs $2. I have sent for it, but some one may have beaten me to it....

Cline.

Feb 23, 1921

Dear Pataway,

It is very late but I will write you a line or two. I got here safe and have been studying all day. My book (Miss Baillie's Works) came to-day. It is a beautiful copy—and has never been used! It is bound in brown Morocco, stamped with gilt design, and with gilt-edged pages.

One of the books came from Harvard too and I have looked over some of it. I must finish it soon in order to get the rest, for they will send only one book at a time....

Cline

March 6, 1921

My own Sweetheart,

I am sending you some plans for the building.[22] All of them are about the size of the H. S. building in amount of floor space. No 1. is a little larger, has about 3,000 sq ft of floor space more. So they should all cost about the same as it did if prices were the same.

I don't know which I like best but I am inclined to *No. 1*. The chapel is in the middle of the building & has two entrances, while in No 3 it is at one end and has only one entrance. It looks more balanced. Then it separates the classes too. It doesn't hurt to have the chapel break through the hall—this is the plan of the Helena building and of Fraser Hall here.[23] Then I like the three stories. I am afraid of these half basements—they always look dirty. Of course they might be all right if they have wooden floors—over the cement. It could easily be fixed like that. I like the No 3. next to No 1, I think.

Have your mother look them over & then change them as you wish. Of course the sizes of some of the rooms may have to be changed for architectural reasons—I just guessed where to put the partitions. Some rooms of course should be large & some small for all classes are not alike in size. I didn't know whether to arrange rooms in this building for chemistry & physics or not...

Cline.

---

22. Cline was working on designs for a new administration and classroom building at the College. Sears, *What Is Your Life?*, 95.

23. The first reference is possibly to a building in Helena, Oklahoma. The second is to a famous building at the University of Kansas that housed the chapel. The Fraser Hall Cline knew was built in 1872 and replaced in 1967.

March 14, 1921

... Have you been reading about the Harmon trial? Clara Harmon's murder of her pretended husband? Jake Harmon is an old K. U. law student—graduated here, I think. He roomed with Stilwells next door. They say he was a mighty fine boy when he was here—frank & affectionate and all the time playing pranks. He dressed up once in woman's clothes (he was very fair & looked like a girl) & fooled Mr. Stilwell, who came in & thought he was some strange lady. But when he got into the oil business down in Oklahoma & made money up into the millions he got wild. I am interested in knowing what they will do with the woman. Miss Stilwell thinks they will turn her loose.

You know, yesterday afternoon Walker & I took a walk out to Haskell Institute, the government Indian school.[24] It is nearly as big a place as the university—something like 10 or 12 buildings. The students were coming from chapel or church as we came past the building & we stopped & watched them march out. (It is [sic] Catholic service, you know). They are under military discipline & an officer stood at the door while the girls marched out by twos. Women officers stood at the door & as so many passed out one of the women took charge of the detachment. The girls marched out first & on a street leading west. After them the boys came out by twos & marched south. Officers, men, took charge of the squads & marched along by their sides & gave commands. All were in uniforms—the boys in khaki & the girls in blue serge....

Cline.

March 20, 1921

My sweetheart Jeanette,

I have finished Romola at last and had to cry over it like a fool, too. Romola is a magnificent woman—one of the finest I have ever found in all my reading. In her innocence and purity, her strong passionate nature, her deep rooted moral principles which cannot be shaken, and her implicit obedience to every demand of duty, she is exactly like you—I interpreted her throughout the story by what you would feel and do in the same place—and the farther I read the more proud I became of you, because I knew you were the

---

24. Founded in 1884 as part of the residential schools initiatives, the Haskell Institute is now Haskell Indian Nations University.

equal of Romola in every virtue. Dear, at times I feel so little beside you—you must not despise me, but you are so infinitely better than I am.

It has rained all afternoon & is still pouring down. I think I'll have to get an umbrella to get through the spring, for it will soon be too warm to wear an overcoat. Still I may be able to make out without it.

I want to begin writing on the second part of my thesis this week & finish a little of it before I come home if possible, but I may not get to it.

Tell your father I casually asked Walker what he thought of Winterrowd as a teacher. They are close friends & he said he would not like to say anything to injure him, but that he was not a teacher at all. He cannot interest his students & he clashes with them & with the other teachers. You of course know how he got along at Lockney.[25] He said when [sic] had been Principal of the H. S. at Paul's Valley they asked him to resign in three months after he came. Walker thinks Winterrowd himself realizes his failure as a teacher & would be slow to go into it again. Of course, Walker has peculiarities but his opinion coincides exactly with the idea I have had of Winterrowd for a good while. If he is all we can get we must make a shift to use him, but I'm afraid of him as a teacher. However if we should get him & he would become dissatisfied as he has done everywhere yet he could do no more than leave, I suppose. But there is still the need of some one qualified for the normal training work of Education.

I am inclined to think the two story building with the half basement may be what we had better plan for. I don't have time now to work out the other plan I had in mind. Maybe when I get home & have nothing else to do I can do it. . . .

Cline.

April 1, 1921.

This is April Fool day—but I'll not fool you this time. The weather is getting warm again. It was colder here than at Harper & there was more snow; some was on the ground when I came back Tuesday morning. I am sorry all the fruit has been killed—still we could not have put up any this year except what ripens after school closes and I get home.

I don't know yet whether I'll be able to come back commencement to deliver the diplomas or not. I'll do it if I can, but I am anxious to get my thesis

---

25. A reference to Lockney Christian College, which ran from 1894 to 1918 in a town south of Amarillo. Ira Winterrowd served as dean there. Young, *History of Christian Colleges*, 148–51.

entirely finished, and that is about the time I am to hand it in. Then comes the preparation for examinations....

It is getting very late again. I have been working up the Gothic material in Miss Baillie & shall begin to write on the second division of my thesis tomorrow. It is the biggest job of all to get the material properly arranged—the outline entirely logical—so many of my divisions necessarily overlap & it will be impossible entirely to separate them....

Cline.

April 4, 1921

... Brother Draper came over this afternoon to talk with me about the battle yesterday. He wanted me to tell Brother Mitchell & Bradley that I'll be glad to talk over the college question with them at a private meeting any time they desire, and that he will help me. He thinks we ought to start a separate meeting, perhaps, if we can get a place. He has seen about a church house which he thinks could be bought for 3 or 4 thousand dollars. There would be about half a dozen of us to begin meeting, but he thinks a church could be built up here, & it is certain there should be one where the State University is located. He is a good man & has his heart set on it. Ask your father what he thinks the Harper brethren would be willing to do toward helping to have a meeting held here & later toward buying the house. If we could put a good man up here for a month or more in a big meeting & then continue the work right on, I think we could build up a church. I believe several of the members of the old congregation would come in with us, & several members of the Christian Church who are disgusted with their picture shows, etc. It ought to be done. If I were to be here for a year or so I would have no hesitation about starting it, but Draper will be away part of the time in meetings and the work might run down with no one to see to it each Sunday. Since I'll be here only till June the burden of the work will be left to Draper. Of course it would be possible, if the Harper church were willing to undertake a partial support of it, to have some one come each Sunday from Wichita or even Harper when Draper could not be here. The car fare from Harper would be only a little over $11 for the round trip. The only difficulty is the time it would take— One could leave Harper at 4 pm Saturday or at 9:30 pm Sat.—and get back at 11:30 a.m. Monday or even at 10 on the Orient. He would have to travel all night two nights in succession. Ask your father what he thinks about it. I wish we could have a church in Lawrence. The Topeka church has said they are willing to help build it up & they have some money, too.

I am inclosing the plans of the school building. I forgot them yesterday & before....

Cline

April 8, 1921.

My Sweetheart,

... It has been raining a little to-night & is cooler.—I haven't heard how the student election came out to-day but there was enough campaigning. Every time I passed from the library to Fraser Hall a dozen boys & girls filled my arms with bills & cards advertising their candidates. I didn't vote—it took too much time & I know *none* of the candidates either & might have voted for the wrong men—There were enough to elect some one without me. As I came across to the library one time a fellow started toward me with a handfull [sic] of cards, but when he got near & looked up, he said "Oh, you're an instructor, I guess," & stopped & went back. From that I suppose instructors are not allowed to vote. At least it saved me from one more deluge of literature—for I was busy all day receiving it & throwing it down. Then came an old fellow with a stick with a sharp nail in the end of it and a sack over his shoulder, picking up the litter from the campus & the street. Everybody was kept busy by the election!—the campaigners, the voters, & the janitors. And mamas & papas will be kept busy hereafter paying the bills for campaign expenses....

Cline

April 9, 1921.[26]

My Sweetheart,

How much I love you it is impossible even to describe—so please just try to imagine *it all*. Fancy, if you can, a sea whose depths have never been touched & whose shores have never been reached—or better still, an infinity of space reaching to the nethermost regions of darkness below and above to

---

26. This letter is written on Harper College letterhead rendering faculty names and academic disciplines as follows: Pres. J. N. Armstrong, Bible; Dean L. C. Sears, English; B. F. Rhodes, History and Government; H. J. Sudbury, Education and Psychology; A. S. Croom, Mathematics; S. A. Bell, Science; J. N. Gardner, Languages; D. L. Cooper, English; Mrs. Harry E. Squire, Expression; Rebecca Anne Rose, Art and Design; Anna Lee Baxter, Music; Dorothy Pittman, Music Assistant; Margaret Harris, Violin; Frank Millard, Prin., Grammar School; Cecil Gardner, 5th and 6th Grades; Mary Hazlet, 3rd and 4th Grades; Lola Plank, Primary.

the light of God's throne—or best of all, the tenderness of a first strong love which seems born to a life eternal—so large, so infinite, & so tender is my love for *meine Frau*. . . .

To-morrow is Sunday. I am anxious to know how the brethren will be? Don't be afraid of their arresting me—I've not turned villain yet & they don't doubt my "goodness of heart" I suppose—They at least say they have nothing against me personally. . . .

Cline.

April 12, 1921.

Dearest Jeanette,

. . . I have great hope of getting through now. I spoke to Whitcomb . . . & he is willing for me to finish & said the department would allow me to hand in my thesis after May 15th if necessary, since only I am to finish. None of the girls have written a page so far & don't intend to graduate this spring. I have about forty pages written or about 8000 words. I am completing my whole outline—not quite finished however. I think I can easily finish the whole thesis by May 15 except for a little revising perhaps and having it typed. I am working on nothing else just now—that is, I am doing the least possible on everything else. I intend to catch up on other things after I see my thesis is going to get through.

It will be impossible for me to come home for commencement, because it will mean a *loss of several* days to me just when I am busiest. Every day now counts—and I cannot afford to throw any of them away. After the 20th of May I'll have the thesis off & then will have my examinations to prepare for. I don't dread them because I can *memorize* my notes & remember them for at least one class hour.

Granny Patties [*sic*] letter was pitiful. She certainly has a hard time with Brother Harding & she seems to be giving way herself. She can get very little real rest as long as she has to watch him all the time. I'll try to write her but I can't say for sure I'll do it. My good intentions often miscarry. . . .

The school is sending out questionnaires to all the seniors asking them about their past occupations, & their plans for the future, their residence & where they intend to live, & above all of what they did in the *war*, where they served, how *long*, etc. I don't know whether they will send the graduate students the same thing or not, I haven't received mine yet. I don't think it would cause me any trouble, however, for my work has been good, & my classification was clear & definite at last. I don't think they would write to Cordell. . . .

Cline

April 20, 1921.

My Sweetheart,

... The paper announces to-day that Edwin *Markham*, the poet of whom I wrote, is to give the commencement address here. It ought to be good. I am glad you will be here to hear it—for I'm counting on you—see? ...

I suppose we'll have to wear caps & gowns—it will be decided to-morrow—I haven't been short of money yet, but I will be when I order that, for they charge $6.25 here. I have not registered yet, but the last day is Friday. Still we may not have to wear caps & gowns—if not, I'll save my $6.25. ...

Cline.

April 21, 1921

... The graduates met & decided, of course, that we must all wear caps and gowns. I ordered mine to-day. The die is cast. I must finish my thesis—I can do it, for it does not have to be in before June 1. I know I can do it. Whitcomb told me to-day to write it off fast & don't say much—I have written far too much on each topic so far. I'll just have to say a few things & pass on. Seems a pity not to tell all a fellow knows after [word(s) missing] has spent a year learn[ing] it! Still what I tell i[s] worth very little if anything.

I need not pay my $10 diploma fee until I graduate or until the committee pass [sic] on my application & grant the degree.

A poor ignorant girl in the Browning class to-day nearly got eaten up raw. Miss Lynn said something a week or more ago about giving us some questions to write a paper on, but she seems to have forgotten it. The girl reminded her! Miss Lynn got the questions—but you should have seen how the [g]irls in the class raked her while Lynn was gone to the office. I felt like hitting her myself—Now we have another paper to write and perhaps a second one before school closes—Had this one been deferred for a short while longer there would have been no danger of a second this term. ...

Cline.

April 22, 1921.

Dear Pataway,

I have nothing to write to-night. I have done almost nothing to-day except work on that miserable thesis. I asked Whitcomb about cutting it down to three chapters, but he doesn't favor the plan—wants me to write only a little on each division but have the entire six chapters. He suggested 3000 words for each chapter which is very little—I have 4000 words in ch 1 & have 7000 for chapter 2 with two or three thousand more that will have to go into ch 2. Well, well, maybe I'll finish it someday. It is like a bite of rare meat the longer I chew on it the bigger it gets & the tougher....

Are any plans being made to raise money for our building? Is the drive to start before school closes or wait until next fall? If it is put off, I'm afraid the building will be put off. It will take a long time to raise the money.[27]

What is being done on the catalog? Is it to be out by the close of school?...

Cline

May 22, 1921

My Sweetheart,

How are you amusing yourself since you can't cook for the five thousand any longer? The old place is pretty lonesome, I imagine.

It's too sultry here to live—only one's afraid of enjoying hotter weather if one dies. Rooms downstairs are so much cooler than these up next to the fire-box.

The meeting closed to-night, so you will not have the enjoyable privilege of hearing the Rt Rev Mr Rhoady [sic]. He again prayed and preached about "companions who have lost their companions" to-day....

Cline.

---

27. Efforts were made to raise funds for the anticipated administration and classroom building. When Harding died, it was decided to name this building after him. But fundraising went slowly and the building was never erected there. Instead, Harper College merged with Arkansas Christian College and funds raised for the Harding building went toward establishing Harding College in Morrilton, Arkansas. Sears, *What Is Your Life?*, 95–96.

May 24, 1921

Sweetheart,

... Dear, it seems awful to me the amount of money it is taking these last weeks. I had to buy those shoes, $9.50, and I was out the full month's rent in the house, instead of only a half as I thought I should be—this came only a few days ago. Then my thesis is going to cost between $25 & $30. Isn't that too bad? And diploma fee is $10. I'll still have at least $6 rooming bill & if you come it may be a little more—not much—& board will cost me about $7 yet. I have counted up every cost I can see, and I think I'll need $25 to get out & have enough to come home on. Perhaps after all it will cost too much for you to come. You could meet me at mother's....

Cline.

May 30, 1921.

My Sweetheart,

Mrs Whitcomb is typing my thesis as fast as she can but doesn't have a third of it done yet. Don't know when it will be ready & don't care. I'm getting so tired of the grind I'm ready to quit. Still have an abominable paper to write for Hopkins....

I shall be so glad when I can start home. I'm about to lose all my patience. I love you all.

Cline.

June 4, 1921.

Dearest,

I am tired enough to—to sleep well to-night. I've been chasing back and forth between my house and Whitcombs and town nearly all day, but at last my thesis is finished and bound. Whitcomb charged me $21 for the typewriting. It was a little high I think but Mrs. Whitcomb worked awfully hard on it to get it finished in time, and got so nervous for fear she would not get it done that it was nearly worth it. It cost $5.50 to have it bound. This leaves me just enough to get home on comfortably....

My work is not yet quite finished. I still have to hand that paper to Hopkins & it is not written. I have about 750 words more to write if I can blow up that more wind. All I am writing is a very profound breeze for I know almost nothing about my subject. But I take great comfort in the fact that the professor knows still less. I am sure of that.

I'll begin to pack up my junk Monday, and Wednesday I'll leave the old place for a long, long time. I'll go to Cottonwood & will write you from there what time I shall reach home. I think I'll leave Cottonwood on the 2 o'clock train and get home Sunday night, June 12....[28]

Do you know I love you? I'll show you when I get home. Kiss my babies for me, & tell Jack Wood I'll be home tomorrow Sunday morning.

Cline.

---

28. Cline's handwritten note on the envelope indicates that he was referring to Cottonwood Falls, Kansas. The reason for the stopover is unclear, his autobiography only mentioning an en route visit to Topeka to talk with state officials about Harper College's accreditation. Sears, *What Is Your Life?*, 94.

Afterword

Unlike the scholarly perspectives presented by Richard Hughes and Liz Parsons, mine is far more personal, both in my perceptions of the correspondents and in my observations about what the authors reveal in the letters. Since I am currently the chief academic officer of Harding University—the role that L. C. Sears once filled at Harding College—and since only five men have held that office in the ninety-year history of the institution, I enjoyed learning more about this man whose picture hangs near my desk and whose spirit lingers in the room. L. C. Sears is a key name in the university's history, remembered and respected on campus and in university lore, but I knew the man only as an elderly gentlemen walking to the campus post office each morning and occasionally seen at the college congregation in my early days at Harding. My longest conversation with Dr. Sears occurred at a dinner Liz hosted in her grandfather's campus home during his last years. When I later had an office in that stone cottage, I realized how little I knew about him and how much I regretted not taking more advantage of his proximity during those few years.

From the letters I learned that Dr. Sears was a very real human being, capable of deep feelings and sincere dedication to God, to loved ones, and to ideals, including the ideals of Christian education. At times the letters showed Dr. Sears and Pataway as typical young people almost embarrassingly in love and struggling to say it without saying it. In fact, Dr. Sears did not declare that he loved Pataway in any of the letters written in the summer of 1915. Instead, the letters present thoughtful discussion and observations about life, morals, human nature, and spiritual truths juxtaposed with playful, almost giddy (for early twentieth-century standards) adolescent emotional communications. At times I felt as if I were looking at the texts on a couple of fourteen-year-olds' cell phones. But at other times I saw a depth of character and Christian commitment that elevated the words to life-changing and life-defining credos. The tentative exploration of personal feelings and relationships is balanced by the dedicated and unquestioned commitment to Christian values, doctrine, education, and life.

No doubt the letters reveal a young couple in the process of falling deeply in love. As I read the passage prompted by Dr. Sears's overhearing someone playing "Il Trovatore" (July 19, 1915), I can almost see the fog and hear the whine of the plane's engine as Bogart tells Ingrid Bergman, "We'll always have Paris." This same young man casually commits to walking eighteen miles to speed his reunion with his love (August 3, 1915) and admitted to studying Pataway's picture for an hour or more (July 24, 1915).

In the most poetic passage in the letters (July 12, 1915), Pataway embraces her imagination that transports her to Norman and, more impressively, Dr. Sears to Cordell to share the evocative scene with her. And she lays claim to the validity of imagination in helping them process their loneliness. Ah, the power of love. But this passage humanizes the young woman whose raw emotions lie barely below the surface of her day and are incarnated by the delightful scene of fireflies on a warm summer evening equally lit by the glow of her feelings for her absent "big brother."

Because of his devotion to Pataway, Cline also vows to lead a righteous life going forward and only wishes that he could undo whatever he has done in the past that might cause her to lose "confidence" in him (June 21, 1915). This sincere, deep commitment to being worthy of her helps define his image of Christian love and Christian relationships. While smacking of idealism and romanticism, it also shows the integrity of these Christians whose earthly life and relationship cannot be separated from their spiritual values and commitments. Dr. Sears determines to be holy as his God is holy in order to love his beloved as Christ loved the church—although this letter was written well before he overtly avows love for his "little sister." Sentiments like these raise the bar from puppy love to *agape* in only a few lines.

Astutely, Dr. Sears intuits that he must tell Pataway's mother, Woodson Harding Armstrong, about his plan to declare his love for Pataway when he returns to Cordell after his summer in Norman (July 18, 1915). This letter is different in tone, reflecting his mature understanding of the import of what is about to happen. He affirms that his letters to Pataway have conveyed his love to her without ever directly asserting it. He concedes that he has held up his end of the promise not to declare love for Pataway. But most of all, he has self-evaluated and knows that it is time to declare his love openly. And he knows that the pathway to that declaration goes through Woodson Armstrong, a wise, solid, careful, direct, and loving mother.

Mrs. Armstrong's response shows both his wisdom and that of his future mother-in-law as she outlines Brother Armstrong's assessment of their relationship and his feelings for his future son-in-law (July 31, 1915). Later, when J. N. Armstrong tells Cline of his plans and gives his reluctant blessing to the young couple (August 16, 1915), Mrs. Armstrong's wisdom is verified. She is a tough, no-nonsense woman, whose direct, thoughtful, and yet sympathetic observations pave the way for Cline and Pataway to move forward with their relationship. In a narrative filled with intriguing personalities, she may be the most interesting of them all.

The letters seem to reveal Dr. Sears as he walked through a door into the "big world," and what he saw at once amazed, chagrined, excited, and challenged him. The letters capture him in the moment between adolescence and adulthood, between student and teacher, between friend and husband, between student and scholar. He observes, compares, evaluates and reports. The letters are better than a journal or a diary because there is an immediate audience, real and personal, with whom he can share his new insights.

For example, Dr. Sears reflects on the power of the fellowship of Christians, the feeling of belonging and acceptance that one feels among Christians, even those who are complete strangers (if such is possible among followers of Christ) (June 20, 1915). This observation rings true today among those of us who travel and visit churches where we find ourselves "at home," accepted, understood, in familiar ritual and practice and teaching.

In the early letters, Dr. Sears is lonely and homesick but he is also appalled and maybe a little fascinated by the new world he is discovering, a world that includes "fallen" women (June 15, 1915; July 19, 1915; July 24, 1915). His values come through as he seeks friendship and avenues of service, he defends the quality of his past education at Cordell, he tries to find his role in the local church, he plans a strategy for his advanced education, he tests his understanding of marriage and male-female relationships through his readings, his entertainments, and his observations of those around him, and he investigates his ability to live and thrive independently.

Dr. Sears often reveals his vision of Christian education that required spiritual priorities be foremost (June 19, 1915). Therefore, he surmises, the size of the institution would have to be limited. He questioned whether the mission could remain intact if the school were larger than two hundred-fifty students or if the school were to become a university. Sitting in his academic seat at Harding University, I have to wonder what Dr. Sears would think today when Harding University currently enrolls over sixty-three hundred students in nearly one hundred majors and over twenty-five graduate and professional programs and still tries to maintain a strong emphasis on spiritual elements.

In another letter, Dr. Sears demonstrates how to teach "Christianly" as we now say at Harding (June 22, 1915). His analysis shows that he sees the greatness of his discipline in the context of his Christian worldview. The ideas are Christian regardless of their origin in the words of Shakespeare; the issue is how they are presented by the instructor. In others, he portrays his focus on how to teach and his desire to improve his teaching (July 4, 1916) and his awareness of the sacrifices of those involved in Christian education (July 19, 1916). Though young and fairly inexperienced, Dr. Sears is engaging in the serious work of defining Christian education, an exercise that continues today for many who celebrate his legacy.

In short, these letters reveal the humanity, the values, the passion, the sincerity, and the dedication of Dr. L. C. Sears and Pattie Hathaway Armstrong Sears and a small group of pioneers of Christian education, in whose shadow I proudly and humbly walk. I am grateful that Liz has made them available to me and to many others.

Larry R. Long
Provost
Harding University

Names Index with Annotations

Agnes (See Bills, Agnes)

Albert, Willie (See also Tomlinson, John)—Mentioned in the letters as marrying John Tomlinson, she was with him in Elk City, Oklahoma, and working as a public school teacher by the 1930 census.

Alice (See O'Neal, Alice Belle)

Amanda (See Rutherford, Amanda)

Amidon, Sam—A Wichita trial lawyer and member of the Democratic Party.

Anderson, E. Marie—A faculty member at the University of Oklahoma.

Armstrong, John Nelson; Ida Woodson Harding; and family (See also Harding family)—J. N. Armstrong was president of several NBST model schools while also teaching, preaching, writing, and editing. His wife, Woodson, was the daughter of James A. and Pattie Harding, key Stone-Campbell Movement leaders.

> *Pattie Hathaway* ("Pataway"; See also Sears, Lloyd Cline)—The only child of the couple, she married Lloyd Cline Sears. While a student in Cordell, Pataway twice won the Lee Brothers scholarship for strong academic performance. She completed her college degree at age forty-two while also working as a teacher and overseer of Harding College's dining hall.

> *J. D.*—Nephew of J. N. Armstrong whom he and Woodson raised. By 1930, the census identifies him as a sewing machine salesman in

Oklahoma City. He married a woman named Myrtle and they had at least two children.

Baillie, Joanna–A Scottish poet and dramatist of the late 1700s and early 1800s who was quite famous during her time.

Baxter, Anna Lee Baxter–Music teacher, Harper College.

Baxter, Batsell–Educated at the Nashville Bible School under David Lipscomb and James A. Harding, he served as dean of Cordell Christian College in 1916. For a time, he was also dean of Thorp Springs Christian College. Later, Baxter held the presidencies of Abilene Christian, David Lipscomb, and George Pepperdine Colleges.

Bell, Samuel Albert; Sarah Catherine (Sallie) Hoover; and family–The progeny of this family were close associates of the Armstrongs. Samuel Albert the elder died in 1913. As a widow, Sallie Bell may have visited her family in Cordell in 1916. She would have been about sixty-three years old and could have been "old Sister Bell."

Robert Clark; Bessie Sparkman; and family–R. C. and Bessie Sparkman met at Nashville Bible School. He later taught with the Armstrongs at Potter Bible, Western Bible and Literary, Cordell Christian, Harper, and Harding Colleges. Bell held additional posts at Thorp Springs Christian, David Lipscomb, and Abilene Christian Colleges. His areas of expertise included Bible, English, and philosophy.[1]

Bell, Samuel Albert; Ora Anne Jones; and family–S. A., the younger brother of Robert Clark, married Ora Anne in Odessa, Missouri, where they were with the Armstrongs. By 1913, S. A. and Ora Anne were in Cordell where he taught Bible, natural and physical sciences, and mathematics. During World War I, he authored a strongly pacifist article that exacerbated local opposition to the school.[2] Ora Anne died at age forty-two, leaving her husband with six children. Although he remarried in 1938, Samuel Albert and Ora Anne are buried near each other in Morrilton, Arkansas where he had been a teacher at Harding College.

Katherine–Born around 1911, she was probably the daughter whom Pataway called "Catharine."

---

1. Baxter and Young, *Preachers of Today*, 33.
2. See the detailed accounting of this in Casey, "Closing of Cordell," 25.

Bell, Clemmie Mae (See also Klingman, Charles)–Younger sister of Robert and Samuel, she married Charles Klingman and went with him as a missionary to Japan. Clemmie Mae died in January of 1916.

Ben, "Uncle" (See Harding family)

Bernice (See Booker family)

Berrigan, Agnes–Special instructor in the Summer School, University of Oklahoma.

Bessie (See also Loftis, Bessie and Hudson, Bessie)–The letters suggest she was to be a Cordell boarder during the 1915–16 academic year. The reference is possibly to Bessie Loftis or Bessie Hudson.

Beth (See Harding, Beth)

Beulah (See Symcox, Beulah)

Bills, "Brother D."–William Dee Bills was born in Sentinel, Oklahoma, and worked as a preacher in Texas, Oklahoma, and California. He also wrote for the *Firm Foundation*.[3]

Bills, William Hambright; Annie; and family–William Hambright was a member of Cordell's board of regents. According to the 1910 census, the Bills lived on Cook Street near the Treeces and Valentines. They also had a farm in Lake Valley.[4]

    John–The eldest child of the family, became a preacher and lived in California.

    Agnes Rebecca (See also Holland, Pearly Bert)–The second child, Agnes, was about the same age as Pataway. She first married Bert Holland who died young. Agnes later married John L. Troyer and moved to Clinton, Oklahoma.

Billups, Richard Alphonzo–An attorney in Cordell.

Bingaman, Alvin–Chairperson of the Washita County Council of Defense, he played a key role in opposing Armstrong's pacifist stance on World War I. He also helped organize the local drive to close Cordell Christian College.[5]

Bishop, "Sister"–Almost certainly Clara Bishop who, with her husband William (a former Nashville Bible School student), served as a missionary in

---

3. Smith, *Gospel Preachers of Yesteryear*, 31–32.
4. Information about this family obtained from descendant, 2013.
5. Casey, "Closing of Cordell," 30.

Japan. William died in 1913, leaving Clara to struggle for her children's welfare and the mission work.[6]

Bixler, Orville Dean (See also Jaquess and Symcox families)—O. D. Bixler attended Western Bible and Literary College when Armstrong was president and later became a student at Cordell. Bixler married Anna Bell Davis and they went to Japan as missionaries in 1918. Anna died in the late 1940s and O. D. thereafter married Delilah Jaquess Symcox, the widow of Ernest Symcox. Bixler died in Tennessee in 1968.

Blackmar, Francis Wilson—Dean of the Graduate School and professor of sociology, University of Kansas. Cline occasionally spelled his name "Blackman."

Bland, Joseph D. and Ethel (See also Burkett family)—J. D. was an elder in the Lexington, Oklahoma Church of Christ. Ethel may have been his second wife, since the 1910 census shows him married to a woman named Mollie. Census data from that same year confirm Ethel was the daughter of Katie Burkett.

Blansett, "Brother"—Possibly James Elbert Blansett who, during the period covered by the letters, appears to have boarded with the Armstrongs. He married a woman named Berta and became a minister in Dallas. Pataway occasionally spelled his name "Blansette."

Booker, Philip W. and Mickie—Census records locate this couple in Lexington, Oklahoma, from about 1900 until at least 1930. Their son, Bernice, would have been about eleven years old at the time of the letters. Pataway spelled Mrs. Booker's name "Mickey."

Boyd, Minor—The letters indicate he was to be a boarder during the 1915–16 academic year. Boyd was from Oregon and served on Cordell Christian College's debate team.

Bradley, "Brother"—Possibly George C. Bradley who, according to census data, was a long-term Lawrence, Kansas, resident. In 1920, he lived on Vermont Street, not far from the University of Kansas and would have been about seventy-three years old.

Brooks, Stratton D.—President of the University of Oklahoma from 1912 to 1923. He earlier served as superintendent of the Boston public school system.

---

6. See an extensive treatment of Clara and William Bishop's work in Daggett, "Lord Will Provide," 294–363.

Buchanan, James Shannon–Dean of Arts and Sciences and professor of history, University of Oklahoma. Buchanan worked on Cordell's accreditation.

Burkett, Katie (See also Bland family)–Census data identify her as being married to a Noah Burkett and having numerous children. The family lived on a farm near Lexington, Oklahoma.

Ethel–The daughter who married Joseph Bland.

Campbell, Dr.–Beyond Cline's reference to him as an Oklahoma optometrist there is insufficient information to identify him fully.

Campbell, L. Q.–Public speaking teacher, University of Oklahoma.

Campbell, Walter S.–Instructor in English, University of Oklahoma.

Carl (See Colson, Carl)

Catharine (See Bell, Katherine)

Christie–Beyond details in the letters, her identity is unknown due to insufficient information.

Colson, Carl (See also Symcox family)–A native Floridian, Carl Colson worked in the Cordell College offices and possibly also for the *Gospel Herald*. He married Mae Symcox and they moved to Cocoa, Florida where Carl worked for Standard Oil.

Cook–Probably T. L. Cook who served on the Cordell Christian College board of trustees.[7]

Cooper, D. L.–English teacher, Harper College.

Covey, Tona and Eva–Tona Covey was a faculty member at Western Bible and Literary College at the time of the letters.[8] By 1930, they were, according to census records, living in Morrilton, Arkansas.

Cox, James M.–The Democratic Party candidate who, with Franklin D. Roosevelt as his running mate, challenged Republican Warren G. Harding for the presidency in 1920.

Croom, Adlai Stevenson (See also Harris, Margaret Price)–A. S. Croom attended Freed Hardeman and Harvard Colleges.[9] He preached for the Churches of Christ and was president of Arkansas Christian College in Morrilton at the time it merged with Harper College. From 1930

---

7. Young, *History of Colleges*, 122.
8. Ibid., 113.
9. http://www.therestorationmovement.com/croom.htm.

to 1931, he served as president of Oklahoma Christian College. A. S. Croom married Margaret Price Harris.

Crumley, Joe William Sr.; Jennie Arnold; and family–Crumley was a member of the Cordell Church who, along with James Harrel and George Fleming, came to oppose Armstrong's pacifist stance during World War I.[10] He was married to Jennie Arnold and they had five children, three of whom Pataway mentioned in her correspondence. These were most likely the ones listed below.[11] Joe died young and his family had a difficult time thereafter.[12] The census of 1920 lists his widow and her children as residing in Cordell.

Harold Vaughn

Zela

Joe Jr.

Dale, Edward Everett–Instructor in History, University of Oklahoma.

Dasher, "Mr."–Most likely Groover B. Dasher who was from Georgia and did some preaching in Kentucky and Texas. According to the census, by 1930 he was living in Morrilton, Arkansas and teaching at Harding College.

Davidson, "Mr." (See also Katie, "Miss")–Possibly Ernest and Katie F. Davidson who were about Cline's age. According to census data, they were living in Liberal, Kansas, in the 1920s and in Cordell by the 1930s.

Davis, "Sister"–A number of Davis families resided in Washita County at the time of the letters. Additionally, a Winnie and Ola Davis from Texas were students at Cordell Christian College. It is not possible to determine which Davis family might be referenced here nor if Winnie and Ola were connected to the woman Pataway mentioned.

Dell–A student at Cordell who was also possibly a boarder, but there is insufficient information to identify him any further.

Dial, D. R.–Dial joined the Cordell College board in 1916 and served as its secretary.[13] He supported Armstrong's pacifist stance and defended the school's administration during the local conflict of 1918.

---

10. Casey, "Closing of Cordell," 28–29.
11. http://www.therestorationmovement.com/crumley.htm.
12. Smith, *Gospel Preachers of Yesteryear*, 119–22.
13. Parks, *Cordell's Christian College*, 17; Sears, *For Freedom*, 157.

Downing, William Bell–Professor of voice and public school music, University of Kansas.

Draper, "Brother and Sister"–Possibly Fred L. and Margaret Draper who were, according to census data, long term residents of Lawrence, Kansas, living on New York Street. The Church of Christ was on New York Street in the 1920s as well. At the time of the letters, Fred and Margaret would have been in their fifties.

Duncan, Leo A.–Born in Cordell, Leo Duncan went on to serve in the navy as a Lieutenant Colonel. By the early 1940s, he was working at the United States Naval Hospital in San Francisco. His wife's name was Mable.

Dunlap, Charles Graham–Professor of English literature, University of Kansas.

Edwin–There is insufficient information to identify him beyond mention of his being a boarder during the 1915–16 academic year.

Ella, "Miss" (See Forster, Ella)

Elmer (See Taylor, Elmer)

Epperson, Leroy B.–He became one of three Cordell students who suffered legal difficulties over claiming conscientious objector status during World War I. When Epperson failed to complete his registration form, he was convicted as a war deserter.[14]

Eunice (See Freeman, Eunice)

Fannie (See Hockaday, Fannie)

Fenton, "Miss"–A Cordell student, but there is insufficient information to identify her any further.

Fleming, "Brother" (See Fleming, Ben)

Fleming, William; Sarah Frances; and family–The letters mention three of this couple's six children.

> *George Alexander Warren*–The eldest child of William and Sarah, G. A. W. became a Cordell businessman and business manager of Cordell Christian College in 1907. He had a difficult relationship with Armstrong that apparently affected events related to World War I.[15]
>
> *Ben*–Younger brother to George. The census record from 1920 locates him in Norman, Oklahoma.

---

14. Casey, "Closing of Cordell," 22; Sears, *What Is Your Life?*, 80.
15. See, e.g., Casey, "Closing of Cordell," 22.

Mark—The sixth child of William and Sarah.

Fogg, William and family—A widower who lived with his children in Cordell near the Wilsons and Crumleys. According to census records, Fogg would have been almost seventy at the time of the letters.

Ella—Several years older than Cline, she taught in the Cordell public schools.

Fred—A Cordell student who was slightly younger than Pataway, he helped Cline with the *Gospel Herald*.[16] He could have been the one referred to as "Brother Fred."

Forrester, Mrs.—Possibly a misspelling of the Forster family name. If not, there is insufficient information to determine her identity.

Forster, Sarah Elizabeth and family (See also Goodrum, Sarah Elizabeth)—Sarah Elizabeth was known as Lizzie when she married William Forster in 1900. He was an elder in the Churches of Christ who died in 1908. Census records from 1910 show Sarah Elizabeth living alone with her children on Market Street in Cordell. Between the 1915 and 1916 sets of letters, Sarah Elizabeth must have married a J. P. Goodrum. Lela and Eleanor Forster appear as Goodrum's step-daughters in the 1920 census.

Lela Jane—The eldest of Sarah Elizabeth's children, she spent her life in Cordell.

Warren D. and Ella—The 1923 Oklahoma City directory identifies him as being the Secretary for C. H. Wright Ready to Wear Stores, while the Cordell Church of Christ anniversary bulletin of some years later mentions him as being in business in Tulsa. Warren married Zou Ella Mamo as the letters attest.

Eleanor—The youngest of the siblings, Eleanor went on to become a business woman in Ft. Smith, Arkansas.

Foster, Harriet (See also Gentry, Ella)—Pataway identified Harriet Foster as the mother of Ella Gentry while census records of 1910 state she was a step-mother. At the time of the letters, Harriet was married to William J. Foster who would have been about sixty-nine years old. Harriet would have been about fifty-three and Ella nineteen.

Fowler, Willard (See also Sears, Goldie Opal)—The husband of Cline's sister, Opal, he had been her music teacher at the state normal school in Helena, Oklahoma.[17]

---

16. Sears, *What Is Your Life?*, 49.
17. Ibid., 33–34.

Fred, "Brother" (See Fogg, Fred and Treece, Fred)

Freeman, Abraham E. Jr.; Sarah; and family–Usually identified in the letters as "Brother Freeman," A. E. Freeman was an original member of the Cordell Christian College board. He came to the town in 1907 to further his children's education. His first wife was Sarah Bray and they had five children before she died. Freeman than married his wife's sister, Vena Bray.[18]

> *William Webb*–The eldest child of Abraham and Sarah, Webb was educated at Potter Bible College and came to Cordell when R. C. Bell left to teach at Thorp Springs. Webb was a popular English and Latin teacher.[19] He also studied at Yale and taught for a time at Abilene Christian College.[20]

Freeman, Wiley H.; Laura; and family–Usually identified in the text as "Dr. Freeman," Wiley H. was the physician who treated Pataway's diphtheria.[21] He and A. E. were brothers. Wiley Freeman and his family moved to Cordell about the same time as did Abraham and just as the college was originally opening.[22] During the college's 1912–13 academic year, Freeman, who was serving as president of the Panhandle District Medical Association at the time, gave special presentations to the students on health-related topics.

> *Katie*–The eldest child of W. H. and Laura Freeman, she was about Cline's age.

Eunice–The second child in the family, she was about Pataway's age.

French (See also Shepherd, Mary)–Claude French, a Canadian immigrant active in the Churches of Christ in Detroit. He was an enthusiastic supporter of Christian education and married Mary Shepherd in 1919.

Gardner, J. N.–Language teacher, Harper College.

Gardner, Richard Neely and Carrie Florence Coop–R. N. Gardner was a longtime associate of the Armstrongs and Hardings. He was with them at Nashville Bible School and left with them to establish Potter Bible College where he taught math and Latin.[23] Both R. N. and his brother, A.

---

18. Smith, *Gospel Preachers of Yesteryear*, 149–51.

19. Parks, *Cordell's Christian College*, 10; Sears, *What Is Your Life?*, 42, 144–45. Casey, "First Graduate Theological Education. Part 2," 139.

20. Sears, *For Freedom*, 126.

21. Ibid., 121–22; Smith, *Gospel Preachers of Yesteryear*, 150.

22. Ibid.

23. Young, *History of Colleges*, 113.

D., went on to work at Western Bible and Literary College. While A. D. left there before 1916,[24] R. N. stayed on and succeeded Armstrong as president. Gardner had two wives, Ann Deering Owsley, who died in 1904 and Florence Coop, whom he married in 1906. The Gardners were still in Odessa in 1918 when R. N. registered for World War I.

Gentry, Ella (See also Foster, Harriet)—A local resident and step-daughter of Harriet Foster, she was most likely also the "Miss Gentry" referred to in the letters.

Gilbert, L. J. and Eulalee—Probably the Lafayette J. and Ella Lee Gilbert who, according to census records, were living less than forty miles from Bowling Green, Kentucky in 1910. L. J. was about four years younger than Paul Harding and served as one of his pall bearers.[25] At the time of the letters, the Gilberts were living in Franklin, Kentucky.

Goodrum, "Sister" (See Forster, Sarah Elizabeth)

"Granny Pattie" and "Grandpa" (See Harding, James and Pattie)

Gussie, "Miss" (See Teague, Gussie Lee)

Hadsell, Sardis Roy—Professor of the English language, University of Oklahoma.

Hamic, William T.; Etha; and family—According to the 1910 census, the Hamic family lived on South Street in Cordell. William was a hardware store clerk.

> *Stella*—The oldest child of the family, Stella would have been about twenty-one at the time of the letters.
>
> *Nina*—The next in line to Stella, Nina would have been about eighteen at the time of the letters.

Hamilton, Elizabeth—Federal census data identify an Elizabeth Hamilton living with her family on West Tonhawa Street, Norman, in 1910 and 1920. She would have been of the age that Cline indicated in his letter.

Hapgood, Norman—American writer and journalist who served as Ambassador to Denmark under President Woodrow Wilson. He appears to have been a student at Harvard Law School while William Vaughn Moody was an undergraduate at Harvard College.

---

24. Ibid., 113, 117.

25. "Funeral of Paul T. Harding," unidentified newspaper obituary in possession of the editor, 1913.

Names Index with Annotations   231

Harding, James Alexander; Pattie Cobb; and family–The couple, both descended from active Stone-Campbell Movement families, married in 1878. Previously, J. A. had been married to Carrie Knight who died in 1876. Harding co-founded the Nashville Bible School with David Lipscomb but was best known as a preacher and debater.

   Leon Knight–Son of J. A. and Carrie, the only one of their three children to survive past infancy. Although he first trained as a physician, his life's work was as a minister serving congregations mostly in Tennessee. He married Annie Bell Wilson and they lived in Henning, not far from Memphis. The couple had no children. Leon died in 1940.

   Ida Woodson (See also Armstrong family)–The first child of J. A. and Pattie, Woodson married J. N. Armstrong, one of her teachers at the Nashville Bible School and became a celebrated teacher and college administrator in her own right.

   Benjamin Franklin–The next in line to Woodson, Ben married Elizabeth (Beth) Griffin and they had a daughter also named Elizabeth.[26] He followed the family model of being a teacher-preacher with academic specialties in German and mathematics. Ben served on the Potter Bible College faculty and remained there for a time even after his father resigned for health reasons.[27] Census data of 1920 record the family as living in Alabama. Benjamin Franklin died in 1944.

   Sue Blackman–Born in 1888, Sue married Charles Paine, whom she met at Potter Bible College. At the time of the letters, J. A. and Pattie Harding had already moved to Atlanta to be with Sue and Charles where he was a physician.[28] Sue died in 1979.

   Gertrude and Charles Jr.–Children of Sue and Charles Paine.

   Paul Travers–Born in 1891, he contracted rheumatic fever at age nine and developed heart ailments thereafter. He was scheduled to teach at Cordell in the fall of 1913, but poor health prevented this. Paul died at age twenty-one, shortly before he was to be married.

Harmon, Clara and Jake–Jake Harmon graduated from the University of Kansas. He became a millionaire oilman and prominent member of the Republican Party. The trial following his murder was covered fairly extensively in the press.[29]

26. Sears, *Eyes of Jehovah*, 214.
27. Young, *History of Colleges*, 115.
28. Sears, *Eyes of Jehovah*, 260.
29. See, e.g., "Clara Smith Surrenders to Sherif [sic]," *Charleston Daily Mail*,

Harrel, James C. and John M.—The Harrel brothers were members of the Cordell Church of Christ. James, an elder in the Church, was a businessman who dealt in real estate and gave the land to the Church in 1905.[30] He also donated the land for Cordell Christian College and served on the school's first board of regents.[31] During World War I, Harrel strongly opposed Armstrong's pacifist stance and helped build local opposition to it.[32]

Harris, Margaret Price (See also Croom, Adlai Stevenson)—Violin teacher at Harper College, she married A. S. Croom in 1922.

Hatchett, Sarah Edna (See also Smith, Oscar)—Born the same year as Cline, she married Oscar in Cordell and the couple spent their lives in Oklahoma. Pataway spelled the last name "Hatchet."

Hells, "Miss"—There is insufficient information to identify her beyond what the letters provide.

Henton, William C.—Cline's landlord during his first summer at the University of Oklahoma, Henton was first married to Mollie, who died at age forty in 1913.[33] Cline's letters indicate that the woman he subsequently married was named Nell.

Hertzler, Dr.—Possibly Ralph H. Hertzler, a well-established physician in Newton, Kansas, according to census data.

Hockaday, William Doniphan; Louise; and family—Along with J. C. Harrel and G. A. W. Fleming, Hockaday was one of the three individuals who helped found Cordell Christian College in 1907.[34] As chair of the college's board of regents, Hockaday strongly defended Armstrong during the conflict over pacifism in World War I.[35]

Fannie—Second child of W. D. and Louise Hockaday.

Sallie Ellis—The youngest child in the family, she married George S. Benson and they spent over a decade in China as missionaries. Benson eventually succeeded Armstrong as president of Harding College.[36]

December 23, 1920.

30. http://www.therestorationmovement.com/harrel,jm.htm.
31. Smith, *Gospel Preachers of Yesteryear*, 168; Young, *History of Colleges*, 122.
32. Parks, *Cordell's Christian College*, 6; Casey, "Closing of Cordell," 22, 28.
33. http://www.findagrave.com/cgi-bin.
34. The idea for the college apparently arose from a conversation around the Hockaday's dining table. Smith, *Gospel Preachers of Yesteryear*, 176.
35. Casey, "Closing of Cordell," 27–31; Casey, "From Religious Outsiders to Insiders," 462.
36. See also Sears, *What Is Your Life?*, 120.

Holland, "Brother and Sister" and family–Possibly Howard Martin and Nora Holland who moved from Missouri to Cordell sometime before 1918. H. M. was, at one time an elder of the Fourth and College Church of Christ.[37] Nora had five sisters according to the 1900 census and these might have been the sisters to whom Pataway referred. Nora Holland died in 1919. In 1920, the census reports that Howard remained in Cordell as a widower living with his son. Alternatively, the reference could be to Charles Holland who lived on a farm in Washita County.

Pearly Bert (See also Bills, Agnes)–A son from Charles Holland's marriage to Mary Williams, he became Agnes Bills's first husband.

Holland, "little boy"–Possibly Atros Lowell, the son of H. M. and Nora Holland. He would have been about seven years old at the time of the letters. Alternatively, one of the boys in Charles Holland's household.

Home, John–A Scottish poet and dramatist of the 1700s.

Homer, "Brother" (See Rutherford, Homer)

Hopkins, Edwin Mortimer–Professor of rhetoric and English language, University of Kansas.

Horace (See Rutherford, Philip Horace)

Hornbaker "boy"–Possibly Forrest R. Hornbaker, who was from a family that census records show as living in Stafford County and who later became a teacher.

Hubert (See Pope, Hubert)

Hudson, "Miss"–Possibly Bessie or Cora Hudson.

Hudson, Thomas; Lillie; and family–According to the 1910 census, they were a farming family living in Hobart, Oklahoma. The Hudsons had three children.

John Allen–Born in Mississippi, he attended Cordell Christian College and became a preacher. Hudson wrote for the *Gospel Advocate* and *Firm Foundation*, and founded the Old Paths Book Club. He was a couple of years older than Cline. Pataway spelled his name "Johnie" although he went by "Johnnie."[38]

Bessie–She was about one year younger than Cline and could have been the potential boarder mentioned in the letters.

Cora–She was about two years Cline's junior.

---

37. *Christian Chronicle*, 3.
38. Smith, *Gospel Preachers of Yesteryear*, 184–86.

Husband, Agnes–Head of Stephens College vocal department.[39]

Ira (See Warlick, Ira)

J. D. (See Armstrong, J. D.)

Jaquess, Stanley; Laura; and family–Federal census records of 1910 list the family as living in Cordell on Church Street.

> *Eula* (See also McCaleb, Cleburne)–The eldest child of Stanley and Laura, she married Cleburne McCaleb.
>
> *Delilah* (See also Symcox, Ernest and Bixler, O. D.)–Her name is spelled multiple ways in various documents. Delilah first married Albert Ernest Symcox and they remained in Cordell at least through the 1920 census. Delilah went on to earn advanced degrees and was a teacher at several different schools, including Oklahoma Christian College in Cordell during the 1920s.[40] A few years after Ernest died, she married O. D. Bixler who was, by then, a widower. Delilah died in 1970 and is buried in Lawnview Cemetery, Cordell.
>
> *Oneida* (See also Bixler, O. D.)–The youngest child of the family, she married Clay Cook and moved to Tennessee. By 1930, however, they had returned to Hobart, Oklahoma, according to census data. Oneida eventually wrote a biography of O. D. Bixler that was published in 1985.

Jayne "girls"–Anna, Ethel, Nora, and Ruby Jayne were all students at Cordell Christian College high school in 1908. Anna and Nora attended the college in 1912–13, so the reference is probably to two or more of these young women.

Johnson, Hiram–United States Senator from California who ran for president as a Republican in 1920 but was defeated for the nomination by Warren G. Harding. He was an isolationist and ultimately voted against forming the League of Nations.

Johnston, William Hamilton–Professor of education and acting director of Summer Session, University of Kansas. Cline spelled the name "Johnson."

Jones, "Sister"–Most likely Laura Jones, mother of Ora Anne Jones. She appears to have been widowed at an early age. Laura Jones was a student at Cordell Christian College. During the 1913–14 year she won the Lee Brothers Scholarship in recognition of her academic performance.

---

39. *Musical Blue Book of America 1916–17*, 197.
40. Parks, *Cordell's Christian College*, 33.

Jordan, David Starr—President of Stanford University, then chancellor until his retirement in 1916. Armstrong cited Jordan's work in defense of small schools.[41]

Katie, "Miss" (See Davidson, "Mr.")

Kerley, Dr. James W.—Although Pataway and Cline usually rendered his name "Kirley," they were almost certainly referring to Dr. James W. Kerley identified in census records and by current Cordell residents. He was a physician in general practice. In 1910 and 1920, the Kerley family lived on College Street.

Kieffer, George W.—A student and teacher at Cordell and other Churches of Christ schools including David Lipscomb College, Kieffer specialized in chemistry and physics.[42] In addition to preaching in Harper, Kansas, during the 1920s and in Morrilton, Arkansas, during the 1930s, Kieffer served as a member of Harding College's board of trustees in the 1950s.[43] He had experience in masonry and it was likely in this capacity that Woodson mentioned him since Kieffer's construction expertise helped finish Cordell's main building basement.[44]

Kirley, Dr. (See Kerley, Dr. James. W.)

Klingman, Charles Christopher (See also Bell, Clemmie Mae; Zahn family)—A second generation German immigrant, Klingman was by 1900 living with the family of Robert A. and Lula Klingman Zahn in Louisville, according to census records. He attended Potter Bible College[45] and eventually married Clemmie Mae Bell. They went to Japan as missionaries in 1908.[46] Charles and Clemmie had four children. After she died, Charles married Marie, Robert Zahn's younger sister. Census data confirm Pataway's observation that Marie was slightly older than Charles.

Ledbetter, Aline—There is insufficient data to determine her identity beyond the information provided by Pataway.

Lee, Albert W.—Lee was an oilman who served on the Cordell board of regents.[47] He and his brother, John, also ran Lee Brothers, a local lumber

---

41. Young, *History of Colleges*, 117.
42. Sears, *For Freedom*, 129, 136. Parks, *Cordell's Christian College*, 1.
43. *Petit Jean*, vol. 23, 18.
44. Parks, *Cordell's Christian College*, 1, 8.
45. Young, *History of Colleges*, 116.
46. Daggett, "Lord Will Provide," 199.
47. Parks, *Cordell's Christian College*, 23. The Lee brothers sold materials to the college. Sears, *For Freedom*, 143. See also Young, *History of Colleges*, 126.

and coal business. Together, they established a scholarship at Cordell Christian College, some recipients of which are noted elsewhere in this index. A. W. Lee's house still stands in Cordell as of this writing.

Leon, "Uncle" (See Harding, Leon)

Lindley, Ernest H.–Chancellor, University of Kansas from 1920 to 1939. The first years of his presidency were particularly notable for the many building projects he encouraged.

Lindsey, Judge Ben B.–A judge with the Denver juvenile court system who refused to give evidence from a confidential conversation with twelve year old Neal Wright. The conversation concerned the acquittal of a murder charge made against the boy's mother, Berta. The boy's father, John Wright, had been shot while attempting to enter the home.[48]

Loftis, Bessie–The census of 1910 identifies Bessie as living with her family in Texola, Oklahoma. She was a little older than Cline and could have been the potential boarder mentioned in the letters.

Lovett, Robert Morss–A fellow student with William Vaughn Moody at Harvard in the 1890s, Lovett and Moody coauthored two books on English Literature.

Luther, "Brother" (See Marshall, Luther)

Luton, R. N.–Originally from Kentucky, he was a Nashville Bible School graduate.

Lynn, Margaret–Associate professor of English literature, University of Kansas.

Mae (See Symcox, Mae)

Manheart, Minnie–The wife of Fred Manheart. According to census records of 1910 and 1920, the Manhearts were longtime residents of Lexington, Oklahoma. She would have been in her thirties at the time of the letters.

Markham, Edwin–An American poet, he gave the commencement address at Cline's graduation from the University of Kansas in 1921.

Marshall, Benjamin; Emily; and family–The Marshalls lived on Cordell's College Street in 1910 according to the census. He served on the college's board of regents.[49]

---

48. "Holds Lindsey Guilty: Judge Declares Him in Contempt for Concealing Boy's Story," *New York Times*, August 4, 1915.

49. Parks, *Cordell's Christian College*, 17.

Luther—The eldest child in the family, Luther was a couple of years older than Cline. By the 1920 census, he was teaching high school in Cordell. Since Pataway's mention of "Brother" Luther implied he was a teacher, she possibly referenced Luther Marshall.

Mary, "Miss" (See Shepherd, Mary)

Maud, "Miss" (See Young, Maud)

McCaleb, Joe—A Cordell Christian College student from Alabama who is mentioned along with Cleburne McCaleb. Although the letters imply a relationship between the two McCalebs, that relationship is unclear.

McCaleb, Robert Cleburne (See also Jaquess, Eula)—Originally from Alabama, Cleburne McCaleb studied expression at Cordell Christian College and was in a group of young preachers with Cline. He graduated in 1914 and married Eula Jaquess. Cline spelled his name "Cleburn." The letters also suggest that Pataway and Cleburne dated, or at least that she was interested in him, prior to dating Cline.

McCarty, Andrew Jackson—A prominent preacher for the Churches of Christ in that era, A. J. McCarty spent much of his life in Texas.

Milholland, Thomas Eugene—About the same age as J. N. Armstrong, Milholland conducted evangelistic meetings in Texas and Oklahoma during the time of the letters.

Mitchell, "Brother"—Possibly James H. Mitchell who, according to the census of 1920, was an attorney living on Tennessee Street in Cordell.

Moody, William Vaughn—A poet and dramatist educated at Harvard and Yale, Moody died ten years before Cline contemplated him as a subject of study.

Müller, George—A German missionary theologian affiliated with the Church of the Brethren, he was very influential on J. A. Harding's thinking. Müller embraced a "trust doctrine" or theory that God would provide all material needs.[50] He was well known for encouraging Christians to care for orphans, personally founding five orphanages in England. These orphanages had no funding scheme other than Müller's practices of prayer and trust.[51]

---

50. Wayland, *Autobiography of George Müller*. See also Daggett, "Lord Will Provide," 40, 53, as well as Hicks and Valentine, *Kingdom Come*, 16, 127-28.

51. Garton, *George Müller and His Orphans*, 15, 54. See also Olbricht, *Reflections on My Life*, 45.

Nichol, Charles Ready—An evangelist, debater, author, and publisher who had attended the Nashville Bible School. He also worked at the *Gospel Advocate*.[52] C. R. Nichol served as president of Thorp Springs Christian College[53] and taught at Abilene Christian and at George Pepperdine Colleges as well.

Nina (See Hamic, Nina)

Normile, "Mrs."—Apparently the woman whose family rented rooms from Cline while he was a student at the University of Kansas.

O'Leary, Raphael Dorman—Professor of English, University of Kansas.

O'Neal, Edward Price; Amanda Elizabeth; and family—Several of the children of this family are referenced in the letters.

George—The first of the O'Neal children to survive into adulthood, he studied at Thorp Springs but returned to Cordell in 1917 to teach education courses. George O'Neal also took an active part in initiatives to revive the school in Cordell after its 1918 closure. Later in life, he served as a church minister and elder.[54]

Nancy A'Delia (See also Short, William Newton)—Sometimes referred to simply as "Delia," she was the second child to survive into adulthood. Delia married William Newton Short in Harper, Kansas, and they served as missionaries in Rhodesia (Zimbabwe) from 1921 to 1980. Although she eventually died in Cordell, she is buried in Bulawayo.

Alice Belle—The immediate younger sibling to Delia. The letters indicate that she dated O. D. Bixler and imply that she dated Cline. Alice married Joseph Marvin Grimes who attended Thorp Springs with George and Nancy A'Delia.

Oneida (See Jaquess, Oneida)

Owen, Thomas—The Oklahoma State Supreme Court Judge who conducted a hearing regarding local opposition to Cordell Christian College's stance on World War I.

Parsons, Andrew Clarkson—Professor of secondary education and high school inspector, University of Oklahoma. He wrote a testimonial for a Cordell Christian College promotional pamphlet.

---

52. Baxter and Young, *Preachers of Today*, 316.
53. Sears, *What Is Your Life?*, 74; Young, *History of Colleges*, 75.
54. Parks, *Cordell's Christian College*, 9, 15.

Paul, "Uncle" (See Harding, Paul)

Paxton, Joseph Francis—Professor of Greek and classical archaeology, University of Oklahoma.

Petty, "Brother and "Sister"—Possibly Clarence and Etta Petty who appear in multiple censuses as living in Cleveland County, Oklahoma.

> *Mary*—Clarence and Etta's daughter who would have been approximately eighteen years old at the time of the letters. She also might have been the "Miss Petty" referenced by Pataway.

Petty, "Miss" (See Petty, Mary)

Phelan, Warren Waverly—Director of the School of Education and professor of psychology and education, University of Oklahoma. Phelan went on to become president of Oklahoma Baptist University in Shawnee.

Pittman, Dorothy—A music assistant, Harper College.

Pope, Hubert—The reference to "Hubert" possibly means Hubert Pope who, according to the 1910 census, was slightly younger than Pataway and whose family lived in Cordell. Sometime within the subsequent decade, the Pope family moved to California but both Hubert and his sister Ola attended Cordell Christian College. So, it is possible that they boarded on campus.

Porter, Earle Sellers—Assistant professor of chemistry, University of Oklahoma.

Puett, Grace—Federal census records of 1900 identify Grace Puett as having been born in Missouri. She became part of the Western Bible and Literary College faculty during the 1913–14 academic year.[55] Grace Puett would have been about twenty years old at the time of the letters.

Ramey, Andrew Robert—Assistant professor of English, University of Oklahoma.

Randolph, Ben—Cline's roommate who took conscientious objector status during World War I and was imprisoned in Ft. Leavenworth as a result.[56] He died in 1921.[57]

Ray, Newton Onzan; Ora; and family—Ora was Armstrong's younger sister. Although the Armstrong family stayed with them in Lexington in 1916, by 1920 the family had moved to Harper, Kansas. Ray became business

---

55. Young, *History of Colleges*, 120

56. See Sears, *For Freedom*, 156, 158–59; Sears, *What Is Your Life?*, 79, and Casey, "Closing of Cordell," 24.

57. Sears, *What Is Your Life?*, 88.

manager of the *Gospel Herald*, taking over for Will Short when he and Delia left for Africa.[58]

Robbie Jo–The eldest child, born about 1913. She appears to have been a Harding College student in the early 1930s.[59]

Margie–Listed as "Marjorie" in the census data, she was born in 1916.

Raymond (See Symcox, Raymond)

Rhodes, Benjamin Franklin; Otie Sparkman; and family (See also Bell, Robert Clark and Bessie)–He taught at Odessa, Cordell, Thorp Springs, Abilene Christian, Harper, and Harding Colleges.[60] She was the younger sister of Bessie Sparkman Bell. The 1910 census records the Rhodes family as living on Lee Street, Cordell. By 1920, they were in Harper, Kansas.

Willis–The eldest child, he was a few years younger than Pataway.

Rice, Ira Young Sr.–A traveling evangelist based in Oklahoma, Rice conducted numerous singing schools particularly in Oklahoma and Texas for many years.[61] He was known for being especially effective with children and youths.[62]

Roady, John Campbell–Federal census data for 1920 record J. C. Roady as being a traveling minister living in Illinois. He appears to have served in both World Wars, with his World War I registration card listing a Churches of Christ affiliation. He also published a few short works about the denomination. Roady worked in regions where Daniel Sommer's influence was strong. Cline spelled his name "Rhoady."

Robinson "girl"–Possibly the daughter of John and Alice Robinson, Cordell residents according to census records.

Rutherford, Philip Horace; Mary; and family–According to the 1910 census the Rutherfords were a farming family in Cordell. The letters mention three of the family's six children.

Homer Harding (See also Shepherd, Mary)–The eldest child, he appears to have dated Pataway.[63] The letters show that he also seriously dated

---

58. Ibid.
59. *Petit Jean*, vol. 7, 47.
60. Benson, "B. F. Rhodes Passes," 476.
61. Rice, *Pressing Toward the Mark*, 22–52. See also http://www.therestoration-movement.com/rice.htm.
62. Smith, *Gospel Preachers of Yesteryear*, 287–88.
63. See Cline's references in Sears, *What Is Your Life?*, 52.

Mary Shepherd. Homer served in World War I[64] and although official records identify him as a "farmer" or "dairyman," Homer taught Latin at Cordell Christian College.[65]

Amanda–A younger sibling to Homer, she was about Pataway's age.

Philip Horace Jr.–The immediate younger sibling of Amanda, he became a farmer.

Sallie Ellis (See Hockaday, Sallie Ellis)

Schevill, Ferdinand–Professor of history, University of Chicago, from 1892 to 1937. He and William Vaughn Moody traveled through Europe together in 1897.

Scott, Angelo C.–Professor and director of extension lectures, University of Oklahoma.

Scroggs, Joseph Whitefield–Director of the Department of Public Information and Welfare and professor, University of Oklahoma.

Sears, James Matthias; Martha Ellen Hunter; and family–He was born in Kentucky and she in Missouri, but they moved to Indiana and then Kansas.[66] James and Martha Ellen had a number of children, several of whom Cline mentioned in the letters.

Mally Ralph–Ralph was a follower of Daniel Sommer as the letters make clear. He worked as an oil distributor.

Goldie Opal (See also Fowler, Willard)–Federal census records from 1910 list Opal and Willard as living in Tishomingo, Oklahoma.

Raymond S. and Elsie

Lloyd Cline (See also Armstrong, Pattie Hathaway)–The principal author of the letters in this collection, Cline was a recipient of the Lee Brothers scholarship while at Cordell. He married Pattie Armstrong, obtained his PhD, and spent most of his career as an English teacher and academic dean at Harding College.

Ruby

Shepherd "boy"–The letters suggest that he was a former Cordell Christian College student but insufficient information exists to identify him any further.

---

64. Ibid., 69, 80. See also Parks, *Cordell's Christian College*, 21.
65. Ibid.
66. Sears, *What Is Your Life?*, 19.

Shepherd, Mary (See also French, Claude and Rutherford, Homer)–The daughter of well-known preacher J. W. Shepherd,[67] Mary was a child when her family worked with the Hardings at the Nashville Bible School. At Cordell she taught the primary grades. She married Claude French in 1919.

Sheppard, James–The letters suggest he was to be a boarder during the 1915–16 academic year but there is insufficient information beyond this to determine his identity.

Short, James Taylor; Flora Ann Epperson; and family–The Shorts reportedly moved to Cordell on behalf of their children's education. Only two of their four children are mentioned in the letters. It is unclear if Flora Ann was related to Leroy B. Epperson.

> *William Newton* (See also O'Neal, Nancy A'Delia)–He worked at the *Gospel Herald*[68] and married Delia O'Neal. They became long-term missionaries to Rhodesia (Zimbabwe). William died in Bulawayo in 1980 and is buried there.
>
> *Sybil Ann*–A younger sibling; Pataway spelled her name "Syble" at one point.

Showalter, George Henry Pryor–Editor and owner of the *Firm Foundation* from 1908 to 1954,[69] Showalter argued that Christians could participate in civil government and even militarily at the conscientious objector level. He based this on the idea that Christians had a responsibility to support the United States during wartime.[70]

Sisson, Louis Eugene–Professor of comparative literature, University of Kansas.

Smith, "Brother" (See also Smith, J. F. and Smith, Keershal)–The context suggests this could have been Earl Smith who appears in a Cordell Christian College Literary Society photo along with Cline and Arthur Tenney. Alternatively, this could reference E. C. Smith who appears in a photo of students in the college's high school program. It is unclear if these two Smiths are one and the same. The reference also could be to J. F. or Keershal Smith.

---

67. Sears, *For Freedom*, 133.
68. Sears, *What Is Your Life?*, 50, 88.
69. Sears, *For Freedom*, 148.
70. Hooper, *Distinct People*, 112.

Smith, Keershal–There is insufficient information to determine his identity, although he appears to have boarded at Cordell Christian College.

Smith, Oscar (See also Hatchett, Edna)–A Cordell Christian College graduate who wrote a testimonial for one of the school's promotional pamphlets, Oscar married Edna Hatchett and went on to become a teacher.

Smith, "Sister"–Most likely Bessie Smith who, in the 1920 census, is listed as being the widowed mother of a young woman named Ola. They lived on Church Street and had a boarder at that time.

Sommer, Daniel–Of German Lutheran heritage, he grew up in poverty and attended Bethany College. In addition to having "a strong cultural bias against cities and large urban churches," Sommer saw "man-made societies" as detracting from Christians' missions by appealing too much to human pride and desire for worldly popularity.[71] Sommer also believed that preachers did not need to go to college and became an impassioned critic of the NBST's liberal arts education efforts.[72] Cline sometimes rendered the name "Somer."

Stafford, "Brother and Sister"–Possibly Joe and Effie Stafford whom census data record as living on College Street, Cordell in 1920.

Steitz, August–Assistant professor of German, University of Oklahoma.

Stilwell family–Kansas census data of 1925 identify a Mary Elizabeth Stilwell living at 1328 Kentucky Street in Lawrence with her widowed mother. Based on Cline's correspondence, it is highly probable that this is the family to whom he referred.

Sudbury, H. J.–A teacher of education and psychology, Harper College.

Sue, "Aunt" (See Harding, Sue)

Sybil (See Short, Sybil)

Symcox, Albert Henry; Nettie; and family–Albert Henry and Nettie lived within Cordell city limits but had about twenty acres that they farmed. For a time, he served on the board of regents[73] and was also an elder at the Cordell Church of Christ.

> *Beulah* (See also Hunt, Clay)–She married Clay Hunt and they moved to Louisville, Kentucky. After Clay died, Beulah returned to Cordell.

---

71. Ibid., 19.
72. http://www.therestorationmovement.com/sommer,d.htm.
73. Parks, *Cordell's Christian College*, 17, mentions him as a board member in 1914.

Raymond—He attended the college in Cordell when it reopened in the early 1920s and later graduated from Abilene Christian College. Raymond became a banker in Cordell and also served as the city's mayor. In the early 1950s he and his wife, Vera, moved to Norman.[74]

Albert Ernest (See also Jaquess, Delilah)—A Cordell graduate and church leader, he became a banker in the town and married Delilah Jaquess. Ernest died in 1941 and is buried in Lawnview Cemetery, Cordell.

Mae (See also Colson, Carl; Taylor, Elmer; and Wright, Clarence)—A few years older than Pataway, Mae apparently worked at the store owned by Clarence Wright. She dated Elmer Taylor but married Carl Colson. Pataway occasionally spelled her name "May."

Talfourd, Thomas Noon—An English lawyer, politician, and author born in the late 1700s.

Taylor, Dr.—Beyond Cline's explanation of his being an optometrist, insufficient information exists to identify him.

Taylor, Elmer (See also Symcox, Mae)—A student from Oklahoma who attended Cordell Christian College in the years before the letters were written.

Teague, Gussie Lee—A Cordell faculty member, she taught English as well as some of the primary grades.

Tenney, Arthur Boutelle—A Cordell faculty member[75] who appears to have boarded with the Armstrongs. He registered for duty in World War I as a Colorado resident, listing his professions as minister and laborer. Pataway and Cline often misspelled his name.

Terry, "Brother"—Possibly Tillman Terry who was a fellow preacher in training with Cline.

Thelma—Possibly Thelma Young who was slightly Pataway's junior. According to 1910 census data, she lived with her family on Temple Street, Cordell, in the same neighborhood as the Joe R. Warlick family.

Tipton, "Brother"—Possibly S. T. Tipton who attended both the high school and Cordell Christian College.

---

74. Information obtained from family member, 2012.
75. Casey, "Closing of Cordell," 28.

Tomlinson, William E.; Serena; and family—He served on Cordell Christian College's board of trustees[76] and was, at one point, treasurer. Federal census data of 1900 locate the family in Roger Mills County, Oklahoma.

    Eula—An older sibling of John, Eula attended Cordell Christian College in the years preceding the letters.

    John—(See also Albert, Willie)—A student in Cordell Christian College's high school, he went on to marry Willie Albert as the letters indicate.

Treece, Bennette and family—Bennette Treece would have been in her fifties at the time of the letters. According to the 1910 census, the Treece family lived on Cook Street, very near the Valentines.

    Jennie May (See also Utley, Homer)—The eldest of the two Treece children, she was a student at Cordell Christian College and married Homer Utley.

    Fred—Slightly older than Pataway, Fred was a student at Cordell Christian College. He went on to serve in World War I. He appears in a c. 1912 group photo with Pataway and could have been the one referred to simply as "Brother Fred."

Tuggle, Percy—A Percy Tuggle, born in 1905, resided in Beckham County near Cordell, according to the 1910 and 1920 censuses.

Utley, Louis; Ella; and family—The head of this household appears in census records sometimes as Louis and sometimes as Levi. He, his wife Ella, and their children appear on the 1900 census as being a farming family in Roger Mills County, Oklahoma. All the children mentioned in the letters attended Cordell Christian College.

    Homer Albert (See also Treece, Jennie)—He married Jennie May Treece and became a preacher in Sedgwick County, Kansas, according to 1930 census data. By the early 1940s, he was working as a minister in Detroit.[77]

    Clyde (See also Warlick, Ira)—The most immediate younger sibling to Homer, Clyde married Elizabeth Seward. The census of 1920 indicates that he worked as a groceryman. Probably in this capacity he hired Ira Warlick as the letters indicate. By 1930, Clyde had a double profession as minister and merchant.

---

76. Young, *History of Colleges*, 122.
77. *Christian Chronicle*, 9.

(Oma) Lou Ella—The youngest of the Utley children, Lou Ella was an art teacher at Cordell Christian College. She married Benton Raymond Westbrooks.

Valentine, James—According to the 1910 census, he was a carpenter in Cordell. His two children attended Cordell Christian College. The Valentines lived on the same street as the Treeces.

Vaughn, William Thomas—The head of Cordell Christian College's grammar school, he was appointed to that position in 1910.[78] Vaughn knew the Armstrongs from his days as a student at Potter Bible College.[79] He appears to have enlisted in World War I while living in Cordell.

Voss, John Henry—Associate professor of German, University of Oklahoma. Cline spelled his name "Vosse."

Walker, "Mr."—A student who appears to have attended school with Cline in Oklahoma and Kansas. The letters reveal that he was married and suggest that he was, at the time, living in Chicago even though he might have earlier attended Lockney Christian College in Texas. Records at the University of Oklahoma indicate that a Lee A., a Robert S., and a Joseph D. all were enrolled full time around 1915–16. But it is unclear if any of these were the Walker to whom Cline referred. So, insufficient information exists to identify him any further.

Wall, Samuel Claude—Wall was a Cordell faculty member who taught penmanship.[80] He also studied at the college and began his preaching career in Cordell.[81]

Warlick, Joseph Rowlett; Ollie D. Blackwell; and family—In 1910, census records show the family living on Valentine Street, Cordell. Sometime between then and the 1920 census they moved to Shawnee. Joe was the younger brother of Henry Warlick who had been involved in the effort to establish Cordell Christian College and who also served on the board of regents.[82]

> *Ira Elmore Warlick* (See also Utley, Clyde)—About two years older than Pataway, he was a student at Cordell Christian College. Ira married Bessie Marie Lassiter.

---

78. Parks, *Cordell's Christian College*, 10; Sears, *What Is Your Life?*, 47.
79. Young, *History of Colleges*, 116.
80. Parks, *Cordell's Christian College*, 4.
81. Smith, *Gospel Preachers of Yesteryear*, 377.
82. Young, *History of Colleges*, 122.

Wells, Elmer C.; Tillie; and family–The family appears to have lived on a farm near Cordell, according to 1920 census information. At one point, Elmer Wells was treasurer of the college's board of regents.[83] All the children attended Cordell Christian College.

Audrey–Since she was Cline's age, she may have been the one mentioned as a possible English teacher.

Wells, "Miss" (See Wells, Audrey)

Westbrooks, Benton Raymond (See also Ultey, Oma Lou Ella)–A Cordell Christian College student, he married Lou Ella Utley. Census records of 1920 and beyond indicate he was a farm laborer.

Whitcomb, Seldon Lincoln–Professor of comparative literature, University of Kansas.

Willard (See Fowler, Willard)

Williams, Claudine–Insufficient information exists to determine her identity beyond what the letters contain.

Williams, Guy Yandall–Associate professor of chemistry, University of Oklahoma.

Wilson, "Brother and Sister" and family (See also Crumley, Joe and Jennie)–Possibly Harvey and Bertha Wilson who lived in Cordell in 1910 according to census records. Two of their children, Harvey Ray and Winnie, were students at the college in years preceding the letters. Federal census data also identify a Charles and Julia Wilson who lived in Cordell on Cook Street near the Crumley family. So the reference could be to either couple.

Winterrowd, Ira–In addition to teaching at Lockney Christian College in Texas, Winterrowd preached at the Fourth and College congregation in Cordell. He later served as president of the school that reopened in Cordell after World War I.[84]

Wood, "Sister" and "Miss"–Census records from 1910 and 1920 identify a number of Wood families in Washita County and surrounding environs. L. B. Wood from Oklahoma was a student in the years preceding the letters but there is insufficient information to know if he was related to the Woods mentioned in the letters.

---

83. Parks, *Cordell's Christian College*, 17.
84. Young, *History of Colleges*, 126; Parks, *Cordell's Christian College*, 26.

Wright, Jefferson David; Maggie; and family–According to the 1910 census, the family lived in Jackson County, Oklahoma.

> Clarence H.–A prominent Cordell merchant, Clarence ran C. H. Wright Stores and later became president of Sun-Ray Oil Company.[85] He was married to a woman named Eva. In 1964, Clarence Wright was inducted into the Oklahoma hall of fame.[86]
>
> Ammon–A younger sibling to Clarence.

Young, Maud–Possibly the daughter of H. D. Young, the town's first merchant.[87] Federal census data of 1900 locate the family in Cloud Chief, Oklahoma, with H. D. being a shopkeeper. Maud would have been about twenty-seven years old at the time of the letters.

Zahn, Charles; Anna Trees; and family–The Zahns were German immigrants who settled in Kentucky. According to census records of 1880, they had a number of children, only two of whom are mentioned in the letters.

> Robert A. (See also Klingman, Charles)–A preacher in various Churches of Christ, he came to Cordell in 1911[88] and served on the college's faculty, teaching German, French, and sight singing.[89] Robert Zahn and J. N. Armstrong were about the same age. It appears that Zahn's wife, Louisa (Lulie), who also taught at the college, was a sibling to Charles Klingman.
>
> Marie–A sibling to Robert, she was slightly younger than Woodson Armstrong.

---

85. Sears, *What Is Your Life?*, 75.
86. http://oklahomaheritage.com/HallofFame.
87. Information obtained from Cordell resident, 2012.
88. Parks, *Cordell's Christian College*, 13.
89. Sears, *For Freedom*, 127; Young, *History of Colleges*, 124.

Bibliography

Adams, James Truslow. *The Epic of America*. Boston: Little, Brown, 1931.
Allen, C. Leonard, and Richard T. Hughes. *Discovering Our Roots: The Ancestry of Churches of Christ*. Abilene, TX: Abilene Christian University Press, 1988.
Armstrong, John Nelson. "A Sad Loss." *Living Message* 4:50 (1926) 787–88.
Bales, James D. "J. N. Armstrong: A Saint Who Greatly Inspired Me." *Twentieth Century Christian* 21:4 (1959) 28–30.
Baxter, Batsell Barrett, and M. Norvel Young. *Preachers of Today: A Book of Brief Biographical Sketches and Pictures of Living Gospel Preachers*. Vol. 2. Nashville: Gospel Advocate, 1959.
Benson, George S. "B. F. Rhodes Passes." *Gospel Advocate* 89:27 (1947) 476.
Bollet, A. J. "Politics and Pellagra: The Epidemic of Pellagra in the U. S. in the Early Twentieth Century." *Yale Journal of Biology and Medicine* 65:3 (1992) 211–21.
Boothe, Wayne. *Washita County*. Images of America. Charleston, SC: Arcadia, 2007.
Burks, David B., ed. *Against the Grain: The Mission of Harding University*. Searcy, AR: Harding University, 1998.
Casey, Michael W. "The Closing of Cordell Christian College: A Microcosm of American Intolerance during World War I." *Chronicles of Oklahoma* 76 (1998) 20–37.
———. "The First Graduate Theological Education in the Churches of Christ. Part 1: Jesse Sewell's and George Klingman's Audacious Synthesis of Spirituality and Academic Excellence at Abilene Christian College." *Restoration Quarterly* 44:2 (2002) 73–92.
———. "The First Graduate Theological Education in the Churches of Christ. Part 2: The Controversy over Webb Freeman's 'Modernism' and the Resulting Collapse of Sewell's Dream." *Restoration Quarterly* 44:3 (2002) 139–57.
———. "From Religious Outsiders to Insiders: The Rise and Fall of Pacifism in the Churches of Christ." *Journal of Church and State* 44:3 (2002) 455–75.
The Christian Chronicle. Special anniversary ed. Cordell, OK: Fourth and College Church of Christ, 1941.

Cordell Christian College Eighth Annual Announcement: 1914-1915. Cordell, OK: Cordell Christian College, 1914.

Cremin, Lawrence A. *The Transformation of the School: Progressivism in American Education 1876-1957*. New York: Knopf, 1961.

Daggett, Shawn Z. "The Lord Will Provide: James A. Harding and the Emergence of Faith Missions in the Churches of Christ, 1892-1913." ThD diss., Boston University School of Theology, 2007.

Eisler, Riane. *The Chalice and the Blade: Our History, Our Future*. San Francisco: Harper & Row, 1988.

Foster, Douglas A., et al., eds. *The Encyclopedia of the Stone-Campbell Movement*. Grand Rapids: Eerdmans, 2004.

Fourth Annual Report. Oklahoma City: Corporation Commission of the State of Oklahoma, 1911.

Garton, Nancy. *George Müller and His Orphans*. Westwood, NJ: Revell, 1963.

Griffith, Terry. *Oklahoma City: Statehood to 1930*. Images of America. Charleston, SC: Arcadia, 2000.

Hicks, John Mark, and Bobby Valentine. *Kingdom Come: Embracing the Spiritual Legacy of David Lipscomb and James Harding*. Abilene, TX: Leafwood, 2006.

Hooper, Robert E. *A Distinct People: A History of the Churches of Christ in the Twentieth Century*. West Monroe, LA: Howard, 1993.

Hughes, Richard T. *Reviving the Ancient Faith: The Story of Churches of Christ in America*. Abilene, TX: ACU Press, 2008.

James Madison University. "What's a Normal School?" http://www.jmu.edu/centennialcelebration/normalschool.shtml.

The Musical Blue Book of America 1916-17. New York: Musical Blue Book, 1916.

Olbricht, Thomas H. "Alexander Campbell as an Educator." In *Lectures in Honor of the Alexander Campbell Bicentennial, 1788-1988*, introduced by James M. Seale, 79-100. Nashville: Disciples of Christ Historical Society, 1988.

———. *Reflections on My Life in the Kingdom and the Academy*. Eugene, OR: Wipf and Stock, 2012.

Parks, Norman L. *Cordell's Christian College: A History*. Cordell, OK: Fourth and College Church of Christ, 1994.

The Petit Jean. Vol. 7. Morrilton, AR: Harding College, 1931.

———. Vol. 23. Searcy, AR: Harding College, 1956.

Rice, Ira Y., Jr. *Pressing Toward the Mark: An Autobiography*. Dallas: Rice, 1998.

Richardson, William J. "Models of Ministerial Preparation among Christian Churches/Churches of Christ and Churches of Christ." *Discipliana* 54 (1994) 49-63.

Sears, Lloyd Cline. *The Eyes of Jehovah: The Life and Faith of James Alexander Harding*. Nashville: Gospel Advocate, 1970.

———. *For Freedom: The Biography of John Nelson Armstrong*. Austin, TX: Sweet, 1969.

———. "James A. Harding: 'He Walked by Faith.'" *Twentieth Century Christian* 21:4 (1959) 10-11.

———. *What Is Your Life? An Autobiography*. Dallas: Temple, 1979.

Sears, Lou Ann. "A Short History of United States Education 1900-2006." http://www.historyliteracy.org/publications.html.

Smith, Loyd, L. *Gospel Preachers of Yesteryear*. Allen, TX: Smith, 1986.

Tyack, David B., and Larry Cuban. *Tinkering toward Utopia: A Century of Public School Reform*. Cambridge: Harvard University Press, 1995.

University of Oklahoma General Catalog 1914–1915. Norman: University of Oklahoma, 1915.

Wayland, H. Lincoln, ed. *Autobiography of George Müller: The Life of Trust*. Grand Rapids: Baker, 1981. Originally published 1861 by Gould & Lincoln.

White County Historical Society. "Harding Timeline." http://www.argenweb.net/white/wchs/Harding_files/Harding_Timeline.html.

Williams, D. Newell, et al., eds. *The Stone-Campbell Movement: A Global History*. St. Louis: Chalice, 2013.

Young, M. Norvel. *A History of Colleges Established and Controlled by Members of the Churches of Christ*. Kansas City: Old Paths, 1949.

Zinn, Howard. *A People's History of the United States 1492–Present*. 1980. Reprint, New York: HarperPerennial, 2003.

Index

accreditation, 12, 48, 50, 74, 153, 162, 171, 200, 215, 225
apocalyptic, 6–7, 27

Baillie, Joanna, 184–85, 188, 193, 195, 199, 204–5, 209, 222
Baptist Church, 54, 80, 150, 239
Belle Isle Park, 65, 70–73
Bethany College, xi, 4, 28, 54, 62, 243
Bible, the, 1–2, 11, 44, 46, 62, 82–83, 109, 147, 151, 175, 180, 190, 192
  Bible schools, 11, 18, 38, 82, 88, 175, 203
Bishop, Clara, 163, 223–24
Bixler, O. D., 54, 63, 96, 224, 234, 238
Brooks, Stratton, 137, 224
Buchanan, James, 12, 156, 225

Campbell, Alexander, ix–xi, 2, 4
Catholicism, Roman, 19, 37, 189–91, 207
Christian Church/Disciples of Christ, 2, 11, 177, 182, 209
Civil War, the, 2, 11, 15, 17, 20, 58
class, socio-economic, xiii, 25–27, 30, 59, 90–91
Columbia University, 139, 176

Conscientious Objector (See also noncombatant service; pacifism), 17, 227, 239, 242
cooperatives, 31
Cordell Christian College, xi–xii, xvii–xviii, 5, 12, 14, 16–17, 35–105, 111–34, 150, 153, 162–66, 174, 211, 222–27, 232–34, 236–39, 241–47
Council of Defense, Washita County, xii, 164–66, 223
Cox, James M., 188, 199, 225

dancing, 28, 70, 178, 183, 202
Darwin, Charles (See also evolution), 28, 59
Democratic Party, 192, 199, 221, 225
Dewey, John, 13
disease, 35, 38, 50, 63, 157
domestic violence (See also gender), 22, 128–29, 131

education (See also normal schools; teaching), x–xiii, 4, 7–15, 18–19, 26, 29, 31, 73, 122, 129, 150, 163, 167, 169, 171–73, 179–81, 184, 185, 189, 192, 194, 197–99,

253

254 Index

education (*continued*)
204, 208, 210, 217–20, 229, 234, 238–39, 242–43
as a discipline, 13–14, 173, 179–81, 192
elementary, 13, 172, 179, 242
pedagogy, 12–13, 85–86, 136, 143, 181
progressive movement, 8, 13
secondary, 13, 47–48, 74, 83, 89, 100, 128, 163, 167, 179, 185, 199, 205, 238
Enlightenment, the, ix, x, 1, 27
evolution (See also Darwin, Charles), 28, 59, 68

Fanning, Tolbert, x, 15
Federal Bureau of Investigation, 17, 165
Firm Foundation, 52, 65, 150, 223, 233, 242
football, 170, 180, 183, 185–87, 192, 194, 196–98, 200–201

gender (See also domestic violence; ladies' aid societies), xiii, 2, 8, 10–11, 19–23, 53, 71, 81, 113, 122, 129, 150
Germany, 58, 61, 139, 147
Gospel Advocate, 17, 52, 233, 238
Gospel Herald, 52, 65, 225, 228, 240, 242
government (See also law), 2, 7, 15–17, 58, 98, 148, 165, 181, 194, 207, 210, 242
Great Awakening, x

Harding College, xii, xviii–xix, 5, 23, 26, 36, 167, 213, 217, 219–22, 226, 232, 235, 240–41
Harding, James Alexander, x–xii, xvii–xviii, 3–11, 15, 18, 20, 23, 25, 27–29, 38, 54, 70, 77, 79, 81, 88, 140, 146–47, 211, 213, 221–22, 231, 237
Harding, Pattie Cobb, x–xix, xvii–xviii, 3, 5, 68–69, 77, 81, 87–88, 92, 102–3, 142, 145, 146–47, 149, 211, 221, 231
Harding, Warren G., 187–88, 199, 225
Harper College, xviii, 5, 12–13, 23, 166–67, 171–72, 175, 205–6, 208, 211
Harvard University, 12, 139, 176, 182, 204, 206, 225, 230, 236–37
Haskell Institute, 26, 170, 207

imagination, 28, 50, 60, 66, 73, 184, 218
industrialization, 8, 28, 40–41, 44
integration, racial, 26, 176–77, 179

Jehovah's Witnesses, 109
Johnson, Hiram, 187, 234
Jordan, David Starr, 12, 58, 235

ladies' aid societies (See also gender; mission societies), 10, 80
law (See also government), 7, 15–16, 48, 50, 84, 98, 130, 144, 152–53, 175, 189, 197, 203, 207
League of Nations, 15, 187–88, 192, 200, 234
liberal arts, 11, 13, 30, 243
Lindley, Ernest H., 173, 187, 236
Lipscomb, David, x, xii, xvii–xviii, 3–4, 6, 8, 10–11, 15, 17, 27, 222, 231
Lipscomb University, xi, xviii, 4, 235
literature, 11, 14, 29, 45, 49, 73, 82, 95, 119, 128, 130, 175–79, 182–84, 200, 204, 227, 236, 242, 247

marriage, 4, 21, 24, 54, 58, 60, 62, 84, 86–87, 92, 94, 162–64, 195, 199, 219
Methodist Church, 182
Mexico, 15, 130, 148
mission, Christian, 7–11, 13–15, 18, 20, 23, 30–31, 219, 223–24, 232, 235, 237, 242
mission societies (See also ladies' aid societies), 11, 22, 26, 243
modernity, 6, 27–32
Moody, William Vaughn, 171, 176–77, 179, 184

Index

Müller, George, 38, 47, 57, 140, 237
music, 11, 19, 23, 28, 32, 59, 70, 119, 132, 178, 181, 190, 198, 204–5, 210
   jazz, 19, 178, 183
   singing, 2, 31, 52, 54–55, 65, 68, 71, 74, 79, 82, 91, 110, 123, 137, 174, 177, 186
mutual edification, 79
Nashville Bible School, xi–xii, xvii–xviii, 4, 7, 9–11, 22, 29–30, 44, 54, 62, 147, 222–23, 229, 231, 236, 242

nationalism, x, 7, 15, 30
noncombatant service (See also Conscientious Objector; pacifism), 17, 165
normal schools (See also education; teaching), 13, 62, 69, 137, 171, 200, 208, 228

orphans, 40, 44, 47, 62, 77, 189, 237
   orphanages, 9, 12, 18, 21, 28, 38, 42, 44–45, 47, 59, 67, 93, 147, 237
Oxford University, 59, 139, 151, 182

pacifism (See also Conscientious Objector; noncombatant service), 16, 30, 223, 232
patriotism, xii, 7, 30, 84, 148
Potter Bible College, xi–xii, xvii–xviii, 9, 11, 31, 54, 147, 229, 231, 235, 246
poverty, x, 17, 24–25, 63, 243
preachers, xii, 4, 8, 19, 26, 42–43, 47, 52–53, 71, 74, 147–48, 150, 173, 177, 192–93, 231, 233, 237, 242–45, 248
   preaching, 23, 31, 52, 68, 79, 98, 123, 155, 177, 180, 190–91, 197

race (See also integration, racial; segregation, racial), ix, xiii, 25–27, 61, 63, 69, 83, 176–77, 179, 207
Republican Party, 187–88, 200, 225, 231, 234
Restoration Movement, 2

Rhodes Scholarship, 12, 138–39
romanticism, 18, 27–29, 218
Roosevelt, Franklin Delano, 187–88, 225
Roosevelt, Theodore, 176

science, 5, 11, 14, 28–29, 126, 181, 198, 210, 222, 225
secularism, 10–11, 13, 29, 82, 137, 148, 167
segregation, racial, 25
Shakespeare, William, xviii, 45, 49, 51, 220
Short, Delia O'Neal, 54, 62, 69, 91, 96, 238, 240, 242
Short, William Newton, 54, 60, 72, 85, 95, 133, 238, 240, 242
socialism, 144
Sommer, Daniel, 4, 26, 128, 150, 175, 182, 240–41, 243
stewardship, 23–25
Stone, Barton, ix–x, 1, 6–7, 19, 25, 27
Stone-Campbell Movement, 1–11, 14, 19–20, 25–27, 29, 33, 62, 221, 231
Story Teller's League, 73
Supreme Court, Oklahoma, 17, 165, 238

taxation, 15
teaching (See also education; normal schools), xiii, xviii, 4–5, 7–8, 10, 12–15, 21, 28–29, 31, 39, 51–52, 59, 65, 70, 73–74, 79, 82, 86, 88–89, 96, 98, 103, 120, 150, 169, 181, 200, 208
theater, 20, 32, 35–36, 50, 68, 98, 107, 173, 179, 184, 189
Thorp Springs Christian College, 62–64, 90, 93, 96, 150, 222, 229, 238, 240
trust theology, 7, 10, 25, 27, 237

University of Chicago, xviii, 174, 177, 179, 184, 241
University of Kansas, xi, xviii, 12, 23, 33, 51, 167–215, 224, 227, 231, 233–34, 236, 238, 242, 246–47

University of Oklahoma, xi, xvii, 12, 35–100, 111–61, 167, 221, 223–26, 230, 232, 238–39, 241, 243, 246–47
urbanization, 13, 28, 31, 243

Vanderbilt University, 7, 83
voting, x, 7, 22, 152, 154, 210

warfare, xii, 98, 130, 148, 165–66, 242
Western Bible and Literary College, xi–xii, xvii–xviii, 14, 128, 222, 224–25, 230, 239

Wilson, Woodrow, 15, 148, 200–201, 230
World War I, x, xii, xviii, 16–17, 58–59, 84, 147, 162, 176, 201, 211, 222–23, 226–27, 230, 238–41, 245–47
worship, ix, 2, 6, 11, 17–19, 79–80, 88

Yale University, 182, 229, 237
YMCA, 168, 171, 180
YWCA, 70, 180

www.ingramcontent.com/pod-product-compliance
Lightning Source LLC
Chambersburg PA
CBHW071244230426
43668CB00011B/1584